ILLUMINATING
the *S*ERMON at the
& TEMPLE
SERMON on the
*M*OUNT

FARMS Publications

Teachings of the Book of Mormon

The Geography of Book of Mormon Events: A Source Book

The Book of Mormon Text Reformatted according to Parallelistic Patterns

Eldin Ricks's Thorough Concordance of the LDS Standard Works

A Guide to Publications on the Book of Mormon: A Selected Annotated Bibliography

Book of Mormon Authorship Revisited: The Evidence for Ancient Origins

Ancient Scrolls from the Dead Sea: Photographs and Commentary on a Unique Collection of Scrolls

LDS Perspectives on the Dead Sea Scrolls

Images of Ancient America: Visualizing Book of Mormon Life

Isaiah in the Book of Mormon

King Benjamin's Speech: "That Ye May Learn Wisdom"

Mormons, Scripture, and the Ancient World: Studies in Honor of John L. Sorenson

Periodicals

Insights: A Window on the Ancient World

FARMS Review of Books

Journal of Book of Mormon Studies

Reprint Series

Book of Mormon Authorship: New Light on Ancient Origins

The Doctrine and Covenants by Themes

Copublished with Deseret Book Company

An Ancient American Setting for the Book of Mormon

Warfare in the Book of Mormon

By Study and Also by Faith: Essays in Honor of Hugh W. Nibley

The Sermon at the Temple and the Sermon on the Mount

Rediscovering the Book of Mormon

Reexploring the Book of Mormon

Of All Things! Classic Quotations from Hugh Nibley

The Allegory of the Olive Tree

Temples of the Ancient World

Expressions of Faith: Testimonies from LDS Scholars

Feasting on the Word: The Literary Testimony of the Book of Mormon

The Collected Works of Hugh Nibley

Old Testament and Related Studies

Enoch the Prophet

The World and the Prophets

Mormonism and Early Christianity

Lehi in the Desert; The World of the Jaredites; There Were Jaredites

An Approach to the Book of Mormon

Since Cumorah

The Prophetic Book of Mormon

Approaching Zion

The Ancient State

Tinkling Cymbals and Sounding Brass

Temple and Cosmos

Brother Brigham Challenges the Saints

Published through Research Press

Pre-Columbian Contact with the Americas across the Oceans: An Annotated Bibliography

New World Figurine Project, vol. 1

A Comprehensive Annotated Book of Mormon Bibliography

ILLUMINATING the SERMON at the TEMPLE & SERMON on the MOUNT

An Approach to 3 Nephi 11–18 and Matthew 5–7

John W. Welch

Foundation for Ancient Research and Mormon Studies
Provo, Utah

Foundation for Ancient Research and Mormon Studies
at Brigham Young University
P.O. Box 7113
University Station
Provo, Utah 84604

Library of Congress Cataloging-in-Publication Data

Welch, John W. (John Woodland)
    Illuminating the sermon at the Temple & sermon on the
mount / John W. Welch.
        p. cm.
    Rev. ed. of: The Sermon at the temple and the Sermon on the
mount. 1990.
    Includes bibliographical references and index.
    ISBN 0-93-489337-3 (pbk. : alk. paper)
    1. Book of Mormon. Nephi, 3rd XI-XVIII—Criticism,
interpretation, etc. 2. Bible. N.T. Matthew V-VII—Criticism,
interpretation, etc. 3. Sermon on the mount—Criticism,
interpretation, etc. I. Welch, John W. (John Woodland) Sermon at
the temple and the Sermon on the mount. II. Title.
    BX8627 .W375 1998
    289.3'22—dc21

                                                    98-35640
                                                    CIP

What Is the Foundation for Ancient Research and Mormon Studies (FARMS)?

The Foundation for Ancient Research and Mormon Studies encourages and supports research and publication about the Book of Mormon: Another Testament of Jesus Christ and other ancient scriptures.

FARMS is a nonprofit, tax-exempt educational foundation affiliated with Brigham Young University. Its main research interests in the scriptures include ancient history, language, literature, culture, geography, politics, religion, and law. Although research on such subjects is of secondary importance when compared with the spiritual and eternal messages of the scriptures, solid scholarly research can supply certain kinds of useful information, even if only tentatively, concerning many significant and interesting questions about the ancient backgrounds, origins, composition, and meanings of scripture.

The work of the Foundation rests on the premise that the Book of Mormon and other scriptures were written by prophets of God. Belief in this premise—in the divinity of scripture—is a matter of faith. Religious truths require divine witness to establish the faith of the believer. While scholarly research cannot replace that witness, such studies may reinforce and encourage individual testimonies by fostering understanding and appreciation of the scriptures. It is hoped that this information will help people to "come unto Christ" (Jacob 1:7) and to understand and take more seriously these ancient witnesses of the atonement of Jesus Christ, the Son of God.

The Foundation works to make interim and final reports about its research available widely, promptly, and economically, in both scholarly and popular formats. FARMS publishes information about the Book of Mormon and other ancient scripture in the *Insights* newsletter, books and research papers, *FARMS Review of Books, Journal of Book of Mormon Studies, FARMS Occasional Papers*, reprints of published scholarly papers, and videos and audiotapes. FARMS also supports the preparation of the *Collected Works of Hugh Nibley*.

To facilitate the sharing of information, FARMS sponsors lectures, seminars, symposia, firesides, and radio and television broadcasts in which research findings are communicated to working scholars and to anyone interested in faithful, reliable information about the scriptures. Through Research Press, a publishing arm of the Foundation, FARMS publishes materials addressed primarily to working scholars.

For more information about the Foundation and its activities, contact the FARMS office at 1-800-327-6715 or (801) 373-5111.

CONTENTS

Setting the Stage

CHAPTER 1

OVERVIEW

No text in the Bible is more important or has had more influence on the history and character of Christianity than the "Sermon on the Mount" in Matthew 5–7. It would be hard to overstate the value of the Sermon on the Mount in shaping Christian ethics and in conveying to the world the teachings of Jesus and of early Christianity. It is known as the Great Sermon, *die Rede von Reden,* an "unparalleled address,"[1] and thousands of books and articles have analyzed it extensively and minutely.[2] It stands unsurpassed as the sermon of the Master *par excellence.*

Embedded in the Book of Mormon, in the account of the first day of Jesus' ministry among the Nephites at the temple in Bountiful (3 Nephi 11–18), are three chapters (12–14) that are substantially the same as the Sermon on the Mount in Matthew 5–7. They stand in the Book of Mormon as a temple text.

The account of what Jesus said that day I call the "Sermon at the Temple." The materials in the two sermons are so profound that no single approach can capture their full meaning and significance. These texts can be studied profitably from several angles. They work together, hand in glove, to give deep insight into the meaning of the Master. When speaking of the shared collective meaning of these texts, I will refer to them together simply as the "Sermon."

In this book I have gathered some thoughts together around one approach to the Sermon on the Mount and the Sermon at the Temple that may be of special interest to Latter-day Saints. I explore the contours of the Sermon through its history, language, and temple context. While I draw upon many particular points from Christian scholars to enrich and corroborate my interpretations, I find that the unique insights afforded by 3 Nephi in the Book of Mormon bring the greatness of the New Testament Sermon on the Mount most dramatically into focus. I view those words of Jesus as a sacred Sermon, as a temple text. The spires and peaks of that monumental Sermon, towering from that everlasting hill, loom even larger than usual when they are understood through the setting of Jesus' Sermon at the Temple.

The present study is divided into three parts. The first part, "Setting the Stage," offers introductory comments to set the stage for exploring the contexts to which the Sermon originally belonged. The next two sections advance ideas to ponder and theories to be considered. These sections are neither exhaustive nor definitive. In exploring a number of possibilities that will hopefully prove to be worth further reflection, they address a variety of issues and audiences.

Following a statement in chapter 2 about the search for a unifying theory of the Sermon on the Mount, the heart of this book, part two, titled "A Sacred Sermon," analyzes the Sermon as more than merely a moral discourse or an eclectic collection of various sayings of Jesus. Here, in chapters 3, 4, and 5, I offer a Latter-day Saint interpretation that illuminates the Sermon in the context of a sacred, ancient temple experience, for that is its setting in the Sermon at the Temple. Seeing the teachings, instructions, doctrines, and commandments of the Sermon on the Mount in this way—in connection with or in preparation for the ceremonial stages and ordinances of covenant making—opens new insights into a unified meaning and comprehensive significance of the otherwise segmented Sermon on the Mount. I invite readers to ponder the prospects of the exceptional view of the Sermon that the Book of Mormon presents to us, for that view has far-reaching implications.

Part three, "Further Studies," offers several additional studies that support and develop the idea of seeing the Sermon as a temple text and shed further light on this material as it appears in the Book of Mormon. The first six chapters in this part come in three pairs.

In chapter 6, I compare the words and phrases in the Sermon at the Temple with those of the Sermon on the Mount to show their points of independence. The subtle differences between these two texts give information about the unique settings for the two presentations and the audiences that Jesus addressed each time he delivered his message. My aim in this chapter is to enhance our understanding and appreciation of the Sermon at the Temple as a solid historical text and, at the same time, to offer further insights into the Sermon as a whole. In chapter 7, I point out a number of elements in the Sermon that were derived from or were present in the common Israelite heritage generally shared by the Jews in Jerusalem and the Nephites in Bountiful. From the comparisons developed in chapters 6 and 7, I strive to show that the Sermon on the Mount materials in

3 Nephi have not simply been spliced naïvely into the text of the Book of Mormon. The Sermon fits into the Book of Mormon context comfortably and appropriately.

In chapter 8, I look at Joseph Smith and the specific text of the Sermon on the Mount in the Book of Mormon. The fact that King James language of the Matthean Sermon appears in 3 Nephi has spawned questions from Book of Mormon critics, and it undoubtedly will continue to raise issues among lay and scholarly readers of the Book of Mormon. What does the text of the Sermon at the Temple tell us about the nature or process of the translation of the Book of Mormon? How may one account for the similarities between the Sermon at the Temple and the King James translation of the Sermon on the Mount? In chapter 9, I add support to the Sermon at the Temple by verifying the essential meaning of certain received translations and by noting one significant variant found in the ancient Greek texts of the Bible. In this pair of chapters, my purpose is to sustain the text of the Book of Mormon as a credible record through textual analysis.

The last pair turns to several issues and insights derived from source criticism and other areas of biblical studies. Chapter 10 asks, what of the synoptic question pursued so thoroughly by critical New Testament scholars? How does the Book of Mormon corroborate the words of Jesus found in the Bible? What stands behind Jesus' great concern over the Temple during his mortal ministry as presented in all four Gospels? Chapter 11 then draws on a growing field in religious studies which seeks to identify possible ritual or ceremonial features standing behind biblical texts. Social scientists find that rituals help religious people create order in their lives, form cohesive relationships, make major transitions, give sacred significance to ordinary elements of daily life, and memorialize their spiritual experiences in many important ways. These have, to some extent, been functions of rituals detected in the Sermon on the Mount, and they are even more explicitly evident in the Sermon at the Temple. My hope is to show how studies of these two sermons can be mutually enriching.

Finally, a few concluding thoughts are given in chapter 12. In the end, when the Sermon is seen as a temple text, as it stands in the Sermon at the Temple, this magnificent scripture is even more powerful and meaningful than typical readers have ever suspected.

This book is a revised edition of my book entitled *The Sermon at the Temple and the Sermon on the Mount*, copublished in 1990 by Deseret Book and the Foundation for Ancient Research and Mormon Studies (FARMS). The invitation of FARMS to reprint this title in paperback afforded me the welcomed opportunity to make a few corrections, clarifications, and several substantive additions that have emerged out of a decade of further research and correspondence. This new edition, however, is largely the same in purpose, style, and approach as the first edition.

I am sincerely grateful to all the staff in the research, editorial, and operations divisions at FARMS. They are deeply devoted friends of the Book of Mormon who have made this revised edition possible by assiduously combing the literature, carefully attending to production details, and sincerely encouraging this project. I remember especially from FARMS the library work of Daniel McKinlay, memos of John Gee, suggestions by Todd Compton,[3] John Sorenson, Stephen Ricks, Donald Parry, Don Norton, and others, and many levels of editorial assistance by Claire Foley, Alison Coutts, Wendy Thompson, Amy Bingham, and Mary Mahan, in addition to the polish that was given to the 1990 edition by Richard Tice and his colleagues at

Deseret Book. I am also ever mindful of the support and feedback given to me by my family. I hope that this book is tangible evidence of my love and appreciation to all who have found joy in this work.

Notes

1. James E. Talmage, *Jesus the Christ* (Salt Lake City: Deseret Book, 1976), 727.

2. Among the general studies of the Sermon on the Mount are Hans Dieter Betz, *The Sermon on the Mount*, ed. Adela Yarbro Collins (Minneapolis: Fortress, 1995); Ulrich Luz, *Matthew 1–7: A Continental Commentary*, trans. Wilhelm C. Linss (Minneapolis: Fortress, 1989); Georg Strecker, *The Sermon on the Mount: An Exegetical Commentary*, trans. O. C. Dean Jr. (Nashville: Abingdon, 1988); Joachim Jeremias, *The Sermon on the Mount*, trans. Norman Perrin (Philadelphia: Fortress, 1963); and Harvey K. McArthur, *Understanding the Sermon on the Mount* (Westport, Conn.: Greenwood, 1978). A valuable annotated listing of hundreds of works on the Sermon on the Mount is Warren S. Kissinger, *The Sermon on the Mount: A History of Interpretation and Bibliography*, American Theological Library Association Bibliography Series, no. 3 (Metuchen, N.J.: Scarecrow, 1975). Extensive bibliographic information is also found in Betz, *Sermon on the Mount*, and Luz, *Matthew 1–7*. From Latter-day Saint circles, see Robert E. Wells, *The Mount and the Master* (Salt Lake City: Deseret Book, 1991); and David H. Yarn Jr., "The Sermon on the Mount," *Ensign*, December 1972, 53–57. For additional references, see *"We Rejoice in Christ": A Bibliography of LDS Writings on Jesus Christ and the New Testament* (Provo, Utah: BYU Studies, 1995), 49–52; see also the bibliography at the end of the 1990 edition of the present book.

3. Todd Compton's review of the 1990 edition of this book is in the *Review of Books on the Book of Mormon* 3 (1991): 319–22.

CHAPTER 2

THE NEED FOR A
UNIFYING INTERPRETATION

Despite the Sermon's acclaimed preeminence and apparent simplicity, it is paradoxically inscrutable. What kind of a text is the Sermon on the Mount? What is its main theme or message? What should it mean to readers today? Is it a coherent speech or a collection of unrelated sayings? Traditional approaches have failed to answer these questions satisfactorily.

The meaning of the Sermon on the Mount seems unfathomable and inexhaustible to most Bible scholars. Despite endless commentaries, the Sermon on the Mount has simply defied summarization. After centuries of New Testament scholarship, no adequate distillation or coherent logic of the Sermon on the Mount has been convincingly identified. As Hans Dieter Betz has summarized, "New Testament scholarship up to the present has offered no satisfactory explanation of this vitally important text."[1] "There is no section of the Bible which has been so quoted (by non-Christians as well as Christians), worked over, commented upon, argued about, taken apart and put together, preached and taught, praised and scorned, as has the Sermon on the Mount."[2]

Seeking Coherence

The Sermon on the Mount has been variously inter-preted since the earliest days of Christianity.[3] It has been viewed practically, ethically, spiritually, ecclesiastically, personally, and ascetically. In modern times, it still remains possible to "understand and interpret the Sermon on the Mount in a thousand different ways."[4]

Every possible tool of critical scholarship has been brought to bear on the Sermon on the Mount, and yet it still eludes and transcends explanation. It has been examined in great detail by textual critics who specialize in compar-ing the early New Testament manuscripts in their variant forms. For example, famous scholars such as Wellhausen, Bultmann, Klostermann, Dodd, and others have asserted that the third beatitude (Matthew 5:5) was not originally part of the text of the Sermon on the Mount since it switches places with the second beatitude in some early New Testament manuscripts, while others argue that such a conclusion is unwarranted.[5]

Analyses of the structural composition of the Sermon have also varied: "Concerning the overall structure of the first Gospel, nothing close to scholarly unanimity has yet been achieved."[6] Dale Allison focuses especially on triadic structures in the Sermon and finds similar three-part struc-tures in the Mishnah.[7] Joachim Jeremias sees basically a three-part structure in the Sermon (covering issues regard-ing the manner of interpreting scripture, controversies con-cerning the righteousness of the Pharisees, and instructions about the new righteousness of the disciples).[8] Luz sees it centering on the Lord's Prayer.[9]

Individual sections are equally baffling. Regarding Matthew 5:21–47, Betz concedes: "There clearly appears to be a rationale behind the six antitheses and their arrangement in the [Sermon on the Mount], but that rationale has so far eluded scholarship."[10] The organizing principle behind Matthew 6:19–7:12 has been declared "most difficult to explain,"[11] even seemingly nonexistent.[12]

Likewise, source criticism has yielded a kaleidoscope of possible designs[13] and authorship. For example, some have proposed that Matthew was personally responsible for writing the five beatitudes in Matthew 5:5, 7–10 that are absent in Luke 6:20–22.[14] The text has been combed for clues of Jewish or Hellenistic influences. David Flusser points out parallels between the *Thanksgiving Scroll* 18:14–15 from the Dead Sea community and Matthew 5:3–5, Erik Sjöberg expounds at length upon the Judaic backgrounds of Matthew 6:22–23, while Betz finds in the same passage Hellenistic ideas and ancient Greek theories of vision.[15]

The theology, meaning, intended uses, and purposes of the Sermon in early Christian piety have been pondered. Betz and Jeremias both see the Sermon on the Mount as an early Christian *didache,* or set of instructions, that was taught to all new converts. In their view (and I basically agree with them on this point), it was used to instruct baptismal candidates or newly baptized Christians.[16] Betz classifies the Sermon on the Mount as an *epitome,* "not intended for outsiders or beginners, but for the advanced students [to help] 'those who have made some advance in the survey of the entire system . . . to fix in their minds under the principal headings an elementary outline of the whole treatment of the subject.'"[17] Krister Stendahl has somewhat similarly concluded that the Gospel of Matthew was produced for use in "a school for teachers and church leaders" and that for this reason its sermon "assumes the form of a manual for teaching and administration within the church."[18]

Daniel Patte extracts from the Matthean Sermon and its context in Matthew 4 distinct views of Christian discipleship.[19]

Moreover, the Sermon on the Mount has been interpreted typologically. One view sees it as reflecting the five dimensions of the early Christian church and the main themes of its ecclesiastical history.[20] These five themes, formulated by Gerhard Ebeling and supposedly exhaustive of early church history, are (1) the mystical ("seeing God," "seek and find"), (2) faith and theology, (3) orthodoxy versus heresy, (4) persecution and mission, and (5) Christian sin and ecclesiastical repentance. Going off in a much different but fascinating typological direction is W. D. Davies, who suggests that the Sermon on the Mount is none other than the new law of God given at a mountain, replicating the giving of the law to Moses on Mount Sinai, set in a five-part structure that mirrors the five books of the Pentateuch.[21]

Questions have been raised about the intended audience of the Sermon,[22] some suggesting that Jesus addressed himself only to the disciples, not to mankind in general.[23] Others have puzzled over which early Christian communities might possibly have played a role in producing the Sermon on the Mount,[24] as well as the potential targets against whom its critical statements may have been aimed.[25]

Beside these various historical treatments, the Sermon on the Mount has been given an astonishingly wide variety of practical applications and interpretations in contemporary theology and religion. For some, the Sermon on the Mount makes nothing less than a demand for ethical perfection;[26] for others, it proclaims a set of ideals impossible to fulfill and is thus "a call to the Mercy Seat."[27] David Greenwood argues that the imperatives in the Sermon should not be thought of as law, for "a good law should be worded in such a way that at least the majority of those on whom it is imposed are capable of obeying it in all normal circumstances," and obviously the high demands of the Sermon on the Mount do not meet this criterion.[28] For Duncan Derrett, the Sermon is nothing short of an ascetic discourse—somber, austere, and even "masochistic."[29] For still others, it preaches an urgent and expedient interim ethic relevant only to the supreme apocalyptic crisis of the world at hand.[30] No wonder Joachim Jeremias has asked,

> What is the meaning of the Sermon on the Mount? This is a profound question, and one which affects not only our preaching and teaching but also, when we really face up to it, the very roots of our existence. Since the very beginning of the church it has been a question with which all Christians have had to grapple, not only the theologians among them, and in the course of the centuries a whole range of answers has been given to it.[31]

This variety of approaches to the Sermon is pervasive. It is also prescriptive, for most of these interpretations reveal far more about the beliefs of the interpreters than about the meaning of the Sermon itself: "What each believes Jesus was, did, and said, determines the method by which each interpreter builds his bridge between Jesus and the twentieth century."[32]

Any study dealing with the Sermon on the Mount, therefore, enters into a soberingly vast field of exegesis and interpretation. Easy answers to any of the questions raised about the Sermon on the Mount are few in number and hard to come by. One way to view this array of opinions is to acknowledge that the living pliability of the Sermon on the Mount is both a great strength and a great weakness. Whoever a person is—from curious investigator, recent initiate, or committed disciple—the Sermon on the Mount can communicate a wide range of ideas and feelings, from technical or practical concerns to pertinent eternal truths and moral imperatives.

Consequently, little consensus has emerged out of this diversity about the original purpose and organization of the Sermon on the Mount: "When one turns to questions about the Sermon's meaning and relevance, there is far from unanimity of opinion."[33] Some have concluded, for example, that the Sermon on the Mount is an eclectic collection of isolated sayings of Jesus, which Matthew or early followers of Christ gathered together without a single theme or organized development. This argument receives some strength from the fact that certain verses in the Sermon on the Mount are also found in other Gospels but in different settings. Others, unsatisfied with that assessment, for it fails to explain the obvious strength of the Sermon as a whole, have attempted to bring all the disparate parts of the Sermon on the Mount under unifying main themes, such as Jesus' fulfillment of the law of Moses, the golden rule, freedom,[34] prayer,[35] love,[36] or the attainment of greater righteousness.[37] The main problem with the unifying approaches offered so far, however, is that no one of them can account completely for all of the text, for each of the suggested distillations selectively ignores many parts of the Sermon that do not happen to fit its particular theme, scheme, or constraints.

Finding Answers in the Temple Context

In the face of this uncertainty, it seems to me that the Sermon at the Temple in the Book of Mormon, with its unifying and coherent understanding of the Sermon on the Mount, provides a welcome new perspective. It offers answers to questions about why the Sermon was given, what was being said, what kind of sermon it was, how all of its parts fit together, and what it all means. When Jesus first appeared to the Nephites at the temple in Bountiful, he instructed and blessed the Nephites for the entire day. His lengthy Sermon at the Temple enhances our understanding of the masterful Sermon on the Mount as much or more than any other source I know.

The Sermon at the Temple does this primarily by disclosing the *context* in which Jesus spoke these words on that occasion, a context in which the Sermon can be completely comprehended, interpreted, and made relevant.

The context of the Sermon on the Mount has long been a major element missing from our understanding of the text. As Jeremias laments, "The instructions of the Sermon have been torn out of their original context,"[38] and thus he and others have sought to supply needed contexts by importing into the Sermon on the Mount the settings of parallel New Testament passages or by hypothesizing how the early Christians developed the Sermon on the Mount for use in their cultic teachings.

The Sermon at the Temple, however, presents an extensive report, offering a coherent view about the missing contextual setting, or, as Jeremias acutely senses, an understanding of what else preceded or accompanied the sayings in the Sermon on the Mount that is necessary to make them comprehensible.[39] Interestingly, Jeremias concludes that the heavy demands of the Sermon on the Mount make sense only if one assumes that the preaching of the gospel preceded and set the stage for those demands.

In Jeremias's view, five things are presupposed by the Sermon on the Mount: it assumes that its audience is already familiar with (1) the light of Christ, (2) the coming of the new age, (3) the expiration of the old law, (4) the unbounded goodness of God, and (5) the designation of the disciples as successors of the prophetic mission. These must be taken as givens in order for the Sermon on the Mount to make sense.[40] Strikingly, these are among the main themes explicitly stated in 3 Nephi 9:19 and 11:3–12:2 as a prologue leading up to the Sermon in 3 Nephi 12–14. That prelude to the Sermon at the Temple reports (1) the brilliant appearance of the risen Christ, "the light and life of the world" (3 Nephi 11:11), (2) the commencement of a new era (see 3 Nephi 11:28–41), (3) the fulfillment of the law of blood sacrifice (see 3 Nephi 9:19), (4) evidence of Jesus' atoning suffering and goodness (see 3 Nephi 11:14–17), and (5) the ordination of disciples as servant-ministers (see 3 Nephi 11:18–22; 12:1). Thus, at the outset, the Sermon at the Temple states explicitly these and other similar background elements that only can be presumed to stand behind the Matthean text.

Knowing more about the immediate context of the Sermon at the Temple then adds many insights to our understanding of this text. Essentially, it serves in the establishment of a righteous people who enter into a covenant to become Christ's sons and daughters, to take upon them his name, and to keep his commandments. Further understanding emerges, in this light, by reading and examining the text closely. The result is an understanding of the Sermon as a whole. While it is, of course, true that we can take individual maxims in the Sermon out of context (such as "turn the other cheek" from Matthew 5:39, or "lay not up treasures on earth" from Matthew 6:19) and make good practical sense of them in many applications, doing this severs these sayings from their surroundings and roots. Cut off, they do not thrive. We can discern a greater range of religious significance, however, when we hear and understand them in the context in which Jesus set them. For those who have ears to hear and eyes to see, the Sermon at the Temple contains more of the fullness of the gospel than anyone has previously imagined, revealing and enriching the profound sacred truths of the Sermon on the Mount.

This contextual information, supplied solely by the Book of Mormon, offers some important keys to the Sermon on the Mount itself—to its internal coherence, purpose, and unity. These keys open new ideas about these words of Jesus, inviting study and reflection for years to come. Just as the Sermon on the Mount has provided fertile ground for spiritual and scholarly research for hundreds of years in Bible studies, the same will undoubtedly be the case with the Sermon at the Temple in Book of Mormon research. The following chapters strive to move in that direction.

Notes

1. Hans Dieter Betz, *Essays on the Sermon on the Mount* (Philadelphia: Fortress, 1985), ix.

2. James H. Burtness, "Life-Style and Law: Some Reflections on Matthew 5:17," *Dialog* 14/1 (1975): 13.

3. Robert M. Grant, "The Sermon on the Mount in Early Christianity," *Semeia* 22/1 (1978): 215–29.

4. Dietrich Bonhoeffer, *The Cost of Discipleship*, trans. E. Mosbacher (New York: Harper and Row, 1970), 115.

5. Robert A. Guelich, "The Matthean Beatitudes: 'Entrance Requirements' or Eschatological Blessings?" *Journal of Biblical Literature* 95/3 (1976): 423 n. 46; see Harvey K. McArthur, *Understanding the Sermon on the Mount* (Westport, Conn.: Greenwood, 1978), 85.

6. Dale C. Allison Jr., "The Structure of the Sermon on the Mount," *Journal of Biblical Literature* 106/3 (1987): 423.

7. Ibid., 423–45.

8. Joachim Jeremias, *The Sermon on the Mount,* trans. Norman Perrin (Philadelphia: Fortress, 1963); see Alfred M. Perry, "The

Framework of the Sermon on the Mount," *Journal of Biblical Literature* 54 (1935): 23.

9. Ulrich Luz, *Matthew 1–7: A Continental Commentary*, trans. Wilhelm C. Linss (Minneapolis: Fortress, 1989), 212.

10. Hans Dieter Betz, *The Sermon on the Mount*, ed. Adela Yarbro Collins (Minneapolis: Fortress, 1995), 201.

11. Ibid., 423.

12. Ibid., 426.

13. Neil J. McEleney, "The Beatitudes of the Sermon on the Mount/Plain," *Catholic Biblical Quarterly* 43/1 (1981): 1–3; and C. M. Tuckett, "The Beatitudes: A Source-Critical Study," *Novum Testamentum* 25 (1983): 193–216.

14. J. Dupont, *Les Béatitudes: Le problème littéraire—Les deux versions du Sermon sur la montagne et des Béatitudes*, 2nd ed. (Paris: Gabalda, 1969), 1:250–64; Hubert Frankemölle, "Die Makarismen (Matt 5:1–12; Luke 6:20–23): Motive und Umfang der redaktionellen Komposition," *Biblische Zeitschrift* 15/1 (1971): 52–75; and N. Walter, "Die Bearbeitung der Seligpreisungen durch Matthäus," *Studia Evangelica* 4 (1968): 246–58.

15. See, for example, D. Flusser, "Blessed Are the Poor in Spirit," *Israel Exploration Journal* 10/1 (1960): 1–13; Erik Sjöberg, "Das Licht in dir: Zur Deutung von Matth. 6,22f Par.," in *Studia Theologica* (Lund, Sweden: Gleerup, 1952), 5:89–105; and Betz, *Essays on the Sermon on the Mount*, 71–87.

16. Betz, *Essays on the Sermon on the Mount*, 55–69; and Jeremias, *Sermon on the Mount*, 22–23.

17. Betz, *Sermon on the Mount*, 79.

18. Krister Stendahl, *The School of Matthew and Its Use in the Old Testament* (Ramsey, N.J.: Sigler, 1990), 35.

19. Daniel Patte, *Discipleship according to the Sermon on the Mount* (Valley Forge, Pa.: Trinity, 1996).

20. Karlmann Beyschlag, "Zur Geschichte der Bergpredigt in der alten Kirche," *Zeitschrift für Theologie und Kirche* 74 (1977): 291–322.

21. W. D. Davies, *The Sermon on the Mount* (Cambridge: Cambridge University Press, 1966), 6–27.

22. Jack D. Kingsbury, "The Place, Structure, and Meaning of the Sermon on the Mount within Matthew," *Interpretation* 41 (1987): 131–43.

23. T. W. Manson, *Ethics and the Gospel* (New York: Scribner's, 1960), 50.

24. Betz, *Essays on the Sermon on the Mount*, 19–22, 65–69; and Stendahl, *School of Matthew*, 13–35.

25. Betz, *Essays on the Sermon on the Mount*, 125–51; and David Hill, "False Prophets and Charismatics: Structure and Interpretation in Matthew 7:15–23," *Biblica* 57 (1976): 327–48.

26. Hans Windisch, *Der Sinn der Bergpredigt* (Leipzig: Hinrich, 1929).

27. This is the view of Robert Frost in McArthur, *Understanding the Sermon on the Mount*, 18.

28. David Greenwood, "Moral Obligation in the Sermon on the Mount," *Theological Studies* 31/2 (1970): 304; see 301–9.

29. J. Duncan M. Derrett, *The Ascetic Discourse: An Explanation of the Sermon on the Mount* (Eilsbrunn: Verlag für Bibel und Religion, 1989), 14.

30. Albert Schweitzer, *The Mystery of the Kingdom of God*, trans. W. Lourie (New York: Dodd, Mead, and Co., 1914), 97–99; see the views summarized by Jeremias, *Sermon on the Mount*, 1–12. McArthur identifies twelve ethical approaches in *Understanding the Sermon on the Mount*, 105–48; Georg Strecker discusses other types of exegesis in *The Sermon on the Mount: An Exegetical Commentary*, trans. O. C. Dean Jr. (Nashville: Abingdon, 1988), 15–23.

31. Jeremias, *Sermon on the Mount*, 1.

32. Irwin W. Batdorf, "How Shall We Interpret the Sermon on the Mount?" *Journal of Bible and Religion* 27 (1959): 213; see 211–17.

33. Warren S. Kissinger, *The Sermon on the Mount: A History of Interpretation and Bibliography*, American Theological Library Association Bibliography Series, no. 3 (Metuchen, N.J.: Scarecrow, 1975), xi.

34. Peter Stuhlmacher, "Jesu vollkommenes Gesetz der Freiheit," *Zeitschrift für Theologie und Kirche* 79 (1982): 283–322.

35. Luz, *Matthew 1–7*, 215.
36. Betz, *Sermon on the Mount*, 205.
37. Kingsbury, "Place, Structure, and Meaning," 136.
38. Jeremias, *Sermon on the Mount*, 30.
39. Ibid., 24–33.
40. Ibid., 26–29.

A Sacred Sermon

CHAPTER 3

THE TEMPLE CONTEXT AND UNITY OF THE SERMON AT THE TEMPLE

While the Sermon at the Temple adds to our understanding of the Sermon on the Mount in several ways, its most important contribution for me is how it unlocks the age-old mystery of the unity of the Sermon. The main reason that the Sermon on the Mount has remained a sealed text for most readers is the problem of discerning what holds it all together. Does the Sermon on the Mount have a single theme or logic, or is it a haphazard collection of disjointed sayings? To this question, the Sermon at the Temple offers clues to a most remarkable answer.

Simply stated, the Sermon at the Temple is a temple text. By "temple text" I mean one that contains allusions to the most sacred teachings and ordinances of the plan of salvation, things that are not to be shared indiscriminately. In addition, temple texts are often presented in or near a temple. They ordain or otherwise convey divine powers through symbolic or ceremonial means, presented together with commandments that are or will be received by sacred oaths that allow the recipient to stand ritually in the presence of God. Several such texts may be found in the scriptures, notably including Jacob's speech at the temple in the city of Nephi (Jacob 2–3) and King Benjamin's speech at the temple of Zarahemla (Mosiah 1–6).[1] The temple setting is an essential element in the fabric of these speeches.

The temple context likewise gives the Sermon its unity and, therefore, an exceptionally rich background against which it can be understood and appreciated. I therefore advance an interpretation of the Sermon that sees it not only as a moral or ethical discourse, but also in a sacred temple setting. I do not diminish the ethical and didactic functions of the Sermon; on the contrary, the moral force of the Sermon is only enhanced by the solemnity of a sacred setting, which encourages listeners to receive its values with deepened commitment.

This view of the Sermon, like any other interpretation, cannot be proved absolutely but can only be set forth for consideration, scrutiny, reflection, and comparison with other possible analyses. And like any other interpretation, my theory undoubtedly has its weaknesses along with its strengths (although, especially in dealing with a text so fundamental and so extensively studied as has been the Sermon on the Mount, telling those two apart is not always easy). Thus, if a reader knows of another interpretation that accounts better for every element in the text of the Sermon than does the approach I am suggesting, I would certainly encourage him or her to entertain that view. But of all the interpretations of the Sermon on the Mount that I have studied, I see the interpretation of it as a temple text as the most coherent and insightful. If my view on this is correct, it has far-reaching implications for how we should understand the Book of Mormon, the New Testament, and early Christianity, as well as the Latter-day Saint temple experience in general.

What follows, therefore, especially in chapter 4, is an interpretive essay. It is more of an exploration than a proof. Before getting to the individual details of that interpretation, I will first discuss in this chapter the general temple elements in the setting of the Sermon at the Temple, for they provide the basis for the ceremonial and covenantal interpretation that follows. This study is both exegetical, drawing meaning out of the text, and interpretive, bringing meaning to the text. I recognize that I offer a new Latter-day Saint interpretation of the Sermon at the Temple and Sermon on the Mount. I have tried to write just the way I think and feel about this material. I would not expect people unfamiliar with the Latter-day Saint temple ceremony or doctrine to see spontaneously or completely what I see. Still, I hope that any reader will be able to view and ponder the familiar landscape of the Sermon on the Mount from that fruitful vantage point, for the Sermon on the Mount can be understood by anyone as a text constituting or accompanying a covenant-making ritual.

Knowing something about the setting of a speech usually enhances our understanding of it. Where, when, and to whom a sermon is delivered often affects what its words intend, why the speaker selects certain phrases, and how its listeners and readers understand those words. Thus in search of greater understanding, biblical scholars have combed the scriptures for clues about the *Sitz im Leben,* or life setting, of many prophetic discourses and cultic expressions. This search has yielded valuable results in biblical studies. This is true also of research into the Book of Mormon.

In general, we know that we only see the tip of the iceberg in the scriptural record. When Jesus appeared to the Nephites in Bountiful in 3 Nephi, he said and did a great many more things than are recorded in 3 Nephi 11–28.

Recall that not "even a hundredth part of the things which Jesus did truly teach unto the people" are reported (3 Nephi 26:6; compare 17:16–17). Since the record is incomplete, readers must thoughtfully ponder the existing materials and carefully draw possible inferences from the known background information, trying to re-create a vivid picture of what transpired. The following background data can be gleaned from the text, all pointing in the direction of a sacred covenant-making context.

As will be seen, the Sermon at the Temple was definitely delivered at the temple, in connection with the issuing of commandments and the making of personal religious commitments, for the purpose of successfully withstanding the final day of judgment. It can probably also be associated with Jesus' other secret, sacred teachings, which, according to tradition, he delivered after his resurrection in Jerusalem. Moreover, all this may have transpired in Bountiful on a traditional holy day of convocation.

The Place

First, the Sermon at the Temple was given in a temple setting—Jesus spoke at the temple in Bountiful (see 3 Nephi 11:1). Since he could have chosen to appear anywhere he wanted (at the marketplace, at the town gate, or any number of other places where people traditionally congregated), and since we may assume that he chose to appear where he did for some reason, his appearance at the temple invites the idea that his words have something important to do with teachings and ordinances found within the temple.

It would not have surprised the Nephites that the Lord would choose to teach them at the temple. From what we know about their temples in the cities of Nephi and Zarahemla, these sacred places were obviously important religious and political centers for teaching (see Jacob 1:17; 2:2), as people were routinely taught within its walls (see Mosiah 2:7); for preaching (see Alma 16:13); for imparting the mysteries (see Mosiah 2:9; Alma 12:9; 13:3, 16); for gathering for ceremonies, coronations, obligatory annual festivals, ordinances, and covenant renewals (see 2 Nephi 6–10; Jacob 2–3; Mosiah 1–6); for making royal proclamations (see Mosiah 2:30; 7:17); and for sacrificing "according to the law of Moses" (Mosiah 2:3).[2] Nephite temples were patterned after the temple of Solomon (see 2 Nephi 5:16) in layout and in many of their functions, but they were not its equal in size or splendor.[3] What Jesus taught them in 3 Nephi 11:8 struck the Nephites as a marvelous transformation of their old temple order into a new one (see 3 Nephi 15:3).

Of course, some things taught in the temple may also be similar to things said outside the temple, and so it is not inconsistent with understanding the Sermon as an esoteric or sacred text that Jesus should also have spoken parts of it on other occasions scattered throughout his public ministry in Palestine (for example, Luke 6 and 11). At the temple in particular, however, a single, systematic presentation of the essence of the gospel is to be expected and is found.

What is stated so explicitly in the Book of Mormon can only be inferred by New Testament scholars of the Sermon on the Mount. The "mount" may have been a quiet hillside in Galilee, but it also may well symbolize the "mountain of the Lord," a scriptural expression referring to the temple mount in Jerusalem itself. The possible connection between the sermon mount and the temple mount has not escaped the notice of biblical scholars. In Israel, the temple became synonymous with God's mountain (for example, Isaiah 2:2 and Micah 4:1 call the temple in Jerusalem the mountain of the Lord's house). Just as God spoke to Moses from Mount Sinai, he continued to speak and act in Israel from his temple-palace on his chosen mount in Jerusalem, and the temple became "the architectural embodiment of the cosmic mountain."[4] Mount Zion in Jerusalem became the most important mountain in the world for the Jews, precisely because the temple was there. That low and undistinguished mound was nonetheless called, in the Bible, the world's tallest mountain, because God dwelt there.

That sacred place was thought to be protected from all evil enemies, who were powerless against that spiritual fortress, and life was said to flow forth from it in fertilizing streams. In this image of the temple, there came together for the ancient mind the linkage of things in heaven (where God sat upon his throne surrounded by his celestial council) and the earth, his footstool. It was a place set apart, and there the divine presence related to the world of man— ordering and stabilizing that world and acting upon it through natural and spiritual forces. At that point, the earth touched the divine sphere, just as mountain peaks reach the sky.[5] Thus, as W. D. Davies concludes, when Matthew reports that Jesus spoke from a mount in Matthew 5–7, "probably no simple geographic mountain is intended. The mountain is the mountain of the New Moses, the New Sinai."[6] Understood this way, we can imagine no more appropriate place than the temple as the site of the Sermon at the Temple. In the Sermon at the Temple, the temple imagery is no longer veiled.

The Covenant-Making Context

The temple in Israel has always been the shrine of the covenant, the home of the ark of the covenant, and the place where the covenant was renewed and perpetuated.

Similarly, the Sermon at the Temple was delivered in a covenanting context. Its teachings were expressly designed to prepare people to enter into a covenant with Christ, for at the end of the Sermon the people sacramentally promised and witnessed that they were willing to do what Jesus had commanded them that day, to take upon them his name, and to partake of emblems to help them remember that he had shown his body to them and shed his blood for them (see 3 Nephi 18:1–11).

Moreover, many aspects of the Sermon at the Temple deal overtly with gospel ordinances. For example, the Sermon on the Mount materials in the Sermon at the Temple appear immediately following Jesus' explanations of baptism, of the gift of the Holy Ghost, and of the rock upon which one should build, namely, the covenantal relationship formed by repentance, baptism, and becoming as a little child (see 3 Nephi 11:38–39).

To a Nephite, the invitation to "become as a little child" (3 Nephi 11:38) would probably have reminded them of their own traditional covenant ritual, for at least since the days of King Benjamin they understood that "because of the covenant" they had made that day at the temple of Zarahemla, they were "called the children of Christ, his sons, and his daughters" (Mosiah 5:7). Becoming a "child of God" may well also have reminded these people of the divine inheritance of the elect as the "sons and daughters" of God (see Mosiah 27:25–26)[7] who enter into God's presence, the theme on which the Sermon on the Mount also ends (see Matthew 7:21; 3 Nephi 14:21). By both beginning (see 3 Nephi 11:39–40) and ending (see 3 Nephi 14:24–15:1) with this theme of entering into God's presence and withstanding the final judgment, the Sermon at the Temple gives added emphasis to the establishment of a covenantal relationship as a main purpose of the entire Sermon.

The metaphorical explanation of how a person must build upon this rock, instead of upon a sandy foundation (see 3 Nephi 11:39–40; 14:24–27), brackets the words of the Sermon on the Mount that appear in 3 Nephi 12–14. The rock is the doctrine of repentance, baptism, and becoming God's child by spiritual rebirth. So we see that obedience to the commandments given in 3 Nephi 12–14 is not merely advisory or ethically desirable. Obedience to these stipulations is to be understood in connection with the making of a covenant through being baptized, receiving the gift of the Holy Ghost, and becoming a child of God fully blessed to inherit the Father's kingdom. These are among the requirements, or terms, of the covenant.

The Laws of the Covenant

Next, the teachings of the Sermon at the Temple were expressly given by way of commandment. Scholars have debated the basic character of the injunctions of the Sermon on the Mount: Do they form a new public order, a set of ideals, a set of commands, a law of the future kingdom but not of the present church, rules applicable only for a brief period before a shortly awaited coming of the kingdom, an existential claim of God on the individual, or general conditions of discipleship?[8] However, in one of the most significant sets of disclosures in the Sermon at the Temple, Jesus refers explicitly, emphatically, and consistently to his words as "commandments" (see 3 Nephi 12:19–20; 15:10; 18:10). They are necessary if the individual is to "come unto Jesus."

Just as the commands and laws promulgated in the making of the covenant at Sinai formed the basis of the

Old Testament, the commandments of the Sermon at the Temple form the basis of this new covenant (or "testament") of Jesus Christ. For this reason, seeing the Book of Mormon as "Another Testament of Jesus Christ" is all the more meaningful, since the word *testament* in Greek literally means "covenant, . . . usually [describing] the entire relationship between God and the children of Israel."[9] As "Another Testament" or "Covenant," the Book of Mormon indeed reestablishes a modern-day understanding of God's commandments, which his people agree to obey by covenant (see D&C 21:1). Accordingly, the Doctrine and Covenants admonishes the Saints to "remember the new covenant, even the Book of Mormon" (84:57).

Seeing the Sermon on the Mount essentially as a set of commandments is not the normal approach of most interpreters, though this view has been proposed by some ruthlessly honest commentators.[10] Interestingly, this view has the support of the early Christian Didache 1:5, 4:13, and 13:7. For example, this so-called Teaching of the Twelve Apostles tells early members of the church to follow Jesus' instructions to give generously (quoting Matthew 5:41–42) and thereby not to "abandon the *commandments* of the Lord"; and it promises that "blessed is the man who gives according to the *commandment*, for he is without blame" (Didache 1:5; italics added). The version of the Sermon in the Joseph Smith Translation, which I consider a third telling of the speech, reflects the same idea in yet another setting (see Matthew 5:21, 50 JST; 6:30 JST).

It remains unpopular, though, to see Jesus' words here as commandments figuring prominently in his doctrine of salvation. This is especially the case among many Protestant scholars who see salvation by grace as primary, if not exclusive. Thus Martin Luther relegated the epistle of James (which declares that "faith without *works* is dead," James 2:26; italics added) to the straw pile[11] and called the Sermon on the Mount "the devil's masterpiece"[12] because in his opinion "the devil so masterfully distorts and perverts *(verdrehet und verkeret)* Christ's true meaning through his Apostle [Matthew] especially in the fifth chapter."[13] To this, Hans Windisch answers, "Let us be honest; let us free ourselves once and for all from that idealistic and Paulinizing exegesis! We must admit that the ethic of the Sermon on the Mount is every bit as much an obedience-ethic as is the ethic of the Old Testament."[14] The Sermon at the Temple confirms this view, and more: Not only is the ethic of the Sermon on the Mount an obedience-ethic, the Sermon on the Mount also belongs every bit as much to the creation of a sacred covenant relationship between Jesus Christ and his people as did the Old Testament commandments, which belong unequivocally to the covenant made between Jehovah and the children of Israel (for example, Exodus 19–24).

The Sacred Teachings of the Forty-Day Literature

A further contextual clue is found in a disclosure by Jesus that may place the teachings of the Sermon in the same class as his postresurrectional teachings to his apostles in Palestine, namely, that of the so-called forty-day literature. After basically rehearsing the Sermon on the Mount to the Nephites, Jesus told them that they had now "heard the things which I taught *before I ascended* to my Father" (3 Nephi 15:1). This may mean that Jesus reiterated the Sermon on the Mount to his apostles once again after his death and before his ascension. Otherwise, he could have said to the Nephites, "Behold, ye have heard the things which I taught *during my ministry* in Palestine." I suspect that Jesus taught his disciples the Sermon, or parts of it, many times during his ministry (for example, when he began preaching in Galilee as reported in Matthew 5, when he sent out the apostles as missionaries as reported in Matthew 5 JST, and after his resurrection as reflected in 3 Nephi) and that his followers grew in understanding each time they heard it repeated.

Hugh Nibley, in several articles entitled "Christ among the Ruins," has demonstrated a number of connections between the Sermon at the Temple and the forty-day literature.[15] Jesus addressed most of his teachings at that time to his apostles and instructed them in their priesthood duties; told them about their premortal existence, the creation of the world, and the purpose of this life; and explained how they could return to the glory of God through obedience to ordinances for the salvation of the living and the dead. He blessed them with an initiation or endowment, generally called the "mysteries," which emphasized garments, marriage, and prayer circles.[16]

Correspondences between this body of literature and the Sermon at the Temple enhance the possibility that the Sermon on the Mount played a role in the Palestinian post-resurrectional ministry as well. For example, I think it likely that the references in the Sermon to "raiment" and "clothe" (see Matthew 6:25 and Matthew 6:28–30) had something to do with what Jesus gave the apostles who were instructed to remain in Jerusalem after the resurrection: "until ye be endued [i.e., endowed, or clothed] with power from on high" (Luke 24:49).[17] This view is corroborated by the fact that Joseph Smith taught that Peter and John received the "fulness of priesthood or the law of God" at the Mount of Transfiguration and that Peter "washed and anointed" all the apostles and received "the endowment" on the day of

Pentecost in Jerusalem.[18] President Heber C. Kimball similarly once remarked that Jesus had "inducted his Apostles into these ordinances [the holy endowments]."[19] Since the esoteric and postresurrectional teachings of Jesus in the forty-day literature contain, above all, hints concerning the sacred mysteries he taught to his apostles prior to his ascension,[20] the postresurrectional context of the Sermon at the Temple invites the conclusion that the materials in the Sermon on the Mount are also at home as part of the sacred or secret teachings of Jesus.

Preparing to Pass the Final Judgment

Another thing the Sermon accentuates is its orientation toward the day of judgment. Its concluding remarks expressly instruct the disciple how to pass through the final judgment, to enter into God's presence "in that day" (3 Nephi 14:21–23; Matthew 7:21–23). This purpose is stated more clearly in the Sermon at the Temple than in the Sermon on the Mount. In the Book of Mormon, Jesus expressly states that the purpose of the Sermon is to assist the disciple in surviving the eschatological day of judgment: "Whoso remembereth these sayings of mine and doeth them, him will I raise up at the last day" (3 Nephi 15:1). The purpose of this statement in the Sermon at the Temple is to encourage remembrance and to stimulate the people to keep the commandments that the Lord has given.

Elsewhere in the Book of Mormon, the first thing done after a covenant ceremony is, likewise, to appoint priests to exhort the people to remember their promises so they may withstand God's day of judgment (see Mosiah 6:1–3; compare 2 Nephi 9:52). The disciple's salvation turns on remembering and doing the things taught in the Sermon. Therefore, one should not think of the standards set forth in the Sermon as unreachable ideals. Observing this specific set of requirements is essential to eternal exaltation, for only thereby can the Lord raise us up at the last day. In this way, the speech embraces both this-worldly and otherworldly concerns. Its requirements impose standards of conduct upon ethical human behavior in this world, but at the same time it reveals the principles whereby the final judgment will proceed, which principles, if followed, will enable a person to survive the final judgment in the next world.

More Than Words Alone

Evidently the presentation of the Sermon at the Temple involved more than words alone. The Nephites heard many things, but they also saw things presented in an unusually powerful way (for example, 3 Nephi 11:15). The amazed reaction of the righteous Nephites may indicate this. Even though they had long anticipated that the law of Moses would be superseded upon the coming of the Messiah, they were astonished at what Jesus taught on this occasion. They "marveled" and "wondered" (3 Nephi 15:2). The apostles in Galilee were likewise "astonished at his doctrine: for he taught them as *one* having authority" (Matthew 7:28–29; italics added). The authority Jesus made evident contributed significantly to their astonishment.

While the amazed reaction of the Nephites can be understood in several ways, it seems possible to me that it had something to do with the idea that what Jesus said and did somehow went beyond mere words or conventional discourse. Jesus presented things to these audiences in a marvelous way. This was not an ordinary lecture or a simple, generic moral sermon. His presentation was far different from the logical thinking of the scribes, which was well-known among the Jews; it also extended beyond the teaching of high moral standards, which had been common among the Nephites throughout their history. Included among the Nephite doctrines had always been powerful prohibitions against disputation, anger, strife, evil thoughts, greed, pride, and neglect of the poor. Why then should similar teachings of Jesus at the temple produce such an amazed reaction? It would seem that their amazement would have something to do with *how* the holy and glorified Jesus taught the principles, not just *what* he taught. The presentation must have been powerful, not just with dynamic intonation or forcefulness, but particularly with divine authority *(exousia)*.

A Traditional Temple Occasion

Finally, one may wonder if Jesus appeared to the Nephites at an auspicious time or on a ritually significant occasion. The record leaves it unclear exactly when Jesus appeared at the temple in Bountiful. Was it shortly after Jesus' death and resurrection at the beginning of the Nephite thirty-fourth year, "soon after the ascension of Christ into heaven" (3 Nephi 10:18), or was it later in that year? Kent Brown and John Tvedtnes have both skillfully presented alternative arguments on this matter. The main question is how to understand the phrase "in the *ending* of the thirty and fourth year" that introduces the verse of 3 Nephi 10:18, and none of the proposed interpretations are conclusive.[21] There are good reasons to think that Christ's appearance did not occur immediately after his resurrection, yet there are equally ample reasons for thinking that it was not at the very end of the thirty-fourth year either.

In light of the inconclusiveness and ambiguity here, it may be more fruitful to consider *what kind* of a gathering was likely involved instead of asking how long after the crucifixion Jesus' appearance in Bountiful was. Had the great multitude gathered together simply for an emergency civilian meeting, or had they assembled for another purpose? Since the Nephites had "gathered together . . . round about the temple" (3 Nephi 11:1) with "men, women, and children" (3 Nephi 17:25), one is reminded of King Benjamin's great covenant-renewal convocation assembly, when all his people gathered "round about" the temple, every man with his family in a traditional Feast of Tabernacles fashion (Mosiah 2:5; compare Deuteronomy 31:9–13)[22] and had "the mysteries of God . . . unfolded to [their] view" (Mosiah 2:9).

Also, since the size of the crowd in 3 Nephi did not increase as the day went on, apparently all these Nephites had gathered for a specific purpose at the beginning of that day. Thus it seems likely that all the people in Bountiful had come to the temple on a scheduled religious festival or holy day. It is evident that these people would have been strict to observe their traditional religious laws, for they were among "the more righteous part of the people" (3 Nephi 10:12; compare 9:13), the wicked having been destroyed. Moreover, the fact that women and children were present supports the idea that their meeting was not simply an emergency session of the city elders to consider the mundane needs for construction repairs and debris removal.[23] Although we cannot be sure what festival it might have been, it seems likely to me that some holy festival was involved at the time the Nephites gathered in 3 Nephi.

Traditionally, all Israelites (and hence Nephites) were instructed to gather at the temple three appointed times each year, namely, for the solemn feasts of Passover, Pentecost, and Tabernacles: "Three times in the year all thy males shall appear before the Lord God" (Exodus 23:17); and "at the end of *every* seven years, . . . in the feast of tabernacles, . . . all Israel [must] come to appear before the Lord thy God" at the temple, "men, and women, and children" (Deuteronomy 31:10–12).

Particularly important for the celebration of the law of Moses and for the renewal of the covenant of Israel with the Lord were two feasts, one called Shavuot in Hebrew (Pentecost in Greek), which came in June fifty days after Passover, and the other called Tabernacles, which followed closely after the Day of Atonement in the fall. These two festivals were each celebrated over a period of seven days, probably reminiscent of the seven days of the Exodus from Egypt and the seven periods of the creation.[24] There is considerable circumstantial evidence that the Nephites, who were strict in their observance of the law of Moses "in all things" (2 Nephi 5:10; see Jarom 1:5; Alma 30:3; 3 Nephi 1:24), observed these essential Israelite festivals.[25] The purposes and themes of these ritual days related closely to covenant-making, law-giving, and prophetic instruction, which are also dominant themes in the Sermon at the Temple.

If the Nephites were assembled on one of these traditional holy days sometime after the signs of Jesus' death had been given, they probably would have wondered what they should do next. We know that they observed the law of Moses until Jesus proclaimed its fulfillment (see 3 Nephi 1:24–25; 15:2–8), but while Jesus' voice, which was heard out of the darkness, had announced the end of the Mosaic law at the time of his death (see 3 Nephi 9:17), no new instructions had yet been given to the Nephites about the law that was to take its place. Indeed, when Jesus spoke to the Nephites in person at the temple of Bountiful, he reiterated the fact that the old law had been fulfilled (see 3 Nephi 12:18; 15:4), but they were still confused in particular about what he meant by this (see 3 Nephi 15:2–3). They "wondered what he would [have them do] concerning the law of Moses" (3 Nephi 15:2). It was inevitable that, sooner or later, as they gathered at their temple, they would have wondered if it was still appropriate for them to continue using their old ritual order. Since it seems unlikely that they would have gone twelve months without addressing the implications of Christ's death for the continuation of their public rites and temple practices, this suggests that his appearance was probably not too long after his crucifixion and ascension.

We do not know how the Nephite ritual calendar in Bountiful related to the Israelite calendar in Jerusalem, for there had been no contact between the two for over six hundred years. It is impossible to determine which of the traditional festivals would have been observed in Bountiful in the months following Jesus' crucifixion. Thus, it could have been around the Nephite time of Passover when Jesus appeared, as John Tvedtnes has suggested, or just before their New Year celebrations, as Kent Brown has proposed. Indeed, a year-rite gathering would make good sense of the occasion in 3 Nephi 11, for at such assemblages kings were typically crowned, laws promulgated, and covenants made or renewed.

If one can assume, however, that the two ritual calendars had not grown too far apart, the feast of Shavuot would have been celebrated in Bountiful a few months after the Passover crucifixion and shortly after the best-known ascension of Jesus from Jerusalem, reported in Acts 1:9–11. Such a scenario would thus make good sense of the reference in 3 Nephi 10:18 to Christ's appearing in Bountiful "soon after" his ascension.[26]

Moreover, that date is close enough after the events of the destruction that the people could still "marvel" and "wonder" about the whole situation as they conversed about Christ and the signs of his death (see 3 Nephi 11:1–2). Such a date accommodates most of the information Kent Brown has gathered about the settled condition of the people at the time of Jesus' appearance, and it also solves John Tvedtnes's major problem by allowing time for records to have been kept between the time of the crucifixion and the appearance in Bountiful. The tension between the words "soon after the ascension" and the phrase "in the ending of the thirty and fourth year" (3 Nephi 10:18) remains unresolved, however, under any theory.

The hypothesis that Christ appeared at the feast of Shavuot in Bountiful also raises many interesting implications. No occasion more relevant than Shavuot can be imagined for the day on which to explain the fulfillment of the old law and the issuance of the new. According to recent scholarship, ancient Israelites may have celebrated, as part of Shavuot, the giving of the law to Moses and the revelation of the Ten Commandments on Mount Sinai.[27] That revelation was received about fifty days after the Exodus from Egypt ("in the third month," Exodus 19:1), although it is uncertain when the similar dates of this theophany and of the early summer festival of Shavuot became associated. The obvious connections between three of the Ten Commandments in Exodus 20 and Jesus' teachings about murder, adultery, and oaths in Matthew 5 and 3 Nephi 12 afford another possible link between the day on which the Nephites would have traditionally celebrated the giving of the Ten Commandments and the time when Jesus taught the new understanding of those very commandments.

In addition, Shavuot was a day for remembering great spiritual manifestations. Thus, the Holy Ghost was manifest as tongues of fire to the Saints gathered for Pentecost (the Greek name for Shavuot) that same year in Jerusalem (see Acts 2:1–4). Shavuot came to be associated with the day on which the Lord came down in smoke and flame on Mount Sinai and appeared to Moses on behalf of the host of Israel. Now Jesus had come down and appeared to all gathered in Bountiful. As the face of Moses had shined radiantly on Sinai, so "the light of [Christ's] countenance did shine upon [his disciples], and behold they were as white as the countenance and also the garments of Jesus" (3 Nephi 19:25).[28] Indeed, the ancient model for Shavuot was the three-day ritual the Israelites observed before the law was given at Sinai (see Exodus 19:15), and Jesus similarly "did teach the [Nephites] for the space of three days" (3 Nephi 26:13; see 3 Nephi 11:1–8; 19:4–15), after which subsequent appearances followed (see 3 Nephi 26:13; 27:2). Thus, while the suggestion that Jesus appeared at Bountiful on Shavuot or any other particular holy day remains tentative, the choice of Shavuot is attractive and symbolically meaningful.

In any event, as the Nephites had washed and presented themselves ritually clean before the Lord at the temple, the question must have forcefully arisen again, as it had a generation earlier when the sign of Jesus' birth was seen (see 3 Nephi 1:24), asking what priestly functions this branch of Israel should continue to perform at its temple now that Jesus had lived and died. Indeed, their conversation "about this Jesus Christ, of whom the sign had been given concerning his death" (3 Nephi 11:2) immediately preceded, if not precipitated, the marvelous manifestation that they experienced.

What Jesus then taught them would have been understood, implicitly if not explicitly, as the new doctrines and ordinances the Nephites were to observe in their temples from that point forward in place of their old temple rituals and performances. Those earlier Nephite ordinances, as I have discussed elsewhere,[29] were after the order of Melchizedek and were given symbolically, "in a manner that thereby the people might know in what manner to look forward to [Christ] for redemption" (Alma 13:2; see v. 16). The new order no longer looked forward to Christ but rather celebrated and looked back on the fulfillment of his atoning sacrifice (see 3 Nephi 11:11).

All this combines to indicate that the Sermon at the Temple is no simple ethical or abstract doctrinal discourse. It is rooted in and around the temple and its covenants and commandments. It prepared those righteous participants to pass successfully by the judgments of God. It instructed them in the new ordinances of the priesthood in a wondrous and marvelous way. Accordingly, we turn our attention next toward an understanding of the possible ritual elements in the Sermon at the Temple.

Notes

1. Discussed in John W. Welch, "The Temple in the Book of Mormon: The Temples at the Cities of Nephi, Zarahemla, and Bountiful," in *Temples of the Ancient World: Ritual and Symbolism,* ed. Donald W. Parry (Salt Lake City: Deseret Book and FARMS, 1994), 297–387. See several sections or chapters in *King Benjamin's Speech: "That Ye May Learn Wisdom,"* ed. John W. Welch and Stephen D. Ricks (Provo, Utah: FARMS, 1998).

2. Discussed extensively in Welch, "Temple in the Book of Mormon."

3. Ibid., 323–26.

4. John M. Lundquist, "What Is a Temple? A Preliminary Typology," in *The Quest for the Kingdom of God: Studies in Honor of George E. Mendenhall*, ed. H. B. Huffmon et al. (Winona Lake, Ind.: Eisenbrauns, 1983), 207; see Donald W. Parry, "Sinai as Sanctuary and Mountain of God," in *By Study and Also by Faith: Essays in Honor of Hugh W. Nibley*, ed. John M. Lundquist and Stephen D. Ricks (Salt Lake City: Deseret Book and FARMS, 1990), 1:482–500.

5. Richard J. Clifford, *The Cosmic Mountain in Canaan and the Old Testament* (Cambridge: Harvard University Press, 1972), 7–8.

6. W. D. Davies, *The Sermon on the Mount* (Cambridge: Cambridge University Press, 1966), 17, acknowledges that "not all scholars accept this view, but it is not to be dismissed cavalierly." Some scholars suggest that there are ten beatitudes, echoing the Ten Commandments of the covenant at Sinai. Hans Dieter Betz, *The Sermon on the Mount*, ed. Adela Yarbro Collins (Minneapolis: Fortress, 1995), 109.

7. H. Riesenfeld, "Guds söner och de heligas församling" (Sons of God and the congregation of the Holy Ones), *Svensk Exegetisk Arsbok* 41–42 (1976–77): 179–88.

8. B. Friesen, "Approaches to the Interpretation and Application of the Sermon on the Mount," *Direction* 10 (1981): 19–25; and Joachim Jeremias, *The Sermon on the Mount*, trans. Norman Perrin (Philadelphia: Fortress, 1963), 1–12.

9. John W. Welch, "Word Studies—Diatheke—Testament," *Newsletter of the Religious Studies Center of Brigham Young University* (June 1987): 5; also in *Ensign*, January 1995, 29.

10. Hans Windisch, *Der Sinn der Bergpredigt* (Leipzig: Heinrichs Verlag, 1929), discussed in Jeremias, *Sermon on the Mount*, 2. See Betz, *Sermon on the Mount*, 187; and Ulrich Luz, *Matthew 1–7: A Continental Commentary*, trans. Wilhelm C. Linss (Minneapolis: Fortress, 1989), 208.

11. Martin Luther called the Epistle of James "ein rechte stroern Epistel" (a right strawy epistle) because it has "no Gospel quality to it." *D. Martin Luthers Werke* (Weimar: Böhlaus, 1906), 6:10.

12. "Das heißt ein Meister Stuck des Teuffels [*sic*]." Ibid., 32:300.

13. Ibid.

14. As paraphrased by Jeremias, *Sermon on the Mount*, 2.

15. Hugh W. Nibley, "Christ among the Ruins," in *Book of Mormon Authorship*, ed. Noel B. Reynolds (Provo, Utah: BYU Religious Studies Center, 1982), 121–41; also in *Ensign*, July 1983, 14–19; reprinted in *The Prophetic Book of Mormon*, ed. John W. Welch (Salt Lake City: Deseret Book and FARMS, 1989), 407–34.

16. Ibid.; see Hugh W. Nibley, "Evangelium Quadraginta Dierum: The Forty-Day Mission of Christ—the Forgotten Heritage," in *Mormonism and Early Christianity* (Salt Lake City: Deseret Book and FARMS, 1987), 10–44; see also John Gee, "Forty-Day Ministry and Other Post-Resurrection Appearances of Jesus Christ," in *Encyclopedia of Mormonism*, 2:734–36.

17. The Greek word *enduō* means "to dress, to clothe someone" or to take on "characteristics, virtues, intentions." For further discussion, see John W. Welch, "Enduō," *Newsletter of the Religious Studies Center of Brigham Young University* (January 1990): 2; reprinted in *Ensign*, April 1993, 29.

18. Andrew F. Ehat and Lyndon W. Cook, *The Words of Joseph Smith* (Provo, Utah: BYU Religious Studies Center, 1980), 211, 246, 285 n. 8, 331; see *Teachings of the Prophet Joseph Smith*, comp. Joseph Fielding Smith (Salt Lake City: Deseret Book, 1979), 158.

19. Heber C. Kimball, in *Journal of Discourses*, 10:241. Robert J. Matthews concludes that this occurred "after the Savior's resurrection" in his *A Sure Foundation: Answers to Difficult Gospel Questions* (Salt Lake City: Deseret Book, 1988), 112.

20. Nibley, "Evangelium Quadraginta Dierum."

21. For detailed discussions of the chronological issues, see S. Kent Brown and John A. Tvedtnes, "When Did Jesus Appear to the Nephites in Bountiful?" with an introduction by John W.

Welch (FARMS, 1989); and S. Kent Brown, *From Jerusalem to Zarahemla* (Provo, Utah: BYU Religious Studies Center, 1998), 146–56.

22. Terrence L. Szink and John W. Welch, "King Benjamin's Speech in the Context of Ancient Israelite Festivals," in *King Benjamin's Speech*, 147–223.

23. Although John A. Tvedtnes, "The Timing of Christ's Appearance to the Nephites," in Brown and Tvedtnes, "When Did Jesus Appear to the Nephites in Bountiful?" asserts that "the gathering of the people at the temple is not evidence that it was festival-time," his reasons for this are not persuasive to me. He claims that the multitude did not gather until the word had gone out that Jesus would appear again on the morrow (see 3 Nephi 19:2), but the crowd is called "a great multitude" even on the first day (3 Nephi 11:1). Those who came for the second day apparently had to travel much of the night to be there (see 3 Nephi 19:3), so their absence on the first day should not preclude it from being considered a festival day observed by those living in the temple-city of Bountiful.

24. Abraham Bloch, *The Biblical and Historical Background of the Jewish Holy Days* (New York: KTAV, 1978), 182.

25. Regarding these holy convocations at the temple that the law of Moses required, see Exodus 23:14–19. Concerning the Book of Mormon, see Szink and Welch, "King Benjamin's Speech in the Context of Ancient Israelite Festivals"; see also FARMS Updates, "The Sons of the Passover," August 1984, and "Abinadi and Pentecost," September 1985, reprinted in *Reexploring the Book of Mormon*, ed. John W. Welch (Salt Lake City: Deseret Book and FARMS, 1992), 196–98, 135–38. For a discussion of the observance of the law of Moses by the Nephites up until the time when that law was fulfilled by the atonement of Christ, see Welch, "Temple in the Book of Mormon," 301–19.

26. John L. Sorenson notes in his study of seasonality in Book of Mormon warfare, however, that if the Nephites celebrated the grain harvest aspect of Shavuot and held this festival fifty days after the grain harvest in Mesoamerica, its date in the New World

would have been sometime in December. See "Seasonality of Warfare in the Book of Mormon and in Mesoamerica," in *Warfare in the Book of Mormon,* ed. Stephen D. Ricks and William J. Hamblin (Salt Lake City: Deseret Book and FARMS, 1990), 445–77.

27. Moshe Weinfeld, "The Decalogue: Its Significance, Uniqueness, and Place in Israel's Tradition," in *Religion and Law: Biblical-Judaic and Islamic Perspectives,* ed. Edwin R. Firmage, Bernard G. Weiss and John W. Welch (Winona Lake, Ind.: Eisenbrauns, 1990), 38–47.

28. I thank my student Daniel Belnap for drawing this connection to my attention.

29. John W. Welch, "The Melchizedek Materials in Alma 13:13–19," in *By Study and Also by Faith,* 2:238–72.

CHAPTER 4

TOWARD AN UNDERSTANDING OF THE SERMON AS AN ANCIENT TEMPLE TEXT

In the limited time Jesus spent with the Nephites, he taught them things of ultimate importance. He gave them a series of commandments, which they then agreed to obey. They were solemnly admonished to "keep these sayings" so that they would "come not under condemnation; for wo unto him whom the Father condemneth" (3 Nephi 18:33). This was serious, sacred business. Although the Savior forbade the disciples to write or speak some of the things they saw and heard (see 3 Nephi 26:18), and while a person can interpret this Christophany in many ways, the recorded material lends itself readily to a ritual or ceremonial understanding. The types of actions, pronouncements, instructions, roles, symbols, images, and injunctions found in the Sermon at the Temple are ritually repeatable. They enshrine and accentuate the ethical components of Jesus' message. By considering the sequence and substance of these materials, we can visualize the outlines—sometimes faintly, other times quite distinctly—of the solemn, ceremony-like experience Jesus presented to those faithful followers he met at the temple.

The temple setting of the Sermon, accordingly, invites us to examine each of its momentous elements with a temple context in mind. In the following pages, I shall explore some fifty elements of the Sermon that I have identified—examining in particular their possible roles in establishing or preparing to establish covenant relationships between God and his people—and consider the capacity of those elements to be ritualized. For corroboration and elaboration, I draw upon a wide range of various ritual aspects of early Christianity, Near Eastern temple typology, continuities between Jesus' Sermon and Israelite temple practices or cultic texts, and modern Latter-day scriptures and teachings. These supplemental points, however, are secondary. The primary objective is to move toward an understanding of the Sermon at the Temple itself and the underlying experience that progressively ties all of its parts together.

A Thrice-Repeated Announcement from Above

The Sermon at the Temple began with a soft, small, piercing voice speaking out of heaven (see 3 Nephi 11:3–5). At first the people could not understand it, but the voice repeated exactly the same announcement three times,[1] and the words were better comprehended as they were repeated. At first, this small piercing voice may have sounded faint and broken; something like this perhaps: "Behold . . . Son, . . . well pleased, in whom I have glorified . . . hear . . ." (3 Nephi 11:7), but the words increased in clarity and were fully understood the last time they were repeated.

Opening the Ears and Eyes

Total silence fell upon the people as they turned their attention toward the sound. On the third hearing of the voice, the people are said to have opened "their ears to hear it; and their eyes were towards the sound thereof; and they did look steadfastly towards heaven, from whence the sound came" (3 Nephi 11:5). Texts referring to the opening of the ears and eyes can mark the beginning of a ritual ceremony (as Mosiah 2:9 expressly does) or the convocation of a solemn assembly (see Joel 1:2; 2:15–16) and can symbolize the commencement of an opening of the mysteries and a deeper understanding of what is truly being said and done.

When the voice came the third time, "they did understand the voice" (3 Nephi 11:6). The effect was to rivet the attention of the crowd on the impending proceedings, which they turned to in awe and silence (3 Nephi 11:8). A formal call to attention serving a comparable function, the *silentium*, typically opened many solemn Old World religious assemblies.[2] Opening the eyes and ears of the people may be compared functionally to an early Christian purificatory anointing of the eyes and ears "that [one] might receive hearing ears of the mysteries of God."[3] Not all people are intended to hear and know the mysteries of God, only those who have ears to hear and eyes to see. For this reason, Jesus spoke parables to the masses in Palestine; yet to his disciples Jesus said that it was given "to know the mysteries of the kingdom of heaven. . . . Blessed are your eyes, for they see: and your ears, for they hear" (Matthew 13:11, 16). Their eyes and ears were opened.

Delegation of Duty by the Father to the Son

The people then understood the words of the Father as he introduced the Son: "Behold my Beloved Son, in whom I am well pleased, in whom I have glorified my name— hear ye him" (3 Nephi 11:7). The Father himself does not personally minister to beings on earth, but does all things by sending the Son as his representative. The Son has the obligation to carry out his stewardship, and on the completion of his assignment, he returns and reports to the Father. Thus, at the conclusion of the Sermon at the Temple, Jesus said, "Now I go unto the Father, because it is expedient that I should go unto the Father for your sakes" (3 Nephi 18:35), whereupon Jesus "ascended into heaven," as the disciples bore record (3 Nephi 18:39).

Coming Down in White Robes

After the Father's words, Jesus then appeared, "descending out of heaven . . . clothed in a white robe" (3 Nephi 11:8). Dramatically, he came down with teachings and instructions from above. Moreover, he came robed in white garments or robes worthy of mention, but not receiving further description at this time—elements rich with possible ritual implementation and significance.[4] The robes are later described as being exceedingly white: "there could be nothing upon earth so white as the whiteness thereof" (3 Nephi 19:25).

Silence

While Jesus came down, the mouths of the people remained shut: "They durst not open their mouths, even one to another, and wist not what it meant" (3 Nephi 11:8). I assume that they remained in this state of profound silence, deep respect, reverence, and awe for several hours, as the two thousand five hundred people (see 3 Nephi 17:25) present stepped forward, one at a time, to touch their Lord (see 3 Nephi 17:25).

Identification by Marks on the Hand

At first the people were confused and cautious, not knowing who had appeared to them. Even though the words of the Father had proclaimed the Son, the people still "thought it was an angel that had appeared unto them" (3 Nephi 11:8). In Hebrew *(mal'āk)*, and also in Greek *(aggelos)*, the word for *angel* and *messenger* is one and the same. Apparently the people were not sure whether they had been greeted by a messenger of light, or perhaps even of darkness, or by the Lord himself.

That confusion was removed only as Jesus "stretched forth his hand" and identified himself, saying, "I am Jesus Christ, whom the prophets testified shall come into the world" (3 Nephi 11:9–10). By these words and the extension of his hands, the people recognized him as the truest messenger, the Lord and Savior Jesus Christ, as had been prophesied. Old Testament prophets had said that the Lord would be known by the marks in his hands: "They shall look upon me whom they have pierced. . . . And one shall say unto him, What are these wounds in thine hands? Then he shall answer, Those with which I was wounded in the house of my friends" (Zechariah 12:10; 13:6). Early Christians also said, in the words of one of the earliest Syriac hymns (ca. A.D. 100), "I extended my hands and approached my Lord, for the expansion of my hands is His sign" (*Odes of Solomon* 42:1).

Falling Down

Upon recognizing the divine visitor as the Lord who had taken upon himself the sins of the world, the multitude "fell to the earth" (3 Nephi 11:12). Bowing down—or more dramatically, full prostration—is not only an instinctive response when coming into the presence of a superior being, but it is also a common element of ritual. Collective group prostration, particularly in a temple context, was more than simply a reaction of people being overcome. It had long been a customary part of the Nephite covenant-making ceremony (see Mosiah 4:1).

Personally Touching the Wounds

The Lord then asked all the people to "arise and come forth . . . that ye may thrust your hands into my side, and also that ye may feel the prints of the nails in my hands and in my feet" (3 Nephi 11:14). All the people then went forth and placed their hands into his side and felt the nail prints in his hands and in his feet, "and did see with their eyes and did feel with their hands, and did know of a surety and did bear record" (3 Nephi 11:15). Thus their knowledge was made sure that he was "the God of Israel, and the God of the whole earth, . . . slain for the sins of the world" (3 Nephi 11:14). They personally felt the signs of his suffering and death. Since two thousand five hundred souls were present at this assembly, no more than a brief contact would have been possible under normal circumstances.

Hosanna Shout and Falling Down a Second Time

The experience continued when, in unison, the company sang out with one accord, "Hosanna! Blessed be the name of the Most High God!" (3 Nephi 11:17), reminiscent of Melchizedek's blessing of Abraham, "Blessed be the most high God" (Genesis 14:20). At this point their mouths were truly opened.[5]

The Hosanna Shout, meaning "Save Now," is puzzling to scholars. It has been alternatively interpreted as an intercessory prayer addressed to God, asking that assistance be given "to his Messiah," or as a "royal supplication addressed to the Messiah," or as "a call of triumphant joy," sometimes chanted as *lulav* branches were waved in the air.[6] "Whatever was the original Hebrew or Aramaic word for Hosanna, it must have conveyed a particular Messianic significance,"[7] associated by some with the anticipated Messianic cleansing of the temple.[8]

The origins of the Hosanna Shout are traceable at least as far back as the familiar *Hallel*, an ancient festival hymn that was especially at home in the temple of Jerusalem: "Save now [Hosanna], I beseech thee, O Lord: O Lord, I beseech thee, send now prosperity. Blessed be he that cometh in the name of the Lord: we have blessed you out of the house of the Lord" (Psalm 118:25–26). This hymn was well-known in ancient Israel, being sung in postbiblical Judaism on the high holy days; it was also used as a liturgical cry in the worship of the early Christian community, particularly at the sacrament of the Lord's supper.[9] Latter-day Saints use the Hosanna Shout at temple dedications.[10] Its aptness to the occasion of novation at the temple in Bountiful is evident. Their praise no longer included psalmodic words directed to the one "who shall come," because now he had come. The fact that the people all cried out in unison indicates that they spontaneously broke forth with a familiar liturgical expression. They then fell down again at Jesus' feet and worshipped him (see 3 Nephi 11:17).

Ordination to the Priesthood

Next, ordaining men to the priesthood in this new dispensation was necessary. Jesus first ordained Nephi, giving him the authority that Latter-day Saints normally associate with the Aaronic Priesthood, namely, the power to baptize the people. The Lord asked him to arise and come forth; he went forth and bowed himself before the Lord and kissed Jesus' feet, whereupon the Lord commanded him to arise. Nephi then arose and stood before Jesus, who ordained him and gave him "power [to] baptize this people when [the Lord] again ascended into heaven" (3 Nephi 11:21). In addition, the Lord called eleven others and similarly ordained them (see 3 Nephi 11:22; 19:4). At the end of the day Jesus would give these twelve the "power to give the Holy Ghost" (3 Nephi 18:37), an authority allowing them to officiate in the higher order of the Melchizedek Priesthood.

Baptism Explained

Jesus then explained the manner of baptism, complete with the specific words of the baptismal prayer, calling the candidate by his own given name (see 3 Nephi 11:23–28). This washing and purifying ordinance stands in this sequence as a necessary first step for every soul desiring to move forward on the path into the kingdom of God. These baptisms were not carried out immediately, but they were performed pursuant to these instructions at the beginning of the next day (see 3 Nephi 19:10–13). Perhaps those baptisms were viewed, among other things, as taking the place of the traditional ceremonial washings that Israelites in Jerusalem practiced before coming up to the temple and that are precedented as early as Exodus 19:10 and Psalm 24:4.

Assuring the Absence of Evil

Jesus next took steps to assure that there were no disputations, contentions, or any influences of the devil among this people (see 3 Nephi 11:28–30). The Sermon at the Temple calls these the influences "of the devil, who is the father of contention" (3 Nephi 11:29). With a simple authoritative statement, Jesus asserted that "such things should be done away" (3 Nephi 11:30). This declaration fills the role of warding off the presence or influence of Satan—a standard element in ritual drama[11]—and I assume that with this Lucifer was assuredly dismissed and for this reason his presence is not indicated again in the Sermon. One of the purposes of Jesus' teaching is to give the righteous the ability to be delivered "from evil," as the Lord's Prayer requests later in the Sermon (see 3 Nephi 13:12). The Greek for this can be read, "deliver us from the Evil One" (see Matthew 6:13). Another power apparently given to the righteous is the ability to "cast out devils" (3 Nephi 14:22), although the Sermon warns that some will exercise this power without authority.

Witnesses Invoked

Jesus then identified three witnesses who would bear record of his doctrine. On this unique occasion, Jesus, God the Father, and the Holy Ghost bore record of the doctrine and of one another (see 3 Nephi 11:35–36). Filling the role of witnesses, necessary in the covenantal process, as is familiar from several other occurrences in scripture (see, for example, Genesis 18:2; Deuteronomy 4:26; 19:15; Joshua 24:22; 2 Nephi 11:3; Mosiah 2:14), these three stand together at the commencement of this dispensation of the new law to the Nephites to witness of the gospel. Among their other functions, witnesses are necessary in the gospel of Jesus Christ to authenticate important ordinances, rites, and ceremonies.[12]

Teaching the Gospel

Having dispelled evil, Jesus' next concern was that all be taught his true gospel. Twice he defined his doctrine in exactly the same terms. It is the gospel of repentance, baptism, and becoming as a little child through which Jesus promises the gift of the Holy Ghost: "Again I say unto you, ye must repent, and become as a little child, and be baptized in my name, or ye can in nowise receive these things. And again I say unto you, ye must repent, and be baptized in my name, and become as a little child, or ye can in nowise inherit the kingdom of God" (3 Nephi 11:37–38). Whoever believes these things and does them, "unto him will the Father bear record of me, for he will visit him with fire and with the Holy Ghost" (3 Nephi 11:35). This doctrine is essential (see 3 Nephi 11:34, 40). Jesus then commanded his ordained disciples to "go forth unto this people, and declare the words which [he had] spoken, unto the ends of the earth" (3 Nephi 11:41). The clear intention is that all people should have an opportunity to receive these things, or, in other words, that the gospel be received by all of Adam's posterity.

Commending His Disciples unto the People

Jesus then turned to the multitude and blessed them, admonishing them to give strict heed to the words of the twelve: "He stretched forth his hand unto the multitude, and cried unto them, saying: Blessed are ye if ye shall give heed unto the words of these twelve whom I have chosen from among you to minister unto you, and to be your servants," and Jesus certified that he had "given [them] power" (3 Nephi 12:1). He blessed all who would believe their instruction and accept the people's words (compare John 17), provided they entered into the covenant of baptism, received the Holy Ghost, and obtained remission of their sins (see 3 Nephi 12:2).

Blessings Promised

Several promised blessings, well-known as the Beatitudes, were then bestowed upon all the people (see 3 Nephi 12:3–12). The repetition of the word *all* and the second person *you* or *ye* in 3 Nephi 12:1–2, 12 in the Book of Mormon Beatitudes emphasizes the fact that the blessings and promises therein were bestowed upon each individual present there. As candidates for Zion, they are typified as humble, compassionate, long-suffering peacemakers, who love righteousness, who will see God's face, and who will be his eternal children:

> Yea, blessed are the poor in spirit who come unto me, for theirs is the kingdom of heaven.
>
> And again, blessed are all they that mourn, for they shall be comforted.
>
> And blessed are the meek, for they shall inherit the earth.
>
> And blessed are all they who do hunger and thirst after righteousness, for they shall be filled with the Holy Ghost.
>
> And blessed are the merciful, for they shall obtain mercy.
>
> And blessed are all the pure in heart, for they shall see God.
>
> And blessed are all the peacemakers, for they shall be called the children of God.
>
> And blessed are all they who are persecuted for my name's sake, for theirs is the kingdom of heaven.
>
> And blessed are ye when men shall revile you and persecute, and shall say all manner of evil against you falsely, for my sake;
>
> For ye shall have great joy and be exceedingly glad, for great shall be your reward in heaven; for so persecuted they the prophets who were before you. (3 Nephi 12:3–12)

These blessings describe and promise the ultimate benefits that the faithful will receive if they obey in righteousness the principles that Jesus is about to deliver to them.

He promises them blessings in nine different respects. Theirs is the kingdom of heaven, the earth, peace, comfort, and mercy; they will also see God, be filled with the Holy Ghost, and be called the children of God. In effect, Jesus blesses their eyes, their hearts, their stomachs, and their appetites; he specifically blesses them further that they may be able to bear up under the persecutions and revilings that will be heaped upon them.

Seeing such blessings in a ritual or temple context is natural. Other texts similar in form to the Beatitudes can be found in several apocryphal, pseudepigraphic, and Greek religious texts[13] that had cultic usages, as well as religious, eschatological, and apocalyptic significance (see, for example, the *Homeric Hymn to Demeter,* lines 480–82; and *4 Ezra* 8:46–54). In *2 Enoch* 42, for example, one reads of an ascent into "the paradise of Edem [*sic*]," where a divine figure appears before Adam and his righteous posterity and rewards them with eternal light and life. Among the nine beatitudes he speaks to them are these: "Happy is the person who reverences the name of the Lord; . . . happy is he who carries out righteous judgment; . . . happy is he who clothes the naked with his garment, and to the hungry gives his bread; . . . happy is he in whom is the truth, so that he may speak the truth to his neighbor; . . . happy is he who has compassion on his lips and gentleness in his heart; happy is he who understands all the works of the Lord, performed by the Lord."[14]

In *2 Enoch* 51–53, one is further taught that "it is good to go to the Lord's temple" three times a day to praise God by speaking a matched list of seven blessings and curses, including: "Happy is the person who opens his lips for praise of the God of Sabaoth; . . . cursed is every person who opens his heart for insulting, and insults the poor and slanders his

neighbor, because that person slanders God; . . . happy—
who cultivates the love of peace; cursed—who disturbs
those who are peaceful. . . . All these things [will be
weighed] in the balances and exposed in the books on the
great judgment day."[15] In ancient sources of this genre, the
word *blessed* "designates a state of being that pertains to
the gods and can be awarded to humans postmortem. In
ancient Egyptian religion the term plays an important role
in the cult of Osiris, in which it refers to a deceased person
who has been before the court of the gods of the nether-
world, who has declared there his innocence, and who has
been approved to enter the paradise of Osiris, even to become an Osiris himself."[16]

It appears that these and other similar texts were regularly used in ancient cultic ceremonies, and thus Hans
Dieter Betz sees a close parallel between the Beatitudes in
the Sermon on the Mount and the initiation rituals of ancient mystery religions, for both "impart to their adherents,
in initiations of the most various kinds, the secrets of the
world beyond and their own lot at present."[17] In other
words, through the blessings of the Beatitudes toward the
beginning of their underlying ceremony, the people are
given a glimpse of the heights to which they may rise—the
kingdoms and qualities—if they are true and faithful and become the people of Zion, the pure in heart (see Matthew 5:8;
D&C 97:21).

Others have seen in the Beatitudes "entrance requirements" for the Kingdom[18] and what Georg Strecker calls
"the conditions that must be fulfilled in order to gain entrance to the holy of holies."[19] This view is supported by the
fact that several of the requirements for entrance into the
temple in Jerusalem are strikingly comparable to certain
phrases in the Beatitudes.

For example, to enter that temple one must be "pure [in] heart" and "seek [the Lord's] face" in order to stand in his holy place (Psalm 24:3–6). When Jesus accordingly blesses "the pure in heart" who shall "see God," he is alluding to those who are worthy to enter the temple. As Betz states, "In terms of the history of religions, the concept implies critical reflection about purity and related rituals."[20] Strecker continues: the "overriding meaning of seeing God and standing before him, as far as the Old Testament is concerned . . . has to do with his mercy-presence in the temple."[21] Strecker hastens to qualify this with the assertion that Jesus "teaches not cultic but eschatological virtues. They refer to entrance not into the earthly temple but into the kingdom of God,"[22] but it seems to me that this assessment is too narrow. The two go hand in hand: To discard the efficacy and the present significance of the temple in earliest Christianity ignores the fact that all aspects of the old were not destroyed, but they simply were fulfilled and became new in Christ.

At the same time, entering the temple also looked forward to entering God's presence in the hereafter. In this regard, the evidence of several Greek Orphic gold leaves is instructive. As Betz points out, following Zuntz,

> The inscriptions on the gold leaves contain quotations of brief sentences, among them a beatitude: "Happy and blessed are you, you will be god instead of human."
>
> One can reach some conclusions about the purpose of these gold leaves and their inscriptions. They were apparently placed into the tombs of deceased mystery-cult initiates, put in the initiates' hand or near their ears. The inscriptions provide the deceased with the decisive formulae that as initiates they have to know as passwords on their way to the Elysian Fields. These formulae were,

one may suppose, revealed to the initiate during an initiation ceremony, and they contain the essential message of salvation that the cult conveys. . . . For the initiate these statements contain indispensable knowledge. . . . They identify their bearer as a beneficiary of the mysteries.[23]

Likewise, the thrust of the first few beatitudes is to be similarly understood: The meek and the poor, according to David Flusser, are the ones who will be "endowed with the supreme gift of divine bliss, with the Holy Spirit."[24] Through the temple, these blessings are both present and future. Such a view is consonant with a powerful passage in the Doctrine and Covenants regarding the Kirtland Temple, which likewise employs the terminology of the sixth beatitude to promise the righteous the blessings of the temple: "Yea, and my presence shall be there, for I will come into it, and *all the pure in heart* that shall come into it *shall see God*" (D&C 97:16). Such realizations call for jubilation. The "double call ['rejoice, and be exceeding glad' (Matthew 5:12)] appeals to the hearers or readers for what amounts to a liturgical response, much like 'hallelujah' or similar exclamations."[25]

The People Are Invited to Become the Salt of the Earth

The Lord next offers the people a special status, with a caution. He says, "I give unto you to be the salt of the earth; but if the salt shall lose its savor . . . the salt shall be thenceforth good for nothing, but to be cast out and to be trodden under foot of men" (3 Nephi 12:13). This is an invitation to enter into a covenant with the Lord, carrying with it a solemn warning that those who violate the covenant will be cast out and trampled under foot (although one is commanded to continue to invite them back; see 3 Nephi 18:32–33). The covenant connection here, for Latter-day Saints, is found most clearly in the Doctrine and Covenants, which explains that those who enter into the everlasting covenant "are accounted as the salt of the earth" (D&C 101:39; compare Numbers 18:19), a theme Elder Delbert L. Stapley developed in his 1964 general conference talk entitled "Salt of the Earth."[26]

Among biblical commentaries, of course, a wide variety of meanings have been attributed to this particular metaphor. Wolfgang Nauck presents evidence, largely from rabbinic sources, that the reference to "salt" in Matthew 5 was "taken from a certain code of instruction for the disciples of Scribes," requiring them to be "modest and (of) humble spirit, industrious and salted, suffering insult and (they should be) liked by all men."[27] The concept of salt, according to his view, demands suffering, purification, and wisdom of the true disciple.

Letting There Be Light

Jesus also gave his covenant people the charge "to be the light of this people" (3 Nephi 12:14). He is the light of the world (see John 8:12), but his true disciples are examples to other seekers. They shine in such a way that when others see they will glorify, not the examples, but the Father in Heaven (see 3 Nephi 12:16). Understood in this way, there is no tension between Matthew 5:14–16 and being seen of men in Matthew 6:2, 5, 16.

Implicit in Jesus' words here about salt, earth, and light may also be hints of certain creation themes: the doctrine of the Two Ways (the separation of opposites, light and dark, and heaven and earth).[28] This teaching was "emphatically brought home in the earliest Christian literature," proclaiming "that there lie before every human being and before the church itself two roads between which a choice must be made. The one is the road of darkness, the way of evil; the other, the way of light."[29] This principle of opposition is fundamental to the Sermon on the Mount. It surfaces again, for example, in the doctrine of the Two Ways in Matthew 7:13. Such creation themes were not confined to wisdom literature in the Bible, but were equally found in ritual. Indeed, some scholars have identified the creation account of Genesis as playing a key role in ancient Israelite temple ritual, although the details remain obscure.[30] In Jesus' words, however, the old symbolism has been imbued with new, additional meaning: Instead of the old imperative, *"Let* there be *light"* (Genesis 1:3; italics added), Jesus now issues the new injunction, *"Let* your *light* so shine before this people, that they may see your good works" (3 Nephi 12:16). Just as the Creator looked at the creation and pronounced his works to be good, Jesus now invites each disciple to become a creator of "good works," that when they are seen, men may glorify God. With this, Jesus is forming a new heaven and new earth, a new creative act and new creation of a new community of righteous people.

A First Set of Laws Explained

Formal instruction to the people begins in earnest as Jesus next turns to teach and explain the essence of three of the Ten Commandments and of the law of Moses, the law administered anciently by the Aaronic Priesthood. He explains that this law has not been destroyed. In its fulfilled form, it still has an essential place in the righteous life: "Think not that I am come to destroy the law or the prophets. I am not come to destroy but to fulfil; for verily I say unto you, one jot nor one tittle hath not passed away from the law, but in me it hath all been fulfilled" (3 Nephi 12:17–18).

Obedience and Sacrifice

First, Jesus teaches the companion principles of obedience to the Lord and of sacrifice. In the Sermon at the Temple, he specifically exhorts the people to obey the commandments that he issues at this time: "I have given you the law and the commandments of my Father, that ye shall believe in me, and that ye shall repent of your sins, and come unto me with a broken heart and a contrite spirit. Behold, ye have the commandments before you, and the law is fulfilled. Therefore come unto me and be ye saved; for verily I say unto you, that except ye shall keep my commandments, which I have commanded you at this time, ye shall in no case enter into the kingdom of heaven" (3 Nephi 12:19–20). He requires the people to exercise faith, repentance, and obedience, which constitutes coming unto him "with a broken heart and a contrite spirit" (3 Nephi 12:19). The offering of a broken heart and a contrite spirit is none other than the new law of sacrifice, as the voice of the Lord had explained earlier from heaven, speaking out of the darkness at the time of the New World destructions following the crucifixion (see 3 Nephi 9:19–20). This new law of obedience and sacrifice superseded the practices of sacrifice under the law of Moses and, in particular, put an end to "the shedding of blood" (3 Nephi 9:19). The same sentiment is expressed in the Gospel of the Ebionites: "I have come to abolish the sacrifices."[31]

Prohibition against Anger, Ill-Speaking, and Ridicule of Brethren

Second, Jesus upgraded the old law against murder into a higher prohibition against becoming angry or speaking derisively or critically about one's brother: "Ye have heard that it hath been said by them of old time, and it is also written before you, that thou shalt not kill, and whosoever shall kill shall be in danger of the judgment of God; But I say unto you, that whosoever is angry with his brother shall be in danger of his judgment. And whosoever shall say to his brother, Raca, shall be in danger of the council; and whosoever shall say, Thou fool, shall be in danger of hell fire" (3 Nephi 12:21–22).

In the brotherhood of a priesthood setting, I interpret this as amounting especially to a prohibition against speaking evil against any other priesthood brother, let alone against God. In effect, it prohibits all manner of evil or unholy speaking against any brother, and thus all the more so against the Lord's anointed leaders. According to the Sermon at the Temple, anyone who is angry with a brother is said to be in danger of *his* judgment (the implication is that the offended person is a "brother" who has power to render judgment). Anyone who calls his brother "Raca" is in danger of being brought before "the council," that is, the elders in charge of administering the kingdom. Those who persist in such misconduct are in danger of hellfire. Since the word "Raca" means "empty-head," the thrust of this injunction is that laughing at a brother's foolishness (that is, what to some may seem to be foolishness) is prohibited.

Such provisions and disciplinary procedures are especially pertinent to a community of covenanters, as the evidence that Manfred Weise and others have marshalled regarding rules of discipline at Qumran and in the earliest Christian community tends to show.[32] According to one of the rules of the Dead Sea community found in the *Manual of Discipline* 7:8, "anger against a fellow-member of the society could not be tolerated under any circumstances," and they applied a punishment "in any case of a member harbouring angry feelings."[33] Indeed, the *Manual of Discipline* 1:16–2:18 concludes its covenant-making ceremony by subjecting those who enter into the covenant unworthily to judgments of the community council and to punishments similar to those mentioned in Matthew 5:21–22. Weise argues that comparable councils were also convened in the early church, as evidenced in 1 Corinthians 5:4–5, 1 Timothy 1:20, and the writings of Ignatius,[34] specifically for the purpose of disciplining those who affronted Christ by insulting those people in whom Christ's spirit dwelt. In Weise's opinion, such deprecations are "not merely chidings in a banal sense, rather they insult to the core the community of God, viz., the covenant-community *(Verbundenheit)* of God. Therein lies their seriousness."[35]

Reconciliation Necessary before Proceeding Further

In 3 Nephi 12:23–24, Jesus interrupts the instruction to explain that if anyone desires to come unto him, he or she should have no hard feelings against any brother or sister: "Therefore, if ye shall come unto me, or shall desire to come unto me, and rememberest that thy brother hath aught against thee—Go thy way unto thy brother, and first be reconciled to thy brother, and then come unto me with full purpose of heart, and I will receive you" (3 Nephi 12:23–24). No disciple can come unto Christ or enter his presence until first being reconciled with his brothers and sisters. One first achieves atonement with one's brothers and sisters, and then one can come with "full purpose of heart" to be received by Christ and thereby be reconciled or atoned with God.

Some scholars have seen this passage as an intrusive interruption in the flow of thought in the Sermon on the

Mount, because it breaks up the rhythm of the antitheses between the old and the new in Matthew 5. It makes good sense, however, in the context of insuring that the listeners are in the proper state of mind to go forward ritually toward the holy altar.[36] Indeed, the Sermon on the Mount tells the disciple to leave his sacrifice on the altar and go and reconcile himself with his brother before proceeding (see Matthew 5:24). In order to facilitate this reconciliation, Jesus admonishes the people to settle all their controversies quickly and to avoid going to court, looking forward instead to another day of divine judgment, which will be far more important than any earthly day in court.

The Sermon on the Mount speaks of leaving one's sacrifice on the altar,[37] because it is addressing an audience prior to the fulfillment of the old law of sacrifice. In prelude to the Sermon at the Temple, however, Christ instructed that the new sacrifice was now to be brought to him (see 3 Nephi 9:20). Since Christ thus became the center of the temple, he fulfills the altar as the locus of reconciliation, but he does not destroy or eliminate it.[38] He still stands behind the idea of the altar where "broken relationships"[39] are atoned and reconciled.

Chastity

The next subject addressed is the law of chastity: "Behold, it is written by them of old time, that thou shalt not commit adultery; But I say unto you, that whosoever looketh on a woman, to lust after her, hath committed adultery already in his heart. Behold, I give unto you a commandment, that ye suffer none of these things to enter into your heart; For it is better that ye should deny yourselves of these things, wherein ye will take up your cross, than that ye should be cast into hell" (3 Nephi 12:27–30). The new law imposes a strict prohibition against sexual intercourse outside of marriage (consonant with Leviticus 18 and 20) and, intensifying the rules that prevailed under the old law, also requires purity of heart and denial of immoral things. "The sanctity of God-ordained marriage is so important for Jesus that already the lustful look" is destructive.[40] Purity in a ritual sense is also at stake.[41] In committing to live by this new law, the righteous bear a heavy responsibility and are symbolically crucified themselves—"wherein ye will take up your cross" (3 Nephi 12:30).

Unlike the Sermon on the Mount, the Sermon at the Temple mentions no penalty concerning the unchaste eye that should be cast out if it offends (see Matthew 5:29). This difficult saying in the New Testament text has been a troublesome point for many biblical commentators, for Jewish attitudes around the time of Jesus were strongly set against any punishment that took the form of bodily mutilation.[42] It is unlikely, of course, that Jesus demanded actual self-mutilation of his disciples, and the Sermon at the Temple invites no such implication, for it does not speak in any way here of actual bodily mutilation; the mode appears to be figurative (see Matthew 5:34 JST: "Now this I speak, a parable concerning your sins"). All references to plucking out the eye or to cutting off the hand that offends are absent in the Book of Mormon text, suggesting that this problematic verse in the Sermon on the Mount, on its face, does not fully reflect Jesus' original intent. Instead, the Sermon at the Temple speaks at this point of a total commitment—of the disciple taking up a symbolic cross, a symbol of capital punishment.

This demands that the righteous strictly exercise the virtue of self-control, and it also reflects a warning that if a person violates the law of chastity, which is of grave importance (see Deuteronomy 22:22; Alma 39:5), the penalty will involve serious consequences. In particular, the disciple must be willing to deny himself these things and, in so do-ing, "cross" himself (Alma 39:9) or, in Jesus' words, "take up your cross" (3 Nephi 12:30). The image this may bring to mind is that of a covenanter taking this obligation very seriously, for hanging or exposing a body on a tree or on a cross was part of the standard punishment under the law of Moses for any person who committed a sin worthy of death. This form of punishment was apparently known to the Nephites through the plates of brass and the writings of the prophet Zenos (see 1 Nephi 19:13–14). Deuteronomy 21:22 speaks of exposing the body of the culprit "on a tree," a practice observed by the Nephites (see 3 Nephi 4:28), which Peter connected with the death of Jesus on the cross (see Acts 10:39). Thus, with this teaching in the Sermon at the Temple concerning the seriousness of the covenant of chastity, one possibly confronts the idea that the disciple must be willing to take upon himself even the very form of mortal punishment that Jesus himself suffered. As a practi-cal matter in early Christianity, the punishment of those violating this covenant of chastity probably took the form of excommunication, understanding the idea of being cut off in Matthew 5:30 as "a communal parable."[43]

Marriages of Covenanters Are Not to Be Dissolved Except for Fornication

In connection with the law of chastity, Jesus teaches these faithful followers the importance of marriage by super-seding the old law of divorcement with the new law of marriage: "It hath been written, that whosoever shall put away his wife, let him give her a writing of divorcement [see Deuteronomy 24:1]. Verily, verily, I say unto you, that whosoever shall put away his wife, saving for the cause of fornication, causeth her to commit adultery; and whoso shall marry her who is divorced committeth adultery" (3 Nephi 12:31–32). Husbands are not to put their wives away, and wives are not to remarry. For centuries, commentators have struggled to understand the intended application of this radical prohibition against divorce. In light of the exceptionally righteous audience that had assembled at the temple in Bountiful, the context of the Sermon at the Temple suggests that this very demanding restriction may have something to do with the spirit and law through which husbands and wives are to be bound together in the eternal covenant relationships involved here. This explains the strictness of the rule, for eternal marriages can be dissolved only by proper authority on justifiable grounds and are sealed up for all eternity (see D&C 132:19). Until they are loosed by proper authority, a person who tries to put aside such a spouse on his or her own authority commits an adulteration of the eternal covenant-marriage relationship.

Oaths to Be Sworn by Saying "Yes" or "No"

Instructions are then given regarding the swearing of oaths (see 3 Nephi 12:33–37), in particular that Jesus' followers should "Let [their] communication be Yea, yea; Nay, nay; for whatsoever cometh of more than these is evil." Some biblical commentators have found this section in the Sermon on the Mount odd because it does not continue logically with the sequence of commandments in the Decalogue, as one might expect Jesus to follow if he were simply giving a commentary on the Ten Commandments of Exodus 20 and Deuteronomy 5. Moreover, it is hard to see this as a demand of love. Instead, instructions are given on how religious commitments are to be made: The swearing of oaths (which often accompanied the making of covenants)[44] should not be by the heavens or by the earth or by one's head, but simply by saying "yes" or "no." That is sufficient. A rabbinic aphorism suggests a similar sentiment: "Let your Yes and No both be righteous. Do not speak with your mouth what you do not mean in your heart."[45] In a ritual context, any more than this is superfluous or perhaps devious; more is not required and is to be avoided. While these words about oaths apply in numerous life settings, they are most pertinent when people are making, or are about to make, solemn oaths to the Lord.

This interpretation holds that Jesus was not opposed to covenantal promises per se, only to oaths sworn in the wrong way. What he objects to is such casuistry that asks whether one is bound if one swears by temple gold but not if one swears by the temple, or whether one is bound to an oath by the offering but not to an oath by the altar (see Matthew 23:16–19). In Matthew 23, which seems to reflect most clearly the historical teaching of Jesus on oaths, "there is no total ban on oaths."[46] Indeed, Jesus' point is that one should look in one's oaths to the deity behind the temple, behind the altar, and in the heavens, who sanctifies them all: "Whoso shall swear by the temple, sweareth by it, *and by him that dwelleth therein;* And he that shall swear by heaven, sweareth by the throne of God, *and by him that sitteth thereon*" (Matthew 23:21–22; italics added). The point is that all oaths are ultimately oaths by and before God: "All oaths directly or indirectly appeal to God; all are therefore binding since they call on him to guarantee their fulfillment."[47] Thus early Christians were in effect told that they should be different from those who swore horrific oaths or from others who regularly swore commercial or legal oaths in the Temple of Herod. They were told to avoid the forms of all such oaths—neither *by* the heaven, nor *by* the earth.

To be sure, some have read the Greek in Matthew 5:34 and James 5:12 as forbidding all oaths or promises of any kind ("swear not *at all*," "swear *no* other oath"), but this does not capture what appears to be the historical intent of Jesus (as reflected explicitly in Matthew 23),[48] and these two texts can be interpreted otherwise: I read the Greek in James 5:12 as telling Christians not to swear any such oath—meaning one that swears by external things, by heaven, or by earth,[49] or by any other such thing *(allon tina)*.[50] The problem lies in bringing in "extralinguistic props" and thereby failing to swear by God, who dwells in those places and sanctifies those vows (see Matthew 23:21–22): "The thing ruled out by the [Sermon on the Mount], therefore, is magic, that is, magical props of all sorts."[51] James admonishes his followers to let their "yes" really be a "yes" and their "no" really be a "no" and to keep their solemn promises, literally "so that they not fall under judgment [of the Lord]." Disciples of Jesus are not to be uncommitted but should let their sacred "word *[logos]* be yes, yes, no, no" (Matthew 5:37). The double yes was "a substitute for an oath."[52] From a Latter-day Saint point of view, the most important commitments a person can ever say "yes" or "no" to are those made in covenants with God.[53] Even the Essenes, who rejected oaths in general, used "the oath at entering the sect."[54]

Love of Enemies

The rules or models of loving one's neighbor, turning the other cheek, suffering humiliation, going the extra mile, giving up one's time and personal belongings, giving the poor more than is asked, loving one's enemies, and doing good to all people are given next:

And behold, it is written, an eye for an eye, and a tooth for a tooth; But I say unto you, that ye shall not resist evil, but whosoever shall smite thee on thy right cheek, turn to him the other also; And if any man will sue thee at the law and take away thy coat, let him have thy cloak also; And whosoever shall compel thee to go a mile, go with him twain. Give to him that asketh thee, and from him that would borrow of thee turn thou not away. And behold it is written also, that thou shalt love thy neighbor and hate thine enemy; But behold I say unto you, love your enemies, bless them that curse you, do good to them that hate you, and pray for them who despitefully use you and persecute you; That ye may be the children of your Father who is in heaven; for he maketh his sun to rise on the evil and on the good. (3 Nephi 12:38–45)

Although the law of the gospel is never expressly defined in scripture, I understand this law to be the law of love and generosity: "Thou shalt love the Lord thy God with all thy heart, and with all thy soul, and with all thy mind. This is the first and great commandment. And the second is like unto it, Thou shalt love thy neighbour as thyself" (Matthew 22:37–39; quoting Deuteronomy 6:5; see D&C 59:5–6). The only place in scripture where the phrase "law of the gospel" appears is in the Doctrine and Covenants, where it is connected with caring for the poor and needy: "If any man shall take of the abundance which I have made, and impart not his portion, according to *the law of my gospel*, unto the poor and the needy, he shall, with the wicked, lift up his eyes in hell, being in torment" (D&C 104:18).

In all dispensations, covenant people have been required to give to the poor and to lend to those who ask. Generosity was required of the children of Israel (see

Deuteronomy 15:7–11) and of the people of King Benjamin (see Mosiah 4:16–26) as a condition of their covenant, qualifying them to receive God's generosity. More than good behavior, however, was required (see Matthew 5:46–47); the covenantal relationship was presupposed. Thus Jesus' commandment that one must "give to him that asketh . . . and from him that would borrow of thee turn not thou away" (Matthew 5:42) not only captures the essence of the law of the gospel regarding love and generosity, but also incorporates a traditional Israelite and Nephite covenantal condition. Indeed, Jesus emphasizes that this law is old as well as new—"those things which were of old time . . . in me are all fulfilled" (3 Nephi 12:46–47)—and it can be seen that this law of the gospel is truly taught in the scriptures of all dispensations.

Transition into a Higher Order

At this point in the Sermon, the disciples have reached a plateau: "Therefore I would that ye should be perfect" (3 Nephi 12:48). The word *therefore* marks a transition in the design of the Sermon: On the one hand, it looks back over the instruction given thus far about the law of Moses, while on the other hand, it looks forward to yet a greater order to be required if the people are to become "perfect."

Although it is certainly presupposed that the word *perfect* has on one important level a straightforward ethical or religious meaning here[55]—reflecting perfect mercy, "undivided obedience to God," and "unlimited love"[56]—there is also a significant possibility that on another level the word carries a ceremonial connotation in this particular text. It seems to me that, in this verse, Jesus is expressing his desire that the disciples now advance from one level to the next, to go on to become "perfect," "finished," or "completed" in their instruction and endowment. In addition to the ritual context of the Sermon, the context usually determining the sense in which the intended "completeness" consists,[57] several reasons support this understanding.

First, the Greek word translated into English as "perfect" in Matthew 5:48 is *teleios*. This important word is used in Greek religious literature to describe several things, including the person who has become fully initiated in the rituals of the religion. *Teleios* is "a technical term of the mystery religions, which refers to one initiated into the mystic rites, the initiate."[58] Other forms of this word are used in Hebrews 5:14–6:1 to distinguish between the initial teachings and the full instruction ("full age," "perfection"); and in Hebrews 9:11 it refers to the heavenly temple. Generally in the Epistle to the Hebrews, its usage follows a "special use" from Hellenistic Judaism, where the word *teleioō* means "to put someone in the position in which he can come, or stand, before God."[59] Thus, in its ritual connotations, this word refers to preparing a person to be presented to come before God "in priestly action"[60] or "to qualify for the cultus."[61] Early Christians continued to use this word in this way in connection with their sacraments and ordinances.[62]

Most intriguing in this regard is the letter of Clement of Alexandria (written ca. A.D. 200) describing the existence of a *second* Gospel of Mark, reporting the Lord's doings as recounted by Peter and going beyond the public Gospel of Mark now found in the New Testament.[63] This so-called Secret Gospel of Mark, according to Clement, contained things "for the use of those who were being perfected [*teleioumenon*]. Nevertheless, [Mark] did not divulge the things not to be uttered, nor did he write down the hierophantic [initiatory priesthood] teaching [*hierophantikēn didaskalian]* of the Lord, but . . . brought in certain sayings of which he knew the interpretation would, as a mysta-gogue, lead the hearers into the innermost sanctuary of that truth hidden by seven veils."[64] The copy was read "only to those who are being initiated *[tous muoumenous]* into the great mysteries *[ta megala mysteria]*."[65] Thus, al-though almost nothing is known about these sacred and secret teachings of Jesus mentioned by Clement (who died A.D. 215), there can be little doubt that such esoteric, ortho-dox teachings existed in Alexandria and that some early Christians had been "perfected" by learning those priest-hood teachings. The suggestion that the words of the Sermon—explicitly inviting its followers to become "per-fected"—may have stood in a similar tradition is, therefore, not without precedent in early Christianity.

Moreover, the cultic use of the Hebrew term *shalom* may provide a concrete link between the Nephites and this Greek and Christian use of *teleios*. John Durham has ex-plored in detail the fundamental meanings of *shalom*, espe-cially in Numbers 6:26 and in certain of the Psalms, and concludes that it was used as a cultic term referring to a gift or endowment to or of God that "can be received only in his Presence,"[66] "a blessing specially connected to the-ophany or the immanent Presence of God,"[67] specifically as appearing in the Temple of Solomon and represented "within the Israelite cult" and liturgy.[68] Baruch Levine simi-larly analyzes the function of the *shelamim* sacrifices as pro-ducing "complete," or perfect, "harmony with the deity, . . . characteristic of the covenant relationship as well as of the ritual experience of communion."[69]

Durham sees this Israelite concept in the word *teleios* in Matthew 5:48.[70] Others concur: "Matthew does not use *teleios* in the Greek sense of the perfect ethical personality, but in the Old Testament sense of the wholeness of conse-cration to God."[71] It tends toward what Hugh Nibley calls the meaning of "living up to an agreement or covenant with-out fault: as the Father keeps the covenants he makes with us . . . . *Teleioi* is a locus technicus from the Mysteries: the completely initiated who has both qualified for initiation and completed it is *teleios*, lit. 'gone all the way,' fulfilling all requirements, every last provision of God's command. The hardest rules are what will decide the *teletios*, the final test—the law of consecration."[72] Thus, although we do not know what word Jesus used when he spoke to the Nephites that has been translated as "perfect" in 3 Nephi 12:48, there is reason to believe that they would have known from their Israelite heritage a word like *shalom* similar in content and function to the Greek word *teleios*.

Accordingly, in commanding the people to "be perfect even as I, or your Father who is in heaven is perfect" (3 Nephi 12:48), it seems that Jesus had several things in mind besides "perfection" as we usually think of it. What-ever he meant, it involved the idea of becoming like God ("even as I or your Father who is in heaven"), which occurs by seeing God (see 1 John 3:2) and knowing God (see John 17:3). These ultimate realities can be represented ceremoni-ously in this world, for as Joseph Smith taught, it is through his ordinances that we are "instructed in doctrine more perfectly."[73]

Finally, the style of the Sermon shifts into a different mode after this invitation to become perfect. The next sec-tion of the Sermon contains no reference to the old law of Moses. If Matthew 5 (or 3 Nephi 12) is about *the law* (Moses), then Matthew 6 (or 3 Nephi 13) distills *the prophets* (represented by the spirit of Elijah; see Matthew 17:3), for the Sermon as a whole embraces both the Law and the

Prophets (see 3 Nephi 12:17; 14:12). Stylistically there is also a sharp contrast between Matthew 5 (or 3 Nephi 12) and Matthew 6 (or 3 Nephi 13), so much so that many biblical commentators have suspected Matthew 6:1–18 of being a later intrusion into the text. That suspicion dissolves, however, if one sees that the text has simply moved on to a new stage of the experience, thus accounting for the different world to which it seems to belong. In this higher level there will be greater emphasis on secret and inward righteousness, as well as controlling the needs of the flesh and this world. Thus the text next presents a second set of requirements by discussing almsgiving, prayer, forgiveness, fasting, and total dedication of all that one has to God. Betz labels Matthew 6:1–18 as "the cultic instruction," because almsgiving, prayer, and fasting are "three ritual acts" that should be performed properly in preparing to "approach the deity."[74]

Giving to the Poor

Almsgiving is the first requirement encountered in connection with the establishment of the higher order (see 3 Nephi 13:1–4). If done in secret *(kryptos)*, giving of one's substance will reap open rewards. This rule is a natural conjunction of the law of the gospel (see D&C 104:18) and the law of consecration (see 3 Nephi 13:19–21, 24, 33). Vermes believes that Jesus' requirement that alms must be given in secret alludes to the "Chamber of Secrets" in the Temple of Herod mentioned in the Mishnah,[75] into which "the devout used to put their gifts in secret and the poor of good family received support therefrom in secret."[76] But giving to the poor has long been a requirement placed upon the Lord's covenant people,[77] and giving in sacred secretness has been generally recognized as "a mark of the truly righteous man."[78] Righteous deeds need not necessarily be performed anonymously. They should be done without pretentiousness; and perhaps even more for a secret, sacred, reason.

King Benjamin emphasized it as one of the main spiritual attributes of a righteous, covenant person: "Ye yourselves will succor those that stand in need of your succor" (Mosiah 4:16). Giving to the poor, he stipulated, is necessary in "retaining a remission of your sins from day to day" (Mosiah 4:26) and is an essential prerequisite for entering into a covenant with God, having "no more disposition to do evil, but to do good continually" (Mosiah 5:2; see 5:5). In order to establish Zion, there are to be no poor among the Lord's people (see Moses 7:18).

The Order of Prayer

After the instructions about praying in public and alone in private (see 3 Nephi 13:5–6), the English pronouns shift from a singular "thou" to a plural "ye," as does also the Greek.[79] This may indicate that the Lord first taught the people how to pray individually in private ("when thou [singular] prayest, enter into thy closet"), then offered instruction in group prayer ("after this manner pray ye [plural]").[80] He then offered the Lord's Prayer: "After this manner therefore pray ye: Our Father who art in heaven, hallowed be thy name. Thy will be done on earth as it is in heaven. And forgive us our debts, as we forgive our debtors. And lead us not into temptation, but deliver us from evil. For thine is the kingdom, and the power, and the glory, forever. Amen" (3 Nephi 13:9–13).

From the earliest Christian times, the Lord's Prayer was "basically a prayer used by a group,"[81] and several early Christian texts document the use of sacred group prayers, with the participants standing in a circle around Jesus at the center.[82] The Lord's Prayer was undoubtedly intended as a pattern or model for group prayers. Jesus probably taught something like it on several occasions and fluidly modified it somewhat each time, as reflected in the fact that no two texts of the prayer are quite the same (see Matthew 6:9–13; Luke 11:2–4; and 3 Nephi 13:9–13; Didache 8 offers yet a fourth, apparently independent, version). The early church father Origen understood the Lord's Prayer to be only a model or outline,[83] and the rabbis similarly expressed "strong prohibitions against reciting a fixed prayer," recommending that in saying a set personal prayer one should vary it a little each time.[84]

Hugh Nibley has seen in the structure of the Lord's Prayer more than a polite request or legal petition.[85] Nibley maintains that the elements of this prayer form an archetype of the "mysteries or ceremonies" that bring down to earth the pattern of heaven ("on earth exactly as it is in heaven"), to which our present linkage "and password is the name" of God ("hallowed be thy name").[86] Like the typical elements of the Greek mysteries, the prayer synoptically covers an *archē* (beginning in heaven, father of spirits), an *omphalus* (history, this world, bread, debts, temptation, and cry for deliverance), and *sphragis* (end of the world, seal, kingdom, and glory).[87]

A further connection between the Lord's Prayer and sacred ritual is evident in the description of the doxology that the children of Israel exclaimed in the temple of Jerusalem on the Day of Atonement. As Strack and Billerbeck explain, after the High Priest had transferred the sins of the people to the scapegoat, driven it into the wilderness, and said the words, "that ye may be clean from all your sins before the Lord" (Leviticus 16:30), then

> the priests and the people, who were standing in the
> Forecourt [of the Temple], when they heard the name of

the Lord clearly uttered, as soon as it came out of the mouth of the High Priest, bowed their knees and threw themselves down and fell on their faces and said, "Praised be the name of his glorious kingdom forever and eternally!" In the Temple [*im Heiligtum*] one did not simply answer "Amen!" How did one answer? "Praised be the name of his glorious kingdom forever and eternally!". . . How do we know that the people answered this way upon each benediction [in the Temple]? The scripture teaches, saying, "He is to be exalted with every praise and adulation."[88]

Thus, in the temple, the people answered a faithful High Priest not with a simple "amen," but also with praises of God—mentioning such divine attributes as his glory, power, kingdom, and everlasting dominion—before the concluding amen. According to the rabbinic sources, this doxological acknowledgment of the kingdom and glory of God was in regular usage in the temple at the time of Jesus, and it was attributed to a much earlier time; it was traditionally believed that these words of praise were spoken by father Jacob to his sons shortly before his death.[89] Thus the extended ending of the Lord's Prayer, "for thine is the kingdom, and the power, and the glory, forever, amen," could well have been recognized by several of Jesus' listeners as a traditional sign of great sanctity and solemnity usually associated with the holiest of temple rituals on the Day of Atonement. Such words may also have signaled an "acclamation," for "perhaps the original function of the 'doxology' in the Lord's Prayer was that of a response by the worshiping congregation."[90]

The stated purpose of Jesus' instruction about prayer is to show his followers how *not* to be "seen of men" (3 Nephi 13:5) or "heard for their much speaking" (3 Nephi 13:7), but how to be seen and heard of God. This is the cry of ages, the prayer that God will hear the words that we speak ("Then hear thou in heaven" [1 Kings 8:32, 34, 36, 39, 43, 45, 49], repeated at least seven times in the dedicatory prayer of the Temple of Solomon). The disciples were then invited to follow suit: "After this manner therefore pray ye" (3 Nephi 13:9–13).

The law of forgiveness is twice reiterated (see 3 Nephi 13:11, 14–15) to emphasize the fact that, under the new law, requests for forgiveness of sin and for deliverance will not be granted unless the disciples forgive one another and hold no hard feelings or unforgiving attitudes toward others, reapplying the prerequisite of 3 Nephi 12:23–24 and Matthew 5:23–24 now to the simple, prayerful petition of one desiring to be "heard" of God (3 Nephi 13:7–8).

Fasting, Washing, and Anointing

A new order of fasting was then taught to add to the preceding instructions on prayer. In addition to requiring a secret inward righteousness in fasting and prayer, true fasting is to be accompanied with the purity of a simple anointing of the head and washing of the face (see 3 Nephi 13:17). Washing the face, the head, the feet, the hands, or other parts of the body is symbolic of becoming completely pure and clean (see John 13:9–10), "clean every whit" (John 13:10). The concept is similar to the desire to become clean from the blood and sins that one encounters in this world (compare 2 Nephi 9:44). When a disciple seeks the Lord in true fasting and prayer in such a condition of inward and outward purity, the Lord promises that he will see and reward the supplicant openly in heaven. The importance of such rituals is evident: "Whether someone's righteousness is safeguarded is therefore decided not by convictions of faith but by the performance of rituals."[91] Fasting served many purposes in early Christianity; among them was preparation to receive ordinances: "Other fasts are to be held one or two days prior to baptism,"[92] according to Didache 7:4. But as Luz points out, due to the cryptic nature of this passage, "The listener himself or herself has to determine what 'washing and anointing' means tangibly."[93]

On three occasions in this section of the Sermon, the disciple is promised that the Lord will see him and reward him (see 3 Nephi 13:4, 6, 18). Clearly, the desire of the disciple is for God alone to hear the words of his cries (compare Solomon's temple language in 1 Kings 8:28, 29, 30, 32, 34, 36, and so on) and for God to recognize and fill his needs. The pattern of repeating things three times, or grouping things in clusters of three, has been identified as a dominant characteristic of the Sermon on the Mount.[94]

A Requirement to Lead a Life of Consecration and Singleness of Heart

The final affirmative requirement advanced in the Sermon is that of singleness of heart in serving God and not Mammon:

> "Lay not up for yourselves treasures upon earth, where moth and rust doth corrupt, and thieves break through and steal; But lay up for yourselves treasures in heaven, where neither moth nor rust doth corrupt, and where thieves do not break through nor steal. For where your treasure is, there will your heart be also. The light of the body is the eye; if, therefore, thine eye be single, thy whole body shall be full of light. . . . No man can serve two masters; for either he will hate the one and love the other, or else he will hold to the one and despise the other. Ye cannot serve God and Mammon" (3 Nephi 13:19–22, 24).

I view this instruction as tantamount in requiring one

to consecrate all that one has and is to the Lord. Jesus commands the disciple, "Lay not up for yourselves treasures upon earth, . . . but lay up for yourselves treasures in heaven." The hearer is also required to have an eye "single" *(haplous)* to the glory of God, which refers not only to being pure[95] but also to "singlemindedness" and "wholehearted dedication," particularly in the sense of being "ready for sacrifice"[96] and being "unbegrudgingly generous"[97] toward the kingdom. The pure eye does not deviate from the course that God has ordained. The duty is to serve a single master: "Ye cannot serve God and Mammon." The slave law language in this section drives home the point: We have been marked as slaves belonging to God and therefore everything we have and are belongs to him; hence, it would be a breach of contract or covenant to serve another lord.[98] Indeed, the Sermon on the Mount presupposes a totally committed community, one that is "prepared to take responsibility for the consequences of the teaching of Jesus, even if it means their lives."[99] By such total, exacting devotion to God, disciples are promised that their "whole body shall be full of light" (3 Nephi 13:22). This assumes that further light and a fulness of light is what the righteous should continually seek.

Care Promised for the Twelve Disciples

At this point in the Sermon at the Temple, Jesus turns to the twelve whom he had ordained and assures them that the Lord will take care of their needs. Their worries are calmed—anxieties that come perhaps less from the ordinary cares of daily human life and more from the feeling of vulnerability that comes when one turns everything completely over to the Lord. The disciples are promised that they shall have sufficient for their needs, just as the Lord's

Prayer in the Sermon on the Mount requests: "Give us this day bread 'sufficient for our needs' *(epiousion)*."[100] As the Lord's anointed, they need not worry about what they shall eat or drink, for they shall have sufficient for their needs. "Worldly concerns are not to be ignored; . . . God will provide what is needed for life's necessities."[101] The promise of food and drink may also foreshadow the Eucharist, another ritual aspect of the Sermon at the Temple focused on especially in the administration of the sacrament in 3 Nephi 18.[102]

Clothing (Endowing) the Disciples

Emphasis in the next section of the Sermon is on the ordained disciple's clothing. They are promised that God will newly clothe them in glorious clothing. As the lilies of the field, so the chosen disciples will be "clothed" by God, even more gloriously than Solomon himself, whose temple was the most splendid of all (see 3 Nephi 13:25, 29–31).

At one level, Jesus promises his disciples that they will have sufficient to wear, but the "clothing" or "raiment" of which Jesus speaks is also richly symbolic. The Greek word for being clothed is *enduō (endumatos,* "raiment," in Matthew 6:25, 28; *endusēsthe,* "put on," in Matthew 6:25). Jesus uses this word in Luke 24:49 shortly after his resurrection when he tells his apostles to remain in the city "until ye be *endued* with power from on high." The English word e*ndue* means "to endow," and it derives from the Greek word *enduō,* which has two meanings, and both are pertinent to the endowment. First is "to dress, to clothe someone," or "to clothe oneself in, put on." The second is, figuratively, to take on "characteristics, virtues, intentions."[103] The meaning of the English word *endue* (or *indue* from the Latin) likewise "coincides nearly in signification with *endow,* that is, to put on, to furnish. . . . To put on something; to invest; to clothe,"[104] and Joseph Smith's diary uses the spellings *endow* or *endue* interchangeably, as for example when Joseph prayed that all the elders might "receive an endument in thy house."[105]

Thus, in this section of the Sermon at the Temple, Jesus can be understood as promising more than garments that offer physical protection for the body (although garments do this too); he speaks of garments that "endow" the disciples with powers and virtues more glorious than Solomon's. Solomon, of course, was the most famous temple builder of ancient Israel, and so this allusion invites the audience in this esoteric setting to think of more than ordinary clothing on this occasion. All of the imagery of royalty and kingship are also suggested here; more is involved than the promise of nourishment to the body or of material well-being: "Is not the life more than meat, and the body than raiment?" (3 Nephi 13:25). All the promised blessings flow from bowing first to God and seeking first his kingdom and his righteousness (see 3 Nephi 13:33). Ultimately, standing before the judgment bar of God, all people will either stand unclean and naked or they shall be "clothed with purity, yea, even with the robe of righteousness" (2 Nephi 9:14).

Preparing for the Judgment

After the promise of this glorious endowment is given, the Savior turns his attention back to the multitude and to the presentation of information about the final judgment and how all may pass through it. He first discloses the principles by which the final judgment will be administered: "Judge not, that ye be not judged. For with what judgment ye judge, ye shall be judged; and with what measure ye mete, it shall be measured to you again. And why beholdest thou the mote that is in thy brother's eye, but considerest not the beam that is in thine own eye? Or how wilt thou say to thy brother: Let me pull the mote out of thine eye—and behold, a beam is in thine own eye? Thou hypocrite, first cast the beam out of thine own eye; and then shalt thou see clearly to cast the mote out of thy brother's eye" (3 Nephi 14:1–5).

Essentially no mortal can stand as a judge of his brother when he himself is flawed, and all people will find themselves judged at the bar of God by the same standard that they have used in judging others. This divine judgment operates universally and impartially, for God is no respecter of persons.[106]

This particular concept of justice—namely, rewarding or punishing a person in a manner that matches his own being or conduct—is mentioned several times in the scriptures as the form of God's justice at the judgment day. For example, Alma 41:13–15 says that God will restore good to the good, evil to the evil, mercy to those who have been merciful. Similarly, forgiveness only comes through the atonement of Christ to those who have forgiven (see Matthew 6:15; 3 Nephi 13:15). Therefore, a primary concern of the true Christian should be to develop one's own character: To be pure ("cast the beam out of thine own eye"), to serve ("see clearly to cast the mote out of thy brother's eye"), to avoid hypocrisy, and to think and act toward others in the way that you would have God render judgment unto you. The judgment process is more reflective than it is projective.

Secrecy Required

Next, the Lord requires that his hearers be willing to keep these holy things secret: "Give not that which is holy unto the dogs, neither cast ye your pearls before swine, lest they trample them under their feet, and turn again and rend you" (3 Nephi 14:6). For most readers, "the original meaning [of this saying] is puzzling."[107] "The logion is a riddle."[108] This saying seems badly out of place or hard to explain for most interpreters of the Sermon on the Mount,[109] for after demanding that the disciple should love his neighbor, even his enemy, it seems inconsistent for Jesus to call these people "dogs" and "swine" and to require his followers to withhold their pearls from them.

The emphasis, however, is clearly on withholding certain things that are "holy" and protecting them as sacred. Drawing on Logion 93 in the *Gospel of Thomas*, Strecker identifies one possibility for the holy thing, "that which is holy" *(to hagion)* in Matthew 7:6, as "gnostic secret knowledge."[110] The implication is that Jesus has given his hearers something more than what the scriptural text publicly reports, something they are required to keep sacred and confidential—an implication consistent with some other interesting conclusions of Jeremias regarding the existence of sacred, secret teachings and practices in primitive Christianity.[111] Similarly, Betz finds it most likely that verse 6 is

> an esoteric saying that the uninformed will never be able to figure out. Finding the explanation is not a matter of natural intelligence but of initiation into secrets. . . . In other words, we are dealing with some kind of secret *(arcanum)*. Indeed, the language reminds us of arcane teaching *(Arkandisziplin)* as it was used in the Greek mystery religions and in philosophy. . . . Originally, then, the [Sermon on the Mount] was meant to be insiders' literature, not to be divulged to the uninitiated outsiders. . . . Remarkably, Elchasai used the same language: "Inasmuch as he considers that it would be an insult to reason that these great and ineffable mysteries

should be trampled under foot or that they should be handed down to many, he advises that they should be preserved as valuable pearls saying this: Do not read this word to all men and guard carefully these precepts because all men are not faithful nor are all women straightforward."[112]

Such a requirement of secrecy is a common feature of ritual initiations or temple ordinances.[113] Indeed, the Didache 9:5 associates this saying in Matthew 7:6 with a requirement of exclusivity, specifically the prohibition not to let anyone "eat or drink of the Eucharist with you except for those baptized in the name of the Lord" (see Didache 14:1–2 connecting Matthew 5:23–25 and the observance of the sacrament). Accordingly, Betz concludes that "the 'holy' could be a ritual."[114] When this body of sacred knowledge is given to the recipients, its elements become or produce a string of precious pearls of great price, "*your* pearls," revelations that one will sell all one has in order to obtain (see Matthew 13:45–46). Once this knowledge is found, one keeps it hidden to protect it (see Matthew 13:44).

The violation of this obligation of secrecy carries or implies harsh penalties and consequences. If it is violated, the pearls will be trampled, and the one who has disclosed the holy thing will be torn to pieces. This reflects the method of punishment prescribed for covenant breakers in Psalm 50: "Those that have made a covenant with me, . . . consider this, ye that forget God, lest I tear you in pieces" (Psalm 50:5, 22). The Sermon text may also warn against apostasy, apostates, or heretics.[115] In a ritual context, such a strict requirement of secrecy is most readily understandable. Of its seriousness the prospective covenanters at Bountiful and in Galilee were expressly forewarned when they were first charged to become the salt of the earth, thereby acquiring great potency but at the same time running the risk of being "trodden under foot" for losing their strength (3 Nephi 12:13; Matthew 5:13).

Moreover, the Joseph Smith Translation confirms that Matthew 7:6 is exactly concerned with the requirement of keeping certain sacred things secret. It adds: "The mysteries of the kingdom ye shall keep within yourselves . . . for the world cannot receive that which ye, yourselves, are not able to bear" (Matthew 7:10–11 JST; on the plural, "holy things," compare the *Gospel of Thomas* 93). As Alma had said in the first century before Christ, "It is given unto many to know the mysteries of God; nevertheless they are laid under a strict command that they shall not impart only according to the portion of his word which he doth grant" (Alma 12:9).

A Threefold Petition

Finally, the listeners are ready to approach the Father. They are told that if they will one at a time ask, seek, and knock (in other words, when a threefold petition is made), "it shall be opened unto [them]" (3 Nephi 14:7). This offer is open to all people (compare Alma 12:9–11). Each one *(pas)* that asks, having been brought to this point of entry, will receive and be received (see 3 Nephi 14:8). In my mind, it makes the best sense of Matthew 7:7 to understand it in a ceremonial context. Actual experience among Christians generally shows that the promise articulated here should not be understood as an absolute one: Many people ask and seek and knock; yet, in fact many of them do not find. Moreover, there is reason to believe that Jesus expected his true followers to seek for something out of the ordinary: An early saying from Oxyrhynchus attributed to Jesus reads, "Let him who seeks not cease seeking until he finds, and when he finds, he will be astounded, and having been astounded, he will reign, and having reigned, he will rest."[116] It is crucial that a person come to the Father correctly (see 3 Nephi 14:21), and for all who seek and ask at this point in their progression—after believing and accepting the requirements in the Sermon that precede this invitation—for them it will be opened.

Seeking a Gift from the Father

Who, then, will be there to open "it" unto the petitioner? The Father. Jesus asked: "Or what man is there of you, who, if his son ask [for] bread, will give him a stone? Or if he ask [for] a fish, will he give him a serpent? . . . How much more shall your Father who is in heaven give good things to them that ask him?" (3 Nephi 14:9–10, 11). Asking for bread is the symbolic equivalent of asking for Jesus, who is the "bread of life" (John 6:48). Asking for a fish, again, is figuratively asking for life through the atonement and salvation of Jesus. The fish was a common pre-Christian symbol of fortune and health that became a familiar symbol of Jesus and baptism very early in Christianity. The promise veiled in such symbolism is that those who properly ask for Jesus will not be stoned (suffer death), nor will they encounter a serpent (Lucifer). Instead, the petitioner will receive good gifts directly from the Father (see 3 Nephi 14:11). The gift is eternal life, "the greatest of all the gifts of God" (D&C 14:7), descending below all things, rising above all heavens, and filling all things (see Ephesians 4:8–10, where *domata*, the Greek word for "gifts" in Matthew 7:11, also appears). The abundant generosity of God providing his people with bread and fish calls to mind the miraculous multiplication of the fish and the loaves (see Matthew 14:15–21), which may foreshadow an actual ritual meal (compare 3 Nephi 18:1–4).

Other People

But one cannot enter into eternal life or heaven alone. In the final analysis, obedience to the law of charity is required to claim the blessings of the Lord, for without charity, the pure love of Christ, we are nothing (see 1 Corinthians 13:2): "Whoso is found possessed of [charity] at the last day, it shall be well with him" (Moroni 7:47). With this virtue in mind, Jesus taught, "Therefore, all things whatsoever ye would that men should do to you, do ye even so to them" (3 Nephi 14:12).

Thus, all followers of the Lord Jesus Christ are responsible to see that other people are shown the way to salvation and eternal life and, where necessary, assisted in every way possible. In other words, Jesus may be commanding Christians not only to do things "to others" but "for others." The sense of the grammar can be read either way. The disciples are told that whatever they would like others to do for them, they should do the same for others, again with reference being made to the law (of Moses) and the spirit of Elijah (the prophets). My conclusion is that Jesus intended here for his disciples to do more than merely engage in the deeds of human kindness normally associated with the Golden Rule. He would want them, above all, to be taught the gospel and be brought to salvation. So he admonishes them to do such things for others, implicitly to teach them the gospel and to perform for them, where necessary, any vicarious ordinances. As Boyd K. Packer has said, "Is it not Christlike for us to perform in the temples ordinances for and in behalf of those who cannot do them for themselves?"[117]

Entering through a Narrow Opening

The necessity of helping others through the gate arises because, as 3 Nephi 14:13–14 makes clear, there is only one gate and one narrow way that leads to life: "Enter ye in at the strait gate; for wide is the gate, and broad is the way, which leadeth to destruction, and many there be who go in thereat; Because strait is the gate, and narrow is the way, which leadeth unto life, and few there be that find it." As 2 Nephi 31:17 indicates, that gate begins with the gateway of repentance, baptism, remission of sins, and the gift of the Holy Ghost. Signposts and markers help guide people to the narrow gate, and instruction about the doctrine of the Two Ways—the path to life or the road to destruction (compare Deuteronomy 30:19 and Jeremiah 21:8)—serves to remind the disciples that it is an undeviating path of truth that leads to life eternal.[118] The image involved here is not that of a door to a house (*thura*), but "the gate of a city or a temple" (*pulē*).[119]

Bearing the Fruit of the Tree of Life

Jesus next points to the imagery of the tree: "Every good tree bringeth forth good fruit; but a corrupt tree bringeth forth evil fruit" (3 Nephi 14:17). Having partaken of the tree of knowledge, man's life becomes a quest to find and righteously partake of the fruit of the tree of life and live forever. Echoes of temple and eschatological imagery are again discernible in the words of Jesus here.

These echoes come from several directions. First, these are no ordinary trees of which Jesus speaks: they are ultimate moral symbols. They either bear "evil" fruit (the Greek word is *ponērous*, "sick, wicked, worthless, degenerate, malicious") and are "corrupt" (*sapron*, meaning "decayed, rotten, evil, unwholesome"), or they are "good" (*agathon*, "fit, capable, of inner worth, moral, right"). Thus, Jesus speaks of eternal trees, symbolic of the final state of one's eternal character, determining whether one will either live or be "hewn down, and cast into the fire" (Matthew 7:19; 3 Nephi 14:19).

Second, these good trees are trees of life. One only lives forever by partaking of the fruit of the tree of life (see Genesis 3:22). Accordingly, the tree is an important feature in the landscape of all temple literature.[120] It is, therefore, natural and logical that Jesus' thoughts should turn to the imagery of the tree of life immediately after he has described the path "which leadeth unto life" (3 Nephi 14:14). In an eternal perspective, that path leads directly to the tree of life (see 1 Nephi 8:20, "I also beheld a strait and narrow path, which came along by the rod of iron, even to the tree by which I stood").

Third, Jesus equates individual people with the tree, for by partaking of the fruit of the tree of life, or by planting the seed of life in oneself, each disciple grows up into a tree of life, as the prophet Alma describes (see Alma 32:41–42). Each good tree of life has a place in God's paradise, growing up unto eternal life and yielding much fruit—powerful imagery also present in the Old Testament Psalms (see Psalm 1:1–3) and in the earliest Christian hymns: "Blessed, O Lord, are they who are planted in Thy land, and who have a place in Thy Paradise; and who grow in the growth of Thy trees" (*Odes of Solomon* 11:18–24). These trees are fruitful, bearing seed and posterity. They are of a kind with Jesus, he being the root and righteous followers becoming the branches (see John 15:1–5; Jacob 5).

Fourth, another temple echo may be heard in the possibility that the cross is also, ironically, a symbol of a tree of life (see 1 Peter 2:24). Each person who is raised up in the form of the tree will have eternal life. Ritually, the early Christians prayed in the "cruciform" position, with their hands raised, "stretched out towards the Lord." This "extension," they said, "is the upright cross."[121] Originally this signified the passion of Christ and was a gesture used in confessing Christ at baptism; it imitated the cross, death, and a mystic unification and life with Christ.[122]

Those who do not become such a tree and bring forth good fruit, however, will be chopped down and thrown into the fire, for they shall be known by their fruits (see 3 Nephi 14:19–20). Evil trees that bring forth bad fruit are the "false prophets" who are sure to come. The Lord assures the disciples that they "shall know them" (3 Nephi 14:20), for he has given them keys of knowledge so that they can test whether these purported prophets have come with truth and goodness.

Entering into the Presence of the Lord

Finally, there will be an encounter with the Lord himself: Some will say to him, "Lord, Lord," and they shall be allowed to "enter into the kingdom of heaven." But many, even good people of the world who have cast out devils and done wonderful works in the name of the Lord, will be turned away, for the Lord will have to acknowledge, "I never knew you; depart from me" (Matthew 7:22–23; 3 Nephi 14:22–23). This strong declaration is precise: "I never knew you," not even once (*oudepote egnōn hymas*).

How is it that the Lord has not known them? Because God knows everything, it cannot be that he is unaware of these people. Also, the problem is not that he knows the petitioners too little to be their advocate in court; on the contrary, he knows them all too well. He must not know them in some other sense. The Hebrew word "know" (*yadaᶜ*) has a broad range of meanings. One of them is covenantal: "You only *have I known* of all the families on earth: therefore I will punish you for all your iniquities" (Amos 3:2).

Amos's words are no longer mysterious. Yahweh had recognized only Israel as his legitimate servants; only to them had he granted the covenant.[123]

Clearly, more than good works alone will be required; and the old covenant with Israel, by which God knew (or recognized) Israel and by which the Israelites knew God (see Hosea 13:4; Jeremiah 24:7), has now become new through the Sermon. Knowing more than simply the just and equitable principles of the noble men of the earth is required in order to enter into the kingdom of heaven. Knowing the Lord through making and keeping this covenant is crucial. Only those who are wise in this sense,[124] who know, remember, and do its requirements, will be recognized and confessed by the Lord at that day, raised up to see God and to inherit celestial glory (see 3 Nephi 15:1).

Lecture on the Portion of God's Covenant with Israel Yet to Be Fulfilled

The Sermon at the Temple continues as Jesus reviews and recapitulates things he had said about the fulfillment of the law of Moses. Some of the people had not understood that all old things "had become new," apparently wondering how this could be, since the covenant promising that the Israelites (including the Nephites) would be gathered before the end had not yet been fulfilled. Jesus explained that the old *law* (v. 5) was ended, but that did not abrogate "things which are to come" (v. 7), especially the parts of the covenant that were "not all fulfilled" (v. 8; see 3 Nephi 15:3–8). He reiterated that his new instructions were given by way of commandment and now constituted the "law and the prophets" (3 Nephi 15:10). Then he spoke to the disciples about their role as a light unto the people, about their relation to the other folds of Christ's sheep, and about the gathering of Israel in complete fulfillment of God's covenants with the House of Israel (see 3 Nephi 15:11–16:20).

Admonition to Ponder

Turning again to the multitude, who now sat or stood "round about" Jesus (3 Nephi 17:1), he told them to go home and "ponder upon the things which [he had] said" (3 Nephi 17:3), for he knew they were weak and could not yet understand the full import and meaning of what he had said. To feel overwhelmed is a typical reaction to the temple or other sacred teachings: They appear simple at first, and we think we understand—but we do not. Only through experience and diligent, prayerful contemplation over time are the mysteries of God unfolded to us (see Alma 12:9).

Healing the Sick

Jesus was about to leave, but when he saw the tears in the eyes of the people looking steadfastly upon him and longing for him to tarry longer with them, he invited the people to bring forward any who were sick, and he healed them (see 3 Nephi 17:5–9). They all bowed down around Jesus and worshipped him, and some went forward to wash his feet with their tears (see 3 Nephi 17:10). These reciprocal spiritual outpourings set other temple precedents for the Nephites: the prayer roll for the sick and the washing of feet are at home in the modern temple as well.

The Parents and the Children

Next, the people were all invited to bring their children forward and set them around Jesus; the multitude gave way so the children could come to the center of the throng, where they surrounded Jesus, and the parents were told to kneel around that group of children. Jesus stood in the middle, with the children around him, and the parents kneeling around them (see 3 Nephi 17:11–13). Jesus himself then knelt and uttered a marvelous prayer. So great were the things they *both saw* and heard that they cannot be written (see 3 Nephi 17:14–17). I suspect that the covenant of secrecy plays a role here, which explains in part why "no tongue can speak, neither can there be written by any man" what Jesus said and did.

I also imagine, although this cannot be known for sure, that Jesus did more than pray, for it seems that he did things that the people saw just as he spoke words that they heard. This produced unspeakable joy. First the parents heard what Jesus prayed *for them*, the parents: "No one can conceive of the joy which filled our souls at the time we heard him pray *for us* unto the Father" (3 Nephi 17:17). The adults were overcome. Jesus asked them all to arise, and he blessed them and pronounced his joy to be full (see 3 Nephi 17:18–20). He then touched the children "one by one, and blessed them, and prayed unto the Father for them" (3 Nephi 17:21). This was done in the presence of God (Jesus), witnesses (the parents who "[bore] record of it"; 3 Nephi 17:21), and angels (who came down and encircled the children with fire and ministered to them; 3 Nephi 17:24). In the end, Jesus turned to the parents and said, "Behold your little ones" (3 Nephi 17:23). It seems to me that Jesus is not just inviting the parents to look at their children and admire them, although that endearing reading is possible. I would suggest that he is saying, "Behold, *your* little ones"—they are *yours*. While it cannot be said exactly what transpired at this time on that extraordinary afternoon, the children apparently now somehow belonged to the parents through the Lord's blessing in a way they had not belonged before.

The Covenant Memorialized and a New Name Given

Next, Jesus sent the disciples for some bread and wine, commanded the people to sit down on the ground, broke bread and blessed the wine, and gave it to his disciples and then to the multitude.[125] With respect to the bread, Jesus instructed his people: "This shall ye do in remembrance of my body, which I have shown unto you. And it shall be a testimony unto the Father that ye do always remember me" (3 Nephi 18:7); the drinking of the wine stood as a "witness" (v. 10) of willingness to keep the commandments that he had given them that day (see 3 Nephi 18:10, 14). The people also received a new name, the name of Christ (as in Mosiah 5:8–12), as they would be "baptized in [his] name" (3 Nephi 18:5, 11) and as they prepared to "take upon them the name of [God's] Son" (Moroni 4:3).

The covenant and ceremonial functions of the sacrament here are evident: The new words of these sacrament prayers would have sounded familiar to these people, for they strongly resemble the old words used by King Benjamin at the end of his coronation and covenant renewal speech when he put his people under covenant to obey God and their new king.[126] Christ's use of traditional Nephite covenantal language is yet one more way all their old things had become marvelously new in this day with Jesus at Bountiful. Moreover, it is known for certain that these eucharistic words of Jesus became liturgical in Nephite religion; his words and phrases became their sacrament prayers, spoken verbatim "according to the commandments of Christ" (Moroni 4:1) as the people continued to renew this ordinance for the next several hundred years.

The ritual application of these words of Jesus raises the presumption that similar uses were made by the Nephites of all or most of the words of Jesus. Although Latter-day Saints do not usually think of the sacrament in connection with its introduction to the Nephites at the temple of Bountiful, this ordinance was kept holy and secret among early Christians in the Old World, and it was regularly administered by the early Saints in the Kirtland Temple in 1836.

Continued Worthiness Required

Jesus' last instructions in the Sermon at the Temple deal with the future. He told the people to watch and pray always in their families that they might remain blessed and faithful (see 3 Nephi 18:15–21). He also gave standards of worthiness to determine who should be allowed to participate in their covenant renewals, forbidding some who are unworthy and including others who will repent (see 3 Nephi 18:22–23, 29–33). In this way, their places of worship and their future ordinances would remain holy and be a continuing means of bringing salvation to the people.

Conferring the Power to Give the Holy Ghost

Finally, Jesus "touched with his hand the disciples whom he had chosen, one by one" and gave them the power to bestow the gift of the Holy Ghost (3 Nephi 18:36–37). Through the events of the day they had progressed from the concerns and powers of the lower to those of the higher priesthood. The words that Jesus spoke in connection with conferring the Holy Ghost are recorded in Moroni 2:2. With this, the day being spent, a cloud overshadowed the multitude, like the cloud that covered the tabernacle of old and gave a sure sign of God's presence at his sanctuary (see, for example, Exodus 40:34–38; Leviticus 16:2, 13; Numbers 9:15–22; Deuteronomy 31:15). Whereupon, Jesus ascended back into heaven.

From Sermon to Ceremony

Thus ended the first day. The incomparable Sermon at the Temple was over. It was a manifestation of divine will and presence never to be forgotten. From this experience come many important things: teachings of immense practical ethical value, an understanding of that which was fulfilled and that which remained yet to be fulfilled, a comprehension of the continuity and transition from the old law to the new, knowledge and testimony of the resurrection and exaltation of Jesus Christ, commandments and covenants, and a basis for religious ritual.

Out of such an experience would naturally flow sacred ceremonies, for it was typical and usual for the temple in Israel "to routinize the momentous, thus rendering it part and parcel of the ongoing religious experience of the individual Israelite and of the people, collectively."[127] Evidently, this also occurred among the Nephites. Several texts from the Sermon at the Temple are known to have been ritually intended and oriented. From the Sermon at the Temple came the Nephite liturgical, priesthood prayers for baptism (see 3 Nephi 11:23–28), for the administration of the sacrament (see 3 Nephi 18:1–14; Moroni 4–5), for the bestowal of the gift of the Holy Ghost (see Moroni 2), and for the ordination of priests and teachers (see Moroni 3).

Main Elements of the Sermon at the Temple

- A thrice-repeated announcement from above
- Opening the ears and eyes
- Delegation of duty by the Father to the Son
- Coming down in white robes
- Silence
- Identification by marks on the hand
- Falling down
- Personally touching the wounds
- Hosanna Shout and falling down a second time
- Ordination to the priesthood
- Baptism explained
- Assuring the absence of evil
- Witnesses invoked
- Teaching the gospel
- Commending his disciples unto the people
- Blessings promised
- The people are invited to become the salt of the earth
- Letting there be light
- A first set of laws explained
- Obedience and sacrifice
- Anger, ill-speaking, ridicule of brethren prohibited
- Reconciliation necessary before proceeding further
- Chastity

- Covenant marriages dissolved only for fornication
- Oaths to be sworn by saying "yes" or "no"
- Love of enemies
- Transition into a higher order
- Giving to the poor
- The order of prayer
- Fasting, washing, and anointing
- Life of consecration and singleheartedness required
- Care promised for the twelve disciples
- Clothing of the disciples
- Preparing for the judgment
- Secrecy required
- A threefold petition
- Seeking a gift from the Father
- Other people
- Entering through a narrow opening
- Bearing the fruit of the tree of life
- Entering into the presence of the Lord
- Lecture on God's covenant with Israel
- Admonition to ponder
- Healing the sick
- The parents and the children
- The covenant memorialized and a new name given
- Continued worthiness required
- Conferring the power to give the Holy Ghost

These known instances of sacred memorialization give reason to believe that more of the Sermon at the Temple, perhaps much more, was ritually understood and transmitted. The words of Jesus (as many as were permissible) were written down, apparently immediately, and checked by Jesus (see 3 Nephi 23:7–9)—further indication that the Nephite disciples gave sacred and meticulous regard to each element of the Sermon at the Temple. Not all is known to us, of course, for the people were taught secret things that were "unspeakable" and "not lawful to be written" (3 Nephi 26:18), and many things were "forbidden them that they should utter" (3 Nephi 28:14). But as much as possible, they went forth and established the Church of Jesus Christ, based on these very "words of Jesus" (3 Nephi 28:34), words that profoundly put all things into perspective and coherence. These things point toward a view of the Sermon at the Temple as a sacred experience that was recorded, revered, repeated, institutionalized, and one that could be ritually represented and reenacted for other audiences. It seems to me that something of this sort indeed occurred, for the disciples went forward to preach abroad not only words and ideas, but also dramatic events, demonstrating things that they not only heard but also saw (see 3 Nephi 27:1).

Notes

1. By way of interest, one may compare the research of Dale C. Allison Jr., displaying the triadic nature of much of the Sermon on the Mount, a feature present also in the Mishnah, in "The Structure of the Sermon on the Mount," *Journal of Biblical Literature* 106 (1987): 429–43.

2. Hugh W. Nibley, *An Approach to the Book of Mormon* (Salt Lake City: Deseret Book and FARMS, 1988), 303 n. 10.

3. Hugh W. Nibley, *The Message of the Joseph Smith Papyri: An Egyptian Endowment* (Salt Lake City: Deseret Book, 1975), 280.

4. Hugh W. Nibley, "Sacred Vestments," in *Temple and Cosmos* (Salt Lake City: Deseret Book and FARMS, 1992), 91–138.

5. For shades of the Egyptian initiatory "Opening of the Mouth" ceremony, see Nibley, *Message of the Joseph Smith Papyri*, 106–13.

6. Various views are summarized in Eric Werner, "'Hosanna' in the Gospels," *Journal of Biblical Literature* 65 (1946): 97–122, esp. 106–11.

7. Ibid., 106.

8. J. Spencer Kennard Jr., "'Hosanna' and the Purpose of Jesus," *Journal of Biblical Literature* 67 (1948): 171–76.

9. G. Kittel, ed., *Theological Dictionary of the New Testament* (Grand Rapids, Mich.: Eerdmans, 1964), 9:683–84; and Eric Werner, *The Sacred Bridge* (New York: Schocken, 1970), 267.

10. Lael J. Woodbury, "Hosanna Shout," in *Encyclopedia of Mormonism*, 2:659.

11. Hugh W. Nibley, *Mormonism and Early Christianity*, ed. Todd M. Compton and Stephen D. Ricks (Salt Lake City: Deseret Book and FARMS, 1987), 360–64.

12. Robert L. Marrott, "Law of Witnesses," in *Encyclopedia of Mormonism*, 4:1570.

13. For further references, see Todd Compton, review of *The Sermon at the Temple and the Sermon on the Mount*, by John W. Welch, in *Review of Books on the Book of Mormon* 3 (1991): 322 n. 2.

14. James H. Charlesworth, ed., *The Old Testament Pseudepigrapha* (Garden City: Doubleday, 1983), 1:168.

15. Ibid., 1:178–81.

16. Hans Dieter Betz, *The Sermon on the Mount*, ed. Adela Yarbro Collins (Minneapolis: Fortress, 1995), 93.

17. Hans Dieter Betz, *Essays on the Sermon on the Mount* (Philadelphia: Fortress, 1985), 30; see 26–33. Betz further relates that "the second line of the macarism in Matt. 5:3 is, therefore, to be regarded as an eschatological verdict reached on the basis of knowledge about the fate of humankind in the afterlife. There is thus a

remarkable parallel within the phenomenology of religion between the ancient Greek mysteries of Demeter and other mysteries, and Jewish apocalyptic. . . . It is for this reason that the verdict awaited at the last judgment, both in the mysteries and in Jewish apocalyptic, can already be rendered in the earthly present" (p. 30).

18. Hans Windisch, *The Meaning of the Sermon on the Mount,* trans. S. MacLean Gilmour (Philadelphia: Westminster, 1951), 26–27, 87–88. Robert A. Guelich, "The Matthean Beatitudes: 'Entrance Requirements' or Eschatological Blessings?" *Journal of Biblical Literature* 95 (1976): 415–34, argues that both factors are present in the Beatitudes, which presuppose the creation of a new relationship between man and God, implicit to which is an eschatological dimension, especially in connection with Isaiah 61.

19. Georg Strecker, *The Sermon on the Mount: An Exegetical Commentary,* trans. O. C. Dean Jr. (Nashville: Abingdon, 1988), 33.

20. Betz, *Sermon on the Mount,* 134.

21. Hermann Strack and Paul Billerbeck, *Kommentar zum Neuen Testament aus Talmud und Midrasch* (Munich: Beck, 1922), 1:206.

22. Strecker, *Sermon on the Mount,* 33; and Betz, *Sermon on the Mount,* 137.

23. Betz, *Sermon on the Mount,* 95–96.

24. D. Flusser, "Blessed Are the Poor in Spirit," *Israel Exploration Journal* 10/1 (1960): 6.

25. Betz, *Sermon on the Mount,* 151.

26. Delbert L. Stapley, "Salt of the Earth," *Improvement Era* 67 (December 1964): 1069–71.

27. Wolfgang Nauck, "Salt as a Metaphor in Instructions for Discipleship," *Studia Theologica* 6 (1953): 165–66; see 165–78; italics deleted.

28. Betz, *Sermon on the Mount,* 522–27.

29. Hugh W. Nibley, *The World and the Prophets* (Salt Lake City: Deseret Book and FARMS, 1987), 185.

30. Discussed in Stephen D. Ricks, "Liturgy and Cosmogony: The Ritual Use of Creation Accounts in the Ancient Near East" (FARMS, 1981). Ricks cites Arieh Toeg, "Genesis 1 and the Sabbath," (in Hebrew) *Bet Miqra* 50 (1972): 290; Moshe Weinfeld, "Sabbath, Temple Building, and the Enthronement of the Lord," (in Hebrew) *Bet Miqra* 69 (1977): 188–89; and Peter J. Kearney, "Creation and Liturgy: The P Redaction of Ex 25–40," *Zeitschrift für die alttestamentliche Wissenschaft* 89 (1977): 375–78. These articles explore the relationships between the creation account and the temple, particularly the instructions for the construction of the tabernacle in Exodus 25–31. See also Hugh W. Nibley, *Temples of the Ancient World: Ritual and Symbolism,* ed. Donald W. Parry (Salt Lake City: Deseret Book and FARMS, 1994), 545–47.

31. Betz, *Sermon on the Mount,* 175.

32. Manfred Weise, "Mt 5:21f—ein Zeugnis sakraler Rechtsprechung in der Urgemeinde," *Zeitschrift der neutestamentliche Wissenschaft* 49 (1958): 116–23; italics deleted.

33. P. Wernberg-Møller, "A Semitic Idiom in Matt. V. 22," *New Testament Studies* 3 (1956): 72; italics deleted.

34. Kittel, *Theological Dictionary,* 7:871, where Ignatius uses the word "council" *(synhedrion)* in reference to a "council of the apostles."

35. Weise, "Mt 5:21f.—ein Zeugnis sakraler Rechtsprechung in der Urgemeinde," 123.

36. Compare Ulrich Luz, *Matthew 1–7: A Continental Commentary,* trans. Wilhelm C. Linss (Minneapolis: Fortress, 1989), 289 n. 62, citing Didache 14:1–2.

37. Matthew 5:24 may tell us something about temple practices in Jerusalem in the first century (Betz, *Sermon on the Mount,* 223).

38. Luz, *Matthew 1–7,* 289.

39. Betz, *Sermon on the Mount,* 205.

40. Luz, *Matthew 1–7,* 296–97.

41. Ibid., 306.

42. J. Schattenmann, "Jesus and Pythagoras," *Kairos* 21 (1979): 215–20.

43. Helmut Koester, "Using Quintilian to Interpret Mark," *Biblical Archaeology Review* 6 (May/June 1980): 44–45; compare 2 Nephi 1:17; 5:20; Mosiah 5:11–12.

44. Kittel, *Theological Dictionary*, 5:460.

45. Quoted in Paul S. Minear, "Yes or No: The Demand for Honesty in the Early Church," *Novum Testamentum* 13 (1971): 11.

46. Ibid., 4.

47. Ibid., 5.

48. Minear finds that the accent originally fell, not on the ban against oaths, but on the demand for radical honesty (ibid., 3).

49. Betz, *Sermon on the Mount*, 271.

50. The Greek grammar in this verse is odd. "By heaven" and "by earth" are in the accusative case, leaving it unclear how to read *allon tina orkon*, which is equally in the accusative: that is, does it mean "an oath by any other thing" or "any kind of oath"? If the sense is "neither by heaven, nor by earth, nor by anything in between," the meaning of James 5:12 is essentially the same as Matthew 23:16–22.

51. Betz, *Sermon on the Mount*, 271.

52. Luz, *Matthew 1–7*, 317.

53. The bilateral covenantal nature of early Christian ordinances such as baptism and the sacrament is not well documented in the Bible, but it is in the Book of Mormon; see Richard L. Anderson, "Religious Validity: The Sacramental Covenant in Third Nephi," in *By Study and Also by Faith: Essays in Honor of Hugh W. Nibley*, ed. John M. Lundquist and Stephen D. Ricks (Salt Lake City: Deseret Book and FARMS, 1990), 2:1–51.

54. Luz, *Matthew 1–7*, 314, citing 1QS v 8–11.

55. On perfection as our eternal goal, having the flaws and errors removed, see Gerald N. Lund, "I Have a Question," *Ensign*, August 1986, 39–41. James E. Talmage, *Jesus the Christ* (Salt Lake City: Deseret Book, 1976), 248 n. 5, minimalizes the concept to "Be ye relatively perfect." See also Walter Bauer, William F. Arndt, and F. Wilbur Gingrich, *A Greek-English Lexicon of the New Testament* (Chicago: University of Chicago Press, 1957), 816–17, giving the meanings of *teleios* as "having attained the end or pur-

pose, complete, perfect," "full-grown, mature, adult," "complete," "fully developed in a moral sense"; E. Kenneth Lee, "Hard Sayings—I," *Theology* 66 (1963): 318–20; and E. Yarnold, "Teleios in St. Matthew's Gospel," *Studia Evangelica* 4 (1968): 269–73, identifying three meanings of *teleios* in Matthew: Pharisaically perfect in keeping the laws, lacking in nothing, and fully grown.

56. This is the preferred meaning suggested in the Protestant view; see Kittel, *Theological Dictionary,* 8:73, 75.

57. Yarnold, "Teleios in St. Matthew's Gospel," 271; and Betz, *Sermon on the Mount,* 322.

58. Bauer, Arndt, and Gingrich, *Greek-English Lexicon,* 817, citing sources and referring to Philippians 3:15 and Colossians 1:28. See Demosthenes, *De Corona* 259, in *Demosthenes,* trans. C. A. Vince (Cambridge: Harvard University Press, 1971), 190–91, where *telousei* is translated as "initiations" into the mystery religions; see also Kittel, *Theological Dictionary,* 8:69.

59. Kittel, *Theological Dictionary,* 8:82; citing Hebrews 7:19 and 10:1.

60. Ibid., 8:83.

61. Ibid., 8:85.

62. H. Stephanus, *Thesaurus Graecae Linguae* (Graz: Akademische Druck und Verlaganstalt, 1954), 8:1961, "gradibus ad sacramentorum participationem, ton hagiasmaton metochen, admittebantur." I thank John Gee for this point.

63. Morton Smith, *Clement of Alexandria and a Secret Gospel of Mark* (Cambridge: Harvard University Press, 1973). For an extended discussion of the Secret Gospel of Mark in comparison with the Latter-day Saint endowment, see William J. Hamblin, "Aspects of an Early Christian Initiation Ritual," in *By Study and Also by Faith,* 1:202–21.

64. Smith, *Clement of Alexandria,* 446; Morton Smith's translation, bracketed phrases added. I have added the word *initiatory* at the suggestion of Todd Compton, based on the idea that "the hierophant at Elevsis was the special 'initiating priest.'" See Todd Compton, review of *The Sermon at the Temple and the Sermon on the*

Mount, by John W. Welch, *Review of Books on the Book of Mormon* 3 (1991): 322.

65. Smith, *Clement of Alexandria,* 446.

66. John I. Durham, "Shalom and the Presence of God," in *Proclamation and Presence: Essays in Honour of Gwynne Henton Davies,* ed. John I. Durham and J. R. Porter (Richmond, Va: John Knox, 1970), 292.

67. Ibid., 281.

68. Ibid., 286–92.

69. Baruch A. Levine, *In the Presence of the Lord* (Leiden: Brill, 1974), 35–36.

70. Durham, "Shalom and the Presence of God," 293 n. 135.

71. G. Bornkamm, G. Barth, and H. Held, *Tradition and Interpretation in Matthew,* trans. Percy Scott (Philadelphia: Westminster, 1963), 101; see Strack and Billerbeck, *Kommentar zum Neuen Testament,* 1:386.

72. Hugh W. Nibley, unpublished notes from his Sunday School class on the New Testament, on Matthew 5:48, in the FARMS Hugh W. Nibley Archive.

73. B. H. Roberts, *History of the Church of Jesus Christ of Latter-day Saints* (Salt Lake City: Deseret News, 1902), 2:312, discussed in Truman G. Madsen, "Mormonism and the New-Making Morality," James E. Talmage Lecture Series, 24 February 1971.

74. Betz, *Sermon on the Mount,* 329–32.

75. Mishnah, *Shekalim* 5:6.

76. Geza Vermes, *Jesus the Jew* (London: Collins, 1973), 78.

77. For a broad and sensitive treatment of this subject in the biblical period, see Léon Epsztein, *Social Justice in the Ancient Near East and the People of the Bible* (London: SCM, 1986).

78. Betz, *Sermon on the Mount,* 344.

79. The second person plural is used in Matthew 6:9 *(hymeis)* and the first person plural runs throughout the prayer itself.

80. In Matthew 6:6 the Greek is also singular while in 6:7–9 it is plural, although in 6:5 the Greek is plural. Betz recognizes the Lord's Prayer as "a group prayer" but finds it hard to place in the context of instruction on personal prayer (Betz, *Sermon on the Mount,* 362–63).

81. Gordon J. Bahr, "The Use of the Lord's Prayer in the Primitive Church," *Journal of Biblical Literature* 84 (1965): 156.

82. Hugh W. Nibley, "The Early Christian Prayer Circle," in *Mormonism and Early Christianity*, 45–99.

83. Bahr, "The Use of the Lord's Prayer in the Primitive Church," 153.

84. Ibid., 157. See Hans Dieter Betz, "The Lord's Prayer" (paper presented at the annual meeting of the Society of Biblical Literature, Chicago, 1988).

85. On Jewish, legalistic prayers, see Joseph Heinemann, *Prayer in the Talmud* (Berlin: de Gruyter, 1977), 193–217, discussing the "law court patterns" in similar prayers, where one presents a plea to the divine judge, gives the facts, defends himself, and asks for judgment in his favor.

86. Hugh W. Nibley, unpublished notes from his Sunday School class on the New Testament, on Matthew 6:9–13, in the FARMS Hugh W. Nibley Archive. Apparently, the hallowed, holy name is something other than Abba, which is not a proper name.

87. Ibid; see Raymond E. Brown, "The Pater Noster as an Eschatological Prayer," in *New Testament Essays* (London: 1965).

88. Strack and Billerbeck, *Kommentar zum Neuen Testament*, 1:423, citing Mishnah, *Yoma* 6:2, and others.

89. Ibid; discussed further in p. 207 below.

90. Betz, *Sermon on the Mount*, 414. Compare Psalm 106:48.

91. Ibid., 352.

92. Ibid., 419.

93. Luz, *Matthew 1–7*, 361.

94. Allison, "Structure of the Sermon on the Mount," 423–45; see 3 Nephi 11:35–36 (Father, Son, Holy Ghost); Matthew 5:22 (angry, Raca, fool); and Matthew 7:7 (ask, seek, knock) for examples of triadic structures.

95. Luz, *Matthew 1–7*, 397.

96. Kittel, *Theological Dictionary*, 1:386; and Strack and Billerbeck, *Kommentar zum Neuen Testament*, 1:431–32.

97. Henry J. Cadbury, "The Single Eye," *Harvard Theological Review* 47 (1954): 71.

98. Betz, *Sermon on the Mount*, 456–57.

99.   Betz, *Essays on the Sermon on the Mount,* 21; see Matthew 5:11–12.

100. This translation is offered by R. ten Kate, "Geef üns heden ons 'dagelijks' brood," *Nederlandisch Theologisch Tijdschrift* 32 (1978): 125–39; see Bauer, Arndt, and Gingrich, *Greek-English Lexicon,* 296–97. The meaning of this cryptic word is widely debated and is by no means certain.

101. Betz, *Sermon on the Mount,* 483.

102. Compare John 4, 6. Discussed also in connection with the miraculous feeding of the multitude in the forty-day literature and in 3 Nephi 20, in Hugh W. Nibley, "Christ among the Ruins," in *Book of Mormon Authorship: New Light on Ancient Origins,* ed. Noel B. Reynolds (Provo, Utah: BYU Religious Studies Center, 1982), 407–34.

103. Bauer, Arndt, and Gingrich, *Greek-English Lexicon,* 263.

104. *Webster's American Dictionary of the English Language* (1828 ed.).

105. Entry for Tuesday, 15 December 1835, in *The Personal Writings of Joseph Smith,* ed. Dean C. Jessee (Salt Lake City: Deseret Book, 1984), 105.

106. Betz, *Sermon on the Mount,* 491.

107. Strecker, *Sermon on the Mount,* 146; and Betz, *Sermon on the Mount,* 494–95.

108. Luz, *Matthew 1–7,* 418.

109. H. C. van Zyl, "'n Moontlike verklaring vir Matteus 7:6" (A possible explanation of Matthew 7:6), *Theologia Evangelica* 15 (1982): 67–82, collapses this saying into Matthew 7:1–5 as a possible solution to the problem.

110. Strecker, *Sermon on the Mount,* 147.

111. Joachim Jeremias, *The Eucharistic Words of Jesus* (New York: Scribner's Sons, 1966), 125–37. P. G. Maxwell-Stuart, "Do Not Give What Is Holy to the Dogs," *Expository Times* 90 (1979): 341, argues that "dogs" has a nonliteral metaphorical sense of "those who are unbaptized and therefore impure, . . . without shame" and that "holy" might originally have meant "what is precious, what is valuable."

112. Betz, *Sermon on the Mount*, 495–96; citations and foot-notes deleted.

113. Stephen D. Ricks, "Temples through the Ages," in *Encyclopedia of Mormonism*, 4:1463–65; and Hugh W. Nibley, "On the Sacred and the Symbolic," in *Temples of the Ancient World*, 553–54, 569–72.

114. Betz, *Sermon on the Mount*, 496.

115. Ibid., 500.

116. Joseph A. Fitzmyer, "The Oxyrhynchus Logoi of Jesus and the Coptic Gospel according to Thomas," in *Essays on the Semitic Background of the New Testament* (London: Chapman, 1971), 371.

117. Boyd K. Packer, "Covenants," *Ensign,* May 1987, 24.

118. The doctrine of the Two Ways was a salient teaching of the early Christians. See, for example, Hugh W. Nibley, *The World and the Prophets,* 183–86; and High W. Nibley, *The Prophetic Book of Mormon* (Salt Lake City: Deseret Book and FARMS, 1989), 462–63, 550–51.

119. Luz, *Matthew 1–7,* 435.

120. John M. Lundquist, "The Common Temple Ideology of the Ancient Near East," in *The Temple in Antiquity: Ancient Records and Modern Perspectives,* ed. Truman G. Madsen (Salt Lake City: Bookcraft and BYU Religious Studies Center, 1984), 53–76; and "Temple, Covenant, and Law in the Ancient Near East and in the Old Testament," in *Israel's Apostasy and Restoration,* ed. Avraham Gileadi (Grand Rapids, Mich.: Baker, 1988), 293–305.

121. *Odes of Solomon* 27:3; 35:7; 37:1, in Charlesworth, *Old Testament Pseudepigrapha,* 2:759, 765–66. "The Odist refers to the early cruciform position for praying." James H. Charlesworth, *The Odes of Solomon* (Oxford: Oxford University Press, 1973), 125 n. 10. See 1 Timothy 2:8: "I will therefore that men pray every where lifting up [raising] holy hands." In the Greek tragedians, *hosioi cheirēs* are "hands which are ritually pure." Martin Dibelius and Hans Conzelmann, *The Pastoral Epistles* (Philadelphia: Fortress, 1972), 44.

122. D. Plooij, "The Attitude of the Outspread Hands

('Orante') in Early Christian Literature and Art," *Expository Times* 23 (1912): 199–203, 265–69. One early artwork shows the figures with "the stigmata Christi in their hands" (p. 268).

123. Delbert R. Hillers, *Covenant: The History of a Biblical Idea* (Baltimore: Johns Hopkins University Press, 1969), 122. See Hillers' discussion of the use of the word *know* in connection with ancient Near Eastern treaty terminology (pp. 120–24).

124. Most often in the words of Jesus, the word for wise man *(phronimos)* describes a person "who has grasped the eschatological condition of man (Mt 7:24; 24:45; 25:2, 4, 8, 9; Lk 12:42)" and not the person who is intelligent or prudent in the practical worldly sense of the word (Fitzmyer, *Essays on the Semitic Background of the New Testament,* 172 n. 21).

125. For further connections between this material and the forty-day literature, see Nibley, "Christ among the Ruins," 407–34.

126. For a full discussion of the relations between the texts of Mosiah 5, 3 Nephi 18, and Moroni 4–5, see my article "The Nephite Sacrament Prayers: From Benjamin's Speech to Moroni 4–5," (FARMS, 1986); summarized in *Reexploring the Book of Mormon,* ed. John W. Welch (Salt Lake City: Deseret Book and FARMS, 1992), 286–89; presented further in "Benjamin's Covenant as a Precursor of the Sacrament Prayers," in *King Benjamin's Speech: "That Ye May Learn Wisdom"* (Provo, Utah: FARMS, 1998), 295–314; and in "From Presence to Practice: Jesus, the Sacrament Prayers, the Priesthood, and Church Discipline in 3 Nephi 18 and Moroni 2–6," *Journal of Book of Mormon Studies* 5/1 (1996): 119–39.

127. Levine, *In the Presence of the Lord,* 52.

CHAPTER 5

SOME PERSONAL REFLECTIONS

In the welter of opinions concerning Jesus' masterful Sermon transmitted by both Matthew and Mormon, I offer a view of the Sermon, especially at the temple in Bountiful, as a rich temple text. I realize that in assembling this view I have relied on circumstantial evidence, contextual inferences, and comparative studies, and have read the Sermon at the Temple in light of a Latter-day Saint's understanding of the temple. Nowhere does Jesus say to us, "I am presenting a temple experience here."[1] In such cases, he says only, "Who hath ears to hear, let him hear" (Matthew 13:9).

I also readily acknowledge that one can understand the Sermon in many other ways. There are many legitimate readings and many good interpretations of this deeply spiritual text. Many elements present in the Sermon are basic to the first principles of the gospel and thus are certainly also relevant to general ethical exhortation, preaching the gospel, personal righteousness, and the covenants of baptism. For example, at baptism one covenants to care for the poor, to comfort those that mourn, and to keep God's commandments (see Mosiah 18:8–10; see also Mosiah 5:3–8; Moroni 4:1–5:2), topics stressed also in the Sermon. So, individual teachings of the Sermon will apply in many gospel settings. Yet I know of no other single interpretation that makes more consistent sense of the Sermon as a whole or gives more meaning to all its parts than does the temple reading. No part is out of place or left out under this approach.

Although I cannot conclusively say through deductive logic that my view of the Sermon at the Temple is correct, I can say that I did not go into this text looking for this result. Whatever subtle bias or predisposition toward the temple may be involved, the pattern that emerges from this text is too natural for me to think that I have imposed it intrusively upon the data. After working for many years on the Sermon on the Mount and the Sermon at the Temple, all these things fell quite suddenly into place, without prodding or coercing. The experience was strong, as the echoes in the text became clearer voices for me. Finding a significant number of details compatible with this view scattered among the writings of various scholars then reinforced the experience.

I also realize now, better than ever before, how imprecise our tools and instruments are as we attempt to map the contours and main features of this rich spiritual landscape. As Jesus said to us, "I perceive that ye are weak" (3 Nephi 17:2); nevertheless, he will bless us in our weakness, and, God willing, our "weak things" may "become strong" (Ether 12:27). I hope that the Spirit will guide all readers who take Jesus' advice to go home and ponder upon the things he said to the Nephites and "prepare [their] minds for the morrow" that he might come again (3 Nephi 17:3). To do this, more than dissecting analysis is called for. The meaning of the Sermon is reduced when it is subsumed under certain focal points only: the truth about God's mysteries is not likely to be found at the end of a syllogism or textual analysis.

Reading the Sermon in light of the temple can enhance our understanding of the Sermon. Equally, experiencing the Latter-day Saint temple in light of the Sermon enhances our understanding of the temple. President Ezra Taft Benson has promised that the Book of Mormon will give intellectual and spiritual unity to the lives of all those who will truly receive it.[2] Perhaps this is one more example of how that promise can be fulfilled.

I hasten to add that people should also notice some differences between the Latter-day Saint temple experience and the Sermon. I do not think that the Nephite temple experience was exactly the same as today's—which itself changes somewhat from time to time. For example, the sequence in which the laws of obedience, sacrifice, chastity, consecration, and so forth are presented is not exactly the same in both, although it is quite close. And the Sermon at the Temple mainly reports the ordinances, laws, commandments, ritual elements, and covenants; little background drama or creation narrative is given. Moreover, the Sermon may have functioned in several respects more to prepare people for specific features of the temple or other ordinances than to conduct them through the experience itself. Nevertheless, the essential elements appear to be there— certainly more than I had ever before thought present in the Book of Mormon, and, as for the rest, the presence of the Lord would have been drama enough.

If the Sermon at the Temple is in some way a ritual text, one must next wonder the same about the Sermon on the Mount. I would not expect scholars unfamiliar with the

Latter-day Saint temple to see—or even imagine—what I think is going on in the Sermon. Still, the number of New Testament scholars willing to recognize the importance of esoteric or sacred ordinances and liturgical or cultic teachings among the early Christians is increasing. I think these scholars should be able to discern a number of possible ritual elements in the Sermon on the Mount.

As we have seen, several ritual-related elements appear specifically with respect to the Sermon on the Mount: the use of macarisms (beatitudes); the requirement that a participant withdraw if he or she has aught against a brother; the instruction about how one is to swear one's oaths; the meaning of *teleios* as being fully introduced into the mysteries; the giving of an exemplary group prayer; connections between the Lord's Prayer and John 17[3] (which connects it with the rituals of the last supper and the upper room); the promise of garments more glorious than Solomon's robes; the insistence upon secrecy; the asking, seeking, knocking, opening, and receiving of a gift; entering into the Lord's presence or rejecting those who are good but lack a certain knowledge; "knowing" God (with its connotations in connection with covenant making generally);[4] the sealing statement that Jesus taught with unusual authority (see Matthew 7:29); the prelude to the Sermon on the Mount in Matthew 3 with the baptism of Jesus, the Father's voice speaking from heaven, a heavenly being descending out of heaven, and in Matthew 4:11 with the expulsion of Satan; the venue of the mount as a new Sinai, a new Temple Mount;[5] the fact that a new covenant resulted, later witnessed by the cup of that new covenant (see Matthew 26:28; 1 Corinthians 11:25; 2 Corinthians 3:6); the recognition that the Sermon was directed only to a small group of disciples;[6] and the possible use of Sermon on the

Mount materials as a cultic or ceremonial reminder in the earliest decades of Christianity in Jerusalem.[7] It requires little familiarity with esoteric texts and basic religious ritual to notice that such are the elements of which ceremony is readily and meaningfully made.

To me, the Sermon at the Temple in this way restores covenantal and sacred meaning to the Sermon on the Mount—meaning that was lost or forgotten, as Nephi had prophesied in 1 Nephi 13:26. I infer from the Book of Mormon that Jesus delivered the Sermon on the Mount to much the same effect in Palestine as in Bountiful as he gave his disciples the new order of the gospel, which they eventually accepted by way of oaths and covenants, with promises and penalties.

In 1 Nephi 13, Nephi explained in some detail how the apostasy from early Christianity would occur. First Nephi 13:24–32 seems to identify *three* stages in this process—not just one.[8]

First, the gentiles would take "away *from the gospel* of the Lamb many parts which are plain and most precious" (1 Nephi 13:26). This stage could have occurred simply by altering the *meaning* of the things taught by the Lord without necessarily changing the words themselves. This change in understanding was the fundamental problem Nephi saw, for the things that would cause many to stumble were those things "taken away out of the gospel" (1 Nephi 13:29).

Second, the gentiles would take away "many covenants of the Lord" (1 Nephi 13:26). This step too could have been taken without deleting any words from the Bible. The knowledge and benefit of the covenants of God would then be lost simply by neglecting the performance of ordinances, priesthood functions, or individual covenants. Then, once the understanding of a text like the Sermon on

the Mount had been changed, the rest was merely paper-
work. The words could even stay the same, yet they would
already have lost their plain and precious meanings.

Only third did Nephi behold that "many plain and
precious things" were consequently "taken away from the
book" (1 Nephi 13:28). Apparently Nephi understood this
step as a consequence of the first two stages, for 1 Nephi
13:28 begins with the word *wherefore*. Thus, things that
were lost from the texts of the Bible were not necessarily a
cause but a result of the fact that, first, the gospel, and
second, the covenants of the Lord had been lost or taken
away.

Understanding this process helps us to see how the
Book of Mormon corrects this situation. Containing the fulness of the gospel (see D&C 20:9), the Book of Mormon
gives a correct understanding of the divinity, mission, and
atonement of Jesus Christ, along with the principles of faith
and repentance, and teaches with unmistakable clarity
other plain and precious parts of the plan of salvation. It
also restores many covenants of the Lord. It provides us
with the words of the baptismal prayer, along with instructions concerning the meaning and proper mode of baptism
(see Mosiah 18; 3 Nephi 11; Moroni 6) and of confirmation
(see Moroni 2). It preserves from ancient times the words
of the sacrament prayers (see Moroni 4–5),[9] makes understandable the covenants of the Lord to the house of Israel,
and teaches the necessity of priesthood authority and the
manner of ordination (see, for example, Moroni 3). In addition, the Book of Mormon restores an understanding of the
covenantal context of the Sermon on the Mount.

Indeed, Nephi prophesied that "the records of [his]
seed," or in other words the Book of Mormon, would be in-
strumental in making known "the plain and precious things

which have been taken away" (1 Nephi 13:40–41), and one of the book's stated purposes is to make known "the covenants of the Lord" (title page). Lehi also prophesied that the Book of Mormon would bring people in the latter days "to the knowledge of [the Lord's] covenants . . . And out of weakness [his people] shall be made strong" (2 Nephi 3:12–13).

For many years, however, the Book of Mormon has been taken lightly by the world. People who harden their hearts "cast many things away which are written and esteem them as things of naught" (2 Nephi 33:2). This has been especially the case with respect to the presence of the Sermon on the Mount in 3 Nephi. In reality, though, what has seemed to many to be an embarrassing problem in the Book of Mormon is no naïve plagiarism but a scripture fully constituted and meaningfully contextualized. If Doctrine and Covenants 84:57 is instructive here, reminding us that the children of Zion are under condemnation until they "remember the new covenant, even the Book of Mormon," it is perhaps not the Book of Mormon's fault that we have not seen the full potential of this Sermon text before.

Notes

1. The temple itself is mentioned explicitly in the Sermon at the Temple only in 3 Nephi 11:11, but one such introduction is typically adequate to firmly establish the setting (compare Mosiah 2:5–8).

2. Ezra Taft Benson, *A Witness and a Warning* (Salt Lake City: Deseret Book, 1988).

3. See W. O. Walker Jr., "The Lord's Prayer in Matthew and in John," *New Testament Studies* 28/2 (1982): 237–56, arguing that John 17 is a midrash on the Lord's Prayer.

4. Delbert R. Hillers, *Covenant: The History of a Biblical Idea* (Baltimore: Johns Hopkins University Press, 1969), 120–24.

5. W. D. Davies, *The Sermon on the Mount* (Cambridge: Cambridge University Press, 1966), 31–32.

6. H. Burkhardt, "Die Bergpredigt—Eine allgemeine Handlungsanweisung?" *Theologische Beiträge* 15 (1984): 137–40.

7. Hans Dieter Betz, *Essays on the Sermon on the Mount* (Philadelphia: Fortress, 1985), 1–16 (on the whole Sermon on the Mount as an epitome of the gospel); 55–69 (on Matthew 6:1–18 as an early Jewish-Christian *didache*).

8. For further discussion see John W. Welch, "The Plain and Precious Things," FARMS Update, January 1987; reprinted as "The Plain and Precious Parts," in *Reexploring the Book of Mormon*, ed. John W. Welch (Salt Lake City: Deseret Book and FARMS, 1992), 37–40.

9. Discussed in detail in John W. Welch, "The Nephite Sacrament Prayers: From King Benjamin's Speech to Moroni 4–5" (FARMS, 1986); reprinted as "Our Nephite Sacrament Prayers," in *Reexploring the Book of Mormon*, 286–89. See also "Benjamin's Covenant as a Precursor of the Sacrament Prayers," in *King Benjamin's Speech: "That Ye May Learn Wisdom,"* ed. John W. Welch and Stephen D. Ricks (Provo, Utah: FARMS, 1998), 295–314; and "From Presence to Practice: Jesus, the Sacrament Prayers, the Priesthood, and Church Discipline in 3 Nephi 18 and Moroni 2–6," *Journal of Book of Mormon Studies* 5/1 (1996): 119–39.

Further Studies

CHAPTER 6

THE SERMON AT THE TEMPLE AND THE SERMON ON THE MOUNT: THE DIFFERENCES

The preceding chapters present an interpretation that in my opinion casts the Sermon at the Temple as a complex, subtle, original, systematic, coherent, and purposefully orchestrated text. Not all people, however, see this text so positively. In fact, most novice readers of the Book of Mormon peruse 3 Nephi 12–14 rather casually, perhaps viewing it as a block of foreign materials unrelated to the surrounding text and bluntly spliced into the narrative of 3 Nephi.

The similarities between the Sermon on the Mount and the Sermon at the Temple have led many to view the Sermon at the Temple more as a liability than an asset to the Book of Mormon. Ever since the publication of the Book of Mormon, one of the standard criticisms raised by those seeking to discredit the book has been the assertion that it plagiarizes the King James Version of the Bible, and the chief instance of alleged plagiarism is the Sermon on the Mount in 3 Nephi 12–14. Mark Twain quipped that the Book of Mormon contains passages "'smouched' from the New

Testament and no credit given."[1] Reverend M. T. Lamb, who characterized the Book of Mormon as "verbose, blundering, stupid,"[2] viewed 3 Nephi 12–14 as a mere duplication of the Sermon on the Mount "word for word" and saw "no excuse for this lack of originality and constant repetition of the Bible," for "we have all such passages already in the [Bible], and God *never does unnecessary things*."[3] "Careful examination proves it to be an unprincipled plagiarist."[4]

These criticisms, however, have been drawn prematurely. Until all the possibilities have been considered, passing judgment with such finality is hasty. Indeed, if the foregoing covenantal interpretation of the Sermon has merit, Jesus could have selected no more appropriate text than the Sermon on the Mount for use at the temple in Bountiful. I am aware of no more valuable contribution to our understanding of the Sermon on the Mount than the insights of the Sermon at the Temple. Instead of being a liability or an embarrassment to the historicity of the Book of Mormon, the text and context of the Sermon on the Mount in the Book of Mormon turn out, in my view, to be among its greatest strengths. Through the Sermon at the Temple, some of the things that have baffled New Testament scholars about the Sermon on the Mount become very plain and precious.

The case of critics like Mark Twain and Reverend Lamb gains most of its appeal by emphasizing the similarities and discounting the differences between Matthew 5–7 and 3 Nephi 12–14. Yet under closer textual scrutiny, these differences turn out to be quite significant. Accordingly, in this chapter I will closely examine differences between the Sermon at the Temple and the Sermon on the Mount. While the substantial similarities between 3 Nephi 12–14 and Matthew 5–7 are readily apparent, the results presented below offer reasons to reject the claim that the Sermon at the Temple is simply a naïve, unprincipled plagiarism of the Sermon on the Mount.

While such writers as B. H. Roberts and Sidney B. Sperry have long cited the differences between these two texts to support the claim that the Sermon at the Temple is not a mindless copy of the Sermon on the Mount,[5] and while some commentators have sensed that the Sermon at the Temple is superior to the Sermon on the Mount in "sense and clearness,"[6] they have not thoroughly articulated the actual extent or nature of the differences. In the following chapters I undertake such an analysis. I examine each variance (for a complete comparison of the two texts, see the appendix) and conclude that there are enough important differences between the Sermon on the Mount and the Sermon at the Temple that the relationship between these texts cannot be attributed to a superficial, thoughtless, blind, or careless plagiarism. On the contrary, the differences are systematic, consistent, methodical, and in several cases quite deft.

For purposes of discussion and testing, the following analyses will assume two things: first, that Jesus began in Bountiful with a speech that he had probably delivered several times in Palestine, for example, when he sent his disciples into the mission field (see Matthew 7:1–2, 9, 11 JST)[7] and again sometime before his ascension (see 3 Nephi 15:1); and second, that he modified that text for delivery to a Nephite audience in Bountiful after his resurrection. Each instance in which the Sermon at the Temple is different from the Sermon on the Mount will be examined against this assumed context to determine whether logical reasons can be found for the differences. The more rational and subtly sensible these differences are, the more respect one should reasonably have for the Sermon at the Temple—and at the same time the less appropriate it becomes to speak disparagingly of the Sermon at the Temple as a plagiarism of the Sermon on the Mount.

A Postresurrectional Setting

Jesus appeared to the Nephites at the temple at Bountiful after his resurrection. Since some of the things he said before his death were superseded by his atonement and resurrection, they needed to be modified when explained to the Nephites to fit into a postresurrectional setting. For example, at the time of the Sermon on the Mount, the fulfillment of the law still lay in the future (see Matthew 5:18). But by the time of the Sermon at the Temple, the law of Moses had already been fulfilled, as Jesus had proclaimed out of the darkness at the time of his death (see 3 Nephi 9:17).

Thus, when Jesus spoke in Palestine he said, "One jot or one tittle *shall* in no wise pass from the law, till all be fulfilled" (Matthew 5:18; italics added), but in Bountiful he affirmed that one jot or tittle *"hath not* passed away from the law, but in me it *hath* all been fulfilled" (3 Nephi 12:18). Similarly, in summarizing the series of antitheticals in 3 Nephi 12:21–45, Jesus drew them together in the Sermon at the Temple with the following conclusion: "Those things which were of old time, which were under the law, in me *are* all fulfilled. Old things *are* done away, and all things have become new" (3 Nephi 12:46–47). In light of the glorified state of the resurrected Jesus at the time of the Sermon at the Temple, he could accurately say, "I would that ye should be perfect even *as* I, or your Father who is in heaven is perfect" (3 Nephi 12:48). Furthermore, there was no need in Bountiful for Jesus to instruct the people to pray, "Thy kingdom come" (Matthew 6:10), a phrase missing from the Lord's Prayer in the Sermon at the Temple (see 3 Nephi 13:9–13), for God's kingdom had already come both in heaven through Christ's victory over death and on earth that day in their midst.

These differences convey significant theological information. First, the Sermon at the Temple clarified that all things under the law of Moses had been entirely fulfilled in Jesus' mortal life, death, atonement, and resurrection. The Sermon on the Mount, on the other hand, never addressed this important question of *when* the law would be fulfilled but left this key issue open, simply saying that nothing would pass from the law "till all be fulfilled" (Matthew 5:18). The issue of when that fulfillment became effective deeply and tragically divided a number of the early Christian communities, as is well documented in the New Testament (see Acts 15; Galatians 5).[8] Second, the Sermon at the Temple speaks from a frame of reference in which Jesus had become glorified with God. Jesus had already ascended to the Father, and thus he could well command his listeners in Bountiful to be perfect as he or as God is perfect (see 3 Nephi 12:48).

A Nephite Setting

When Jesus addressed the Nephites at Bountiful, he spoke in terms they would understand. The change in setting from Palestine to Bountiful accounts for several differences between the Sermon on the Mount and the Sermon at the Temple. Instead of "farthing" (as appears in the King James English of Matthew 5:26), Jesus mentions a "senine" (3 Nephi 12:26), a Nephite unit of exchange. Although this change might appear to be a superficial change or an artifice, there is subtle substance to it. Jesus

undoubtedly had several meaningful reasons for mentioning the senine when he spoke to the Nephites.

First, it was not just one of many Nephite measures but
was their basic measure of gold (see Alma 11:5–19). Through
it one converted values of precious metals into the measure-
ment "of every kind of grain" (Alma 11:7). It was also the
smallest Nephite measure of gold (see Alma 11:8–10). Thus,
when Jesus told the Nephites that they might be held in
prison, unable to pay "even one senine" (3 Nephi 12:26), he
was referring to a relatively small amount, equal to one
measure of grain. It was also likely not just the smallness
that Jesus had in mind, for otherwise he could have spoken
of a "leah" (Alma 11:17), their smallest measure of silver.
The senine was especially important because it was the
amount paid to each Nephite judge for a day's service at
law (see Alma 11:3). Evidently, the losing party in a lawsuit
was liable to pay the judges one senine each, a burden that
would give potential litigants all the more reason to "agree
with thine adversary quickly while thou art in the way with
him" (3 Nephi 12:25). One should note that the Greek phrase
en tēi hodōi, "in the way," in Matthew 5:25, idiomatically
refers to the commencement of a lawsuit.[9]

Another subtle yet important difference is found in
3 Nephi 12:35: there is no mention of Jerusalem. Of course,
no Nephite would be inclined to swear "by Jerusalem, . . .
the city of the great King" (Matthew 5:35) since the Nephite
view of Jerusalem was rather grim. But more than that,
omitting this phrase may be closer to what Jesus originally
said in Palestine as well. While Jerusalem was known anciently as "the city of the great King" (Psalm 48:2; *tou
basileōs tou megalou* in the Septuagint, 47:2), numismatic
evidence shows that the precise phrase "great King"
(*basileōs megalou*) was a special political title in the Roman

world that was not used in Palestine until after Jesus' death. This title was given to the client-king Herod Agrippa I as a result of a treaty *(horkia)* granting him several territories in and around Galilee in A.D. 39 and 41, an event he commemorated with coins in his name bearing this distinctive, honorific title.[10] On the basis of this information, it has been suggested that Jesus' saying about oaths *(horka)* may have originally contained no reference to Jerusalem, "the city of the great King," since Herod Agrippa may not have been politically entitled to that title until after Jesus' ministry. While there is no way to be sure about this suggestion, especially since such words were also available to Jesus in the text of Psalm 48:2, the absence of the phrase *the city of the great King* in the Sermon at the Temple would prove consistent with this obscure numismatic information.

A further difference is that there is no mention of rain in 3 Nephi 12:45, whereas Matthew 5:45 says that the Lord makes the sun rise and also the rain fall on the just and the unjust. It is unknown why the Sermon at the Temple does not mention rain in this verse. Perhaps this difference reflects less anxiety in Nephite lands over regular rainfall or less judgmental attitudes in Mesoamerica toward the heavenly origins of rain.

Finally, the Nephites had had no experience with the hypocrites of Matthew 6:2, who cast their alms with the sounding of (or into) trumpets, and thus Jesus did not speak to the Nephites of what such hypocrites "do," but what they "will do" (3 Nephi 13:2). For the Nephites, such behavior was hypothetical or figurative, not familiar.

An Audience Dependent upon Written Law

The Nephites relied heavily on the written law. Their ancestors treasured the plates of brass, also relying heavily upon those written records for specifications regarding the law of Moses and how they should keep it. Being cut off from most sources of oral or customary Israelite law, the Nephites saw the law primarily as a written body (see 1 Nephi 4:15–16) and viewed any change in the written law with deep suspicion (see Mosiah 29:22–23). The Jews in Jerusalem in Jesus' day, on the other hand, had an extensive body of oral law to accompany the written Torah, and the oral law was very important in the pre-Talmudic period of Jewish legal history.

Accordingly, in the Sermon on the Mount Jesus said repeatedly to the Jews in the old world regarding the laws of "the Sinai generation,"[11] "Ye have *heard* that it was *said* . . ." (Matthew 5:21, 27; see 33, 38, 43; italics added). To the Nephites, however, such a statement would not have carried as much weight as a reference to the written law. Thus, in the Sermon at the Temple Jesus consistently cited the written law, saying, "Ye have heard that it hath been said by them of old time, and it is also written before you" (3 Nephi 12:21), "it is written by them of old time" (3 Nephi 12:27), "again it is written" (3 Nephi 12:33), "behold, it is written" (3 Nephi 12:38), and "behold it is written also" (3 Nephi 12:43).

An Explicit Covenant-Making Setting

As has been explained extensively thus far, the Sermon at the Temple was delivered in a covenant-making context. Several significant differences between the two sermons reveal and reflect this important dimension. In the Sermon at the Temple Jesus gave the injunctions and instructions as "commandments" (3 Nephi 12:20), and the people received them by entering into a covenant with God that they would always remember and keep those commandments that

Jesus gave to them that day (see 3 Nephi 18:7, 10). Just as the children of Israel entered into a covenant to obey the law of Moses as it was delivered to them at Sinai, the Nephites at Bountiful received their new dispensation of law by way of a covenant that superseded the old law, as the Sermon at the Temple openly explains. Consistent with this overt setting, the Sermon at the Temple contains unique phrases that belong to the sphere of covenant making.

First, Jesus' words in the Sermon at the Temple were given to the Nephites as commandments. No such designation appears in the Sermon on the Mount, and thus biblical scholars inconclusively debate whether Jesus' teachings in the Sermon on the Mount were intended as celestial ideals, as ethical or religious principles, or as social commentary. The Sermon at the Temple, however, leaves no doubt that the words Jesus spoke at Bountiful were intended to create binding obligations between God and his people. Jesus issued laws of the gospel, which all those who entered into the covenant that day were to obey. The people were required to come unto Jesus and be saved by obedience to the "commandments, which I have commanded you at this time" (3 Nephi 12:20).

Second, those who will be received into the kingdom of heaven are those who come unto Christ (see 3 Nephi 12:3, 20). The phrase *come unto me* appears five times in the Sermon at the Temple (see 3 Nephi 12:3, 19, and 20, and 23 twice), but it never occurs in the Sermon on the Mount. Coming unto Christ, according to the Sermon at the Temple, requires repentance and baptism (see, for example, 3 Nephi 18:32; 21:6; 30:2), and coming unto him is thus in essence a covenantal concept. Only those who "come unto [Christ] with full purpose of heart" through his prescribed ordinances will be received or allowed to enter into his presence

(3 Nephi 12:24; compare 14:21; 15:1). The use of the phrase *come unto Christ* is consistent with the covenantal context of the Sermon at the Temple, and this connection is strengthened by the likelihood that the Hebrew phrase translated "come before the Lord" probably has cultic meanings of standing before Jesus' presence in the temple at Jerusalem.[12] Stephen D. Ricks suggests that the phrase *come unto me* in the Sermon at the Temple may be conceptually equivalent to the Old Testament expression translated "stand in the presence of the Lord," which is thought to be temple terminology. Along the same lines, John I. Durham presents evidence that the *shalom* described the complete blessedness that is "the gift of God, and can be received only in his Presence." He further notes that "the concept of the Presence of God was certainly of vital importance to the Old Testament cult."[13]

Emphasis on the Desires of the Heart

Although the Sermon on the Mount already demands of its adherents an extraordinarily pure heart (see, for example, Matthew 5:8, 28; 6:21), the Sermon at the Temple adds two more references to the heart. The first is expressly connected with the covenant-making process, requiring any person desiring to come to Christ to do so "with full purpose of heart" (3 Nephi 12:23–24; compare 2 Nephi 31:13; Jacob 6:5; 3 Nephi 10:6; Acts 11:23). This instruction replaces the saying in the Sermon on the Mount about bringing one's gift to the temple altar (see Matthew 5:23–24).

The second such addition sharpens the instruction regarding adultery by issuing the following commandment: "Behold I give unto you a commandment, that ye suffer none of these things to enter into your heart" (3 Nephi

12:29; compare Psalm 37:15). Likewise, the Sermon at the Temple prohibits any anger in the heart at all (see 3 Nephi 12:22), not allowing even justifiable anger, which is allowed in the traditional Matthean text (see Matthew 5:22).

Undoubtedly, these statements about the heart would have been intensely poignant in the minds of the Nephites, since the only thing they knew about the new law at the time the Sermon at the Temple began was the fact that the old ritual law had been replaced by a new law of sacrifice requiring exclusively the sacrifice of "a broken heart and a contrite spirit" (3 Nephi 9:20). The added emphasis on the heart would have been especially instructive to those Nephite listeners, given their pressing need to understand this new law that focused so strongly on the sacrifice of the heart.

A More Immediate Relation to God

In several passages in the Sermon at the Temple, subtle changes bring the divine influence more explicitly to the surface. When one is "filled" in the Sermon at the Temple, the beatitude is not left unspecified, as in the Sermon on the Mount (see Matthew 5:6), but it reads "filled with the Holy Ghost" (3 Nephi 12:6). One suffers, not just "for righteousness' sake," but "for [Jesus'] name's sake" (Matthew 5:10; 3 Nephi 12:10). The murderer is in danger not just of "the judgment," but of "the judgment of God" (Matthew 5:21–22; 3 Nephi 12:21–22). And when one comes to Christ after first being reconciled to his brother, Christ himself is the one who "will receive" him (3 Nephi 12:24). Such expressions give the Sermon at the Temple a somewhat more intimate, personal connection with the divine than is conveyed in the Sermon on the Mount. The shorter version of the beginning of the Lord's Prayer in the Sermon at the Temple places greater "emphasis on the believer's special relation to God, to heaven," and to the position of indebt-edness "at the center" of that relation.[14] This characteristic is consistent with the Sermon at the Temple being delivered by Jesus in his divine and glorified state, and with the Matthean instruction being given by the Master to his clos-est circle of disciples.

Absence of Unseemly Penalties

In two places, penalties mentioned in the Sermon on the Mount are conspicuously absent in the Sermon at the Temple. First, the Sermon on the Mount teaches that any-one who "shall break one of these least commandments, and shall teach men so, he shall be called the least in the kingdom of heaven" (Matthew 5:19), but the Sermon at the Temple mentions no such punishment or criticism. Second, where the Sermon on the Mount says, "If thy right eye offend thee, pluck it out, . . . and if thy right hand offend thee, cut it off" (Matthew 5:29–30), the Sermon at the Temple simply gives the commandment "that ye suffer none of these things to enter into your heart" (3 Nephi 12:29).

Interestingly, the Sermon on the Mount has been sub-jected to considerable criticism by commentators on ac-count of these two passages in Matthew 5. In the one case, some have argued that the drastic, eternal punishment of one who breaks even the least commandment seems grossly disproportionate to the crime and too uncharacter-istically legalistic for Jesus to have said.[15] In the second case, the suggestion of bodily mutilation seems wholly in-consistent with the extraordinary Jewish respect for the hu-man body—an attitude that Jesus undoubtedly shared—and seems at odds with the other statement in the Sermon on the Mount that one should cast the beam from one's eye but not cast away the eye (see Matthew 7:5).[16] None of these problems arises, however, in the Sermon at the Temple. Indeed, the absence of these passages may even support the idea that these two passages were not originally parts of the Sermon on the Mount but were interpolated from Mark 9:43–48, as some commentators have suspected.

Of course, penalties are not entirely absent from the Sermon at the Temple. The strict injunction to "give not that which is holy unto the dogs, neither cast ye your pearls before swine, lest they trample them under their feet, and turn again and rend you" is present in both the Sermon at the Temple and the Sermon on the Mount (Matthew 7:6; 3 Nephi 14:6). While this passage has presented great problems to interpreters of the Sermon on the Mount who wonder why Jesus would in one breath say "love your enemies" (Matthew 5:44) and call other human beings "swine" and "dogs,"[17] this situation can be explained quite naturally, as has been discussed in chapter 4, in connection with a requirement of secrecy in a covenant-making context.

Holy and sacred things are not to be shared or broadcast indiscriminately. Doing so was punished in the ancient world by severe penalties, often mentioned in connection with oath swearing and covenant making. Thus, scholars may be correct in suggesting that the specific penalties mentioned in the Sermon on the Mount (see Matthew 5:19, 29–30) were not originally there (the Sermon at the Temple presents those passages quite differently) but would go too far by concluding that penalties had no role in the teachings of Jesus at all.

A Church Organizational Setting

The Sermon on the Mount gives no clues about how its followers were organized ecclesiastically or about their institutional positions or relationships. The Sermon on the Mount, for all that we know about it from the Gospel of Matthew, could stand independently as a code of private conduct, quite apart from any religious society or organization. Nothing said expressly in or about the Sermon on the Mount tells us how early Christian communities used the Sermon on the Mount or how its parts related to the various officers and functionaries in that movement. Yet scholars such as Hans Dieter Betz have concluded that the Sermon must have occupied a prominent place in the religious and liturgical life of the early Jewish Christians in Jerusalem.[18]

Betz's proposition in general is more than confirmed in the Sermon at the Temple by the fact that it was delivered in connection with the establishment of a group of disciples who would lead the new church of Christ (see 3 Nephi 11:18–22; 12:1; 18:36–37; 26:17–21). Several differences between the Sermon on the Mount and the Sermon at the Temple (and often also the JST) make this organizational setting explicit:

1. At Bountiful, Jesus ordained and called priesthood leaders. The discourse in 3 Nephi 12 begins with two ecclesiastical beatitudes not found in the Sermon on the Mount: "Blessed are ye if ye shall give heed unto the words of these twelve whom I have chosen; . . . again, more blessed are they who shall believe in your words because that ye shall testify that ye have seen me, and that ye know that I am" (3 Nephi 12:1–2).

2. All believers were instructed to enter into a covenant of baptism, thereby becoming members of Christ's church (see 3 Nephi 11:21–27, 34, 38; 12:1; 18:5). As a result of this entry, to them it was given to be the salt of the earth: "*I give unto you to be* the salt of the earth" (3 Nephi 12:13), a trans-

ferral and causal connection unstated in the Sermon on the Mount's simple declaration, "*Ye are* the salt of the earth" (Matthew 5:13).

3. The two commissions "I give unto you to be the light of this people" and "Let your light so shine before this people" (3 Nephi 12:14, 16) seem to refer most clearly to relationships among or exemplary roles of the believing covenant people (see 3 Nephi 12:2; 13:25; 15:12), who later in the Sermon clearly are called "the people of my church" (3 Nephi 18:5; compare 20:22; 27:24, 27). With similar language in an earlier dispensation, the Lord had also given covenant Israel its calling and mission: "I will also give thee for a light to the Gentiles" (Isaiah 49:6).

4. The fact that the words in 3 Nephi 13:25–34 were addressed solely to "the twelve whom he had chosen" (3 Nephi 13:25) and the acknowledgement that the offended brother in 3 Nephi 12:22–24, as discussed above, had the priesthood power to judge ("whosoever is angry with his brother shall be in danger of *his* judgment") are two other places in the Sermon at the Temple where that text distinctively presupposes or discloses ecclesiastical or organizational elements.

A Greater Universality

Consistent with Jesus' open invitations to all mankind in the first parts of the text (see 3 Nephi 11:23; 12:2), the word *all* is introduced into the Sermon at the Temple five times in the Beatitudes (see 3 Nephi 12:4, 6, 8, 9, 10). While this may seem a small addition, its repetition creates a crescendo of emphasis on the universality of the gospel and on the absolute desire of Jesus for all people to receive its blessings. In the Sermon at the Temple, "all" those present went forth and touched the Savior (3 Nephi 11:15–16), "all" came forth with their sick to be healed (3 Nephi 17:9), "all" bowed (3 Nephi 17:9–10), and "all" saw, heard, and witnessed (3 Nephi 17:25; 18:24). The Sermon at the Temple is consistently emphatic that "all" participated, not just a small group of disciples who were separated from the multitudes, as in the Sermon on the Mount (see Matthew 5:1).

The Absence of Anti-Pharisaical Elements

It has been argued that the Sermon on the Mount passed through the hands of an anti-Pharisaical community of early Christians who were struggling to separate themselves from and who were having strained relations with their mother Jewish faith and the established synagogues in Jerusalem.[19] Indeed, anti-Pharisaism can be seen as one of the main tendencies of Matthew, and hence its manifestations in the Sermon on the Mount have been advanced as evidence of Matthean influence on or composition of the Sermon on the Mount.

Interestingly, the evidences scholars think they see of these anti-Pharisaical comments in the Sermon on the Mount are not found in the Sermon at the Temple. The saying "except your righteousness shall exceed the righteousness of the scribes and Pharisees" (Matthew 5:20) is not present in 3 Nephi. A very different and important statement in 3 Nephi 12:19–20 about obedience and sacrifice appears instead. Likewise, the unflattering comparison between good men the world over and the publicans, both of whom love their friends (see Matthew 5:46–47), is wholly absent in 3 Nephi 12. Warnings against hypocrisy are present in both the Sermon at the Temple and the Sermon on the Mount (see Matthew 6:2, 5, 16; 7:5; 3 Nephi 13:2, 5, 16; 14:5), but these admonitions in the Sermon at the Temple are not aimed specifically at the Pharisees.

The Absence of Possible Antigentile Elements

It has been similarly argued that the Sermon on the Mount as it stands in the Gospel of Matthew was redacted slightly by a Jewish-Christian who held an antigentile bias.[20] The evidence for this view comes from three passages. Whatever weight one may accord to such evidence in critical studies of the New Testament, in each of the three cases the perceived antigentile elements are unproblematic for or absent from the Sermon at the Temple, as one would expect in a discourse delivered to a group of people who registered no personal contacts with any gentiles.

Accordingly, the references to publicans in Matthew 5:46–47 are absent in 3 Nephi 12, and the words "for after all these things do the Gentiles seek" (Matthew 6:32) do not appear in 3 Nephi 13:32. The discussion of vain repetitions put up to God by the "heathens" (*ethnikoi*, Matthew 6:7), which is mentioned in the Sermon at the Temple, is a general comment that need not be a later antigentile intrusion into the Sermon on the Mount. In any event, the problem of vain, repetitive apostate prayers was well-known to the Nephites from Alma's shocking encounter with the practices of the Zoramites (see Alma 31:12–23).

The Absence of Alleged Anti-Pauline Elements

It has also been suggested that certain portions of the Sermon on the Mount are anti-Pauline.[21] Again, because of differences between the Sermon at the Temple and the Sermon on the Mount, either the purported anti-Pauline materials are lacking in the Sermon at the Temple or it is highly doubtful that the supposed anti-Pauline elements are in fact anti-Pauline.

The most likely deprecation of Paul in the Sermon on the Mount is the passage that condemns anyone who teaches people to ignore even the least of the commandments in the law of Moses—he will be called "the least in the kingdom of heaven" (Matthew 5:19). Paul is the obvious figure in early Christianity who taught and promoted the idea that Christians need not observe the law of Moses, and his ideas met with considerable hostility among both Jews and certain Christians. Since Paul was known as "the least" of the apostles (1 Corinthians 15:9), it seems quite plausible that early Christians would have seen in Matthew 5:19 a direct criticism of Paul's position, if not of Paul himself; it is easier to believe this appellation was added to the Sermon on the Mount *after* Paul had called himself "the least" than to think he would have called himself by that name, knowing that this appellation had become part of an early Jewish-Christian prolaw tradition. If the text of the Sermon on the Mount solidified around the 50s A.D. when Paul's debate was raging, it is possible that Matthew 5:19 was altered somewhat in light of that controversy (the crucial phrase is also absent in Matthew 5:21 JST). If that was the case, one would not expect to find Jesus at Bountiful using anti-Pauline words twenty years earlier in the Sermon at the Temple. In fact, no anti-Pauline elements can be found or suggested in the differently aimed text of 3 Nephi 12:17–19.

Some commentators have concluded that other passages in the Sermon on the Mount are anti-Pauline, but in those further cases the evidence seems even weaker. The concern about destroying or fulfilling the law is too general to be identified exclusively with Paul. Concern over destroying the law, or the role of the law of Moses in the messianic age or in the world to come, was a general Jewish problem, not just an issue raised by Paul's views of salvation.[22] Questions posed to Jesus about tithing, ritual purity, healing on the Sabbath, and many other such things show that people in early Christianity were concerned with this precise issue from the beginning of Jesus' ministry. Concerns about how and when the law of Moses would be fulfilled were equally problematic in Nephite religious discourse for six hundred years, from the time of Lehi and Nephi until the coming of Jesus at Bountiful (see, for example, 2 Nephi 25:24–27; 3 Nephi 1:24; 15:2). It is therefore fitting that Jesus explained his relationship to the old law in both the Sermon on the Mount and the Sermon at the Temple.

Warnings against false prophets (see Matthew 7:15) need not refer covertly to Paul but probably reflect long-standing Israelite concerns and rules (see Deuteronomy 18:20–22). The mere presence in the Sermon on the Mount of the criticism against those who call "Lord, Lord" (*kurie, kurie*, Matthew 7:21) does not appear to be evidence that this condemnation was included as a polemic against Paul in a theological anti-*kurios* statement, as some have suggested,[23] for the same phrase appears in the Sermon on the Plain in Luke 6:46, and Luke can scarcely be accused of being an anti-Pauline collaborator. Similarly, the text that advises people to build their house upon the rock (see Matthew 7:24) is also argued as supporting Peter (the rock) as opposed to Paul; but, again, Luke's inclusion of this statement in Luke 6:47–49 discredits this view, since Luke would not likely have discredited his companion Paul.

While the Sermon on the Mount in its present form may have passed through the hands of an early Christian anti-gentile, anti-Pauline community, most traces of such influences are scant. Even to the extent that such influences may be discernible, the absence from the Sermon at the Temple of the chief bits of evidence of an anti-Pauline hand in the Sermon on the Mount supports the view that the Sermon at the Temple preserves a reading that predates any such influences on the text.

Other Differences

A number of other differences between the Sermon on the Mount and the Sermon at the Temple are worth mentioning. There seems to be a slightly greater emphasis in the Sermon at the Temple on eschatological judgment at the last day. Futurity is stronger in the Sermon at the Temple than in the Sermon on the Mount: for example, "ye *shall* have great joy" (3 Nephi 12:12), and "the salt *shall* be thenceforth good for nothing" (3 Nephi 12:13).

The Sermon at the Temple seems slightly more personal because *who* has been substituted for *which* on several occasions (see, for example, 3 Nephi 12:6, 10, 45, 48; 13:1, 4, 6, 9), but it is unknown whether this first appeared on the original manuscript of the Book of Mormon or as a correction to the printer's manuscript. While these changes are minor, they add to the overall intimacy of Jesus' words in the Sermon at the Temple. His audience at Bountiful is not a faceless crowd. Unlike the Sermon on the Mount, 3 Nephi even names some of the people who were there to receive him and his words (see 3 Nephi 19:4).

The Sermon at the Temple achieves greater clarity by explicitly stating certain things that the Sermon on the Mount simply assumes: for example, "it" in Matthew 5 is replaced in the Sermon at the Temple with the explicit antecedent "the earth"(3 Nephi 12:13); a cryptic instruction in Matthew 5:30 is explained and motivated with the elaboration "wherein *ye will* take up your cross" (3 Nephi 12:30); the Sermon at the Temple adds the understood injunction "I say that I would that *ye should* do alms unto the poor" (3 Nephi 13:1), which goes beyond the direction on how not to give alms; and a rhetorical question in Matthew 6:30 is given with promissory force in the Sermon at the Temple, "even so *will he* clothe you, if ye are not of little faith" (3 Nephi 13:30). These changes strengthen the imperative force of Jesus' statements, especially those that change negative, self-evident statements into positive commands or promises.

Finally, several reasons may be suggested why Jesus dropped the petition "Give us this day our daily *[epiousion]* bread" (Matthew 6:11) in the Sermon at the Temple. Perhaps the petition did not fit the circumstances because Jesus knew he would spend the entire day with these people and would not take time for lunch. Perhaps it was omitted because Jesus wanted to supply a unique sacramental bread at the end of the day (see 3 Nephi 18:1). Perhaps it was dropped because Jesus is the bread of life, and the people had already received their true sustenance that day in the appearance of Jesus.

Unfortunately, the meaning of the word *epiousion* (daily? continual? sufficient? essential? for the future?) is obscure,[24] but one of the earliest interpretations of it (supported by the early fragmentary *Gospel of the Hebrews*) was eschatological: "*mahar* [the Hebrew that Jerome assumed stood behind the Greek *epiousion*] meant not only the next day but also the great Tomorrow, the final consummation. Accordingly, Jerome is saying, the 'bread for tomorrow' was not meant as earthly bread but as the bread of life" in an eschatological sense.[25] If the several scholars who refer this petition "to the *coming* Kingdom and its feast"[26] are correct, Jesus might have considered this petition unsuitable in the context of the Sermon at the Temple, since the kingdom had in one sense already come. His appearance at that time in Bountiful was a realized eschatological event. Assuming that this is the meaning of *epiousion*, this deletion would fall into the same category as the other differences, mentioned above, that reflect the postresurrectional setting of the Sermon at the Temple.

In sum, one can readily compare the texts of the Sermon on the Mount and the Sermon at the Temple. There are many differences between the two texts. Although to the casual observer most of these points seem insignificant or meddlesome, a closer examination shows that most of these variations are quite meaningful and subtle. The differences are consistent with the introduction of the Sermon into Nephite culture, with its covenant-making context, and with dating the text to a time before the suspected factional alterations or additions were made to the Sermon on the Mount. All this, in my opinion, speaks highly for the Sermon at the Temple as an appropriate, well-thought-out, and pertinent text, and it supplies considerable evidence that the Sermon at the Temple was not simply plagiarized superficially from the Sermon on the Mount. The differences reflect deeper circumstances and well-considered truths.

Of course there are many similarities between the two texts, and in large sections no differences occur. These similarities are consistent with Jesus' open acknowledgement that he taught the Nephites "the things which I taught before I ascended to my Father" (3 Nephi 15:1). His gospel is one gospel, no more nor less (see 3 Nephi 11:40). The Sermon at the Temple is, therefore, not only appropriately similar to but also meaningfully different from the Sermon on the Mount. The more I know of those differences, the more I am impressed that achieving this subtle balance was not something that just casually happened.

Notes

1. Samuel L. Clemens, *Roughing It* (New York: Harper, 1913), 1:119.

2. M. T. Lamb, *The Golden Bible* (New York: Ward and Drummond, 1887), iii.

3. Ibid., 187–89; italics in original. In response to a similar expression, B. H. Roberts countered, "I am led to believe that you have been so absorbed, perhaps, in tracing out the sameness in the expressions that you have failed to note the differences to which I allude, for you make the claim of strict identity between the Book of Mormon and King James' translation too strong." B. H. Roberts, "Bible Quotations in the Book of Mormon; and Reasonableness of Nephi's Prophecies," *Improvement Era 7* (January 1904): 184.

4. Lamb, *Golden Bible*, 212. To the same effect, see Ronald V. Huggins, "Did the Author of 3 Nephi Know the Gospel of Matthew?" *Dialogue: A Journal of Mormon Thought* 30/3 (1997): 137–48.

5. Roberts, "Bible Quotations," 184; Sidney B. Sperry, *Problems of the Book of Mormon* (Salt Lake City: Bookcraft, 1964), 105–6. James E. Talmage, *Jesus the Christ* (Salt Lake City: Deseret Book, 1976), 725, 729, sees a greater emphasis in the Sermon at the Temple than in the Sermon on the Mount on the adoration of Jesus but otherwise considers the two sermons to be virtually identical, both containing "the same splendid array of ennobling precepts" and "the same wealth of effective comparison" (p. 727).

6. Roberts, "Bible Quotations," 191.

7. I will not discuss in detail the differences between the Sermon at the Temple, the Sermon on the Mount, and the Joseph Smith Translation. For a three-column chart comparing these three texts, see the appendix to the 1990 edition of this book. In the interests of simplicity and pertinence to the present study, the appendix in this volume compares in two columns the texts of the King James Bible and 3 Nephi 12–14. For discussions of the JST's

features, see Robert A. Cloward, "The Sermon on the Mount in the JST and the Book of Mormon," in *The Joseph Smith Translation: The Restoration of Plain and Precious Things*, ed. Monte S. Nyman and Robert L. Millet (Provo, Utah: BYU Religious Studies Center, 1985), 163–200; and W. Jeffrey Marsh, "Prophetic Enlightenment on the Sermon on the Mount," *Ensign*, January 1999, 15–21. The fact that the Sermon at the Temple and the Joseph Smith Translation are not identical to each other shows, from one Latter-day Saint point of view, that Jesus delivered the Sermon several times, and thus one should not necessarily expect to find a single "correct" version of the text.

8. Raymond E. Brown, *The Churches the Apostles Left Behind* (New York: Pauline, 1984).

9. Frank Zimmermann, *The Aramaic Origin of the Four Gospels* (New York: KTAV, 1979), 47. Georg Strecker, *The Sermon on the Mount: An Exegetical Commentary*, trans. O. C. Dean Jr. (Nashville: Abingdon, 1988), 69, points out that the expression soon took on a broader meaning, however, than merely "the way to the courthouse." See Hans Dieter Betz, *The Sermon on the Mount*, ed. Adela Yarbro Collins (Minneapolis: Fortress, 1995), 226.

10. The coins of Herod Agrippa I (A.D. 37–44) bearing the inscription *ORKIA BASILEOS MEGALOU AGRIPA* are catalogued in Ya'akov Meshorer, *Ancient Jewish Coinage* (Jerusalem: Amphora, 1982), 2:45, 47, 56, 246; and *Jewish Coins of the Second Temple Period* (Chicago: Argonaut, 1967), 139–40; see Ernst W. Klimowsky, *On Ancient Palestinian and Other Coins: Their Symbolism and Metrology* (Tel Aviv: Israel Numismatic Society, 1974), 105–6. For this information, I am indebted to Dennis C. Duling of Canisius College for his paper presented at the Society of Biblical Literature annual meeting in Chicago, November 1988.

11. Ulrich Luz, *Matthew 1–7: A Continental Commentary*, trans. Wilhelm C. Linss (Minneapolis: Fortress, 1989), 278.

12. John I. Durham, "Shalom and the Presence of God," in *Proclamation and Presence*, ed. John I. Durham and J. R. Porter (Richmond, Va.: John Knox, 1970), 290, 292; see Baruch A. Levine, *In the Presence of the Lord* (Leiden: Brill, 1974).

13. Durham, "Shalom and the Presence of God," 290, 292.

14. Vernon K. Robbins, "Divine Dialogue and the Lord's Prayer: Socio-Rhetorical Interpretation of Sacred Texts," *Dialogue: A Journal of Mormon Thought* 28/3 (1995): 133.

15. Luz, *Matthew 1–7*, 267–72.

16. On the question of whether this mutilation was to be understood literally or as hyperbolic speech, especially in light of similar rabbinic sayings whose actual execution is debated legalistically and philosophically, see Betz, *Sermon on the Mount,* 238–39.

17. William F. Albright and Christopher S. Mann say this applies to alien and heathen people. Albright and Mann, *Matthew* (Garden City, N. Y.: Doubleday, 1971), 84. Samuel T. Lachs links the Samaritans with the dogs and the Romans with the swine: "Who are the dogs and the swine in this passage? It is well-known that they are both used as derogatory terms for the Gentiles." Lachs, *A Rabbinic Commentary on the New Testament* (New York: KTAV, 1987), 139.

18. Hans Dieter Betz, *Essays on the Sermon on the Mount* (Philadelphia: Fortress, 1985), 1–16, 55–69.

19. Ibid., 19.

20. Ibid., 21.

21. Ibid., 20–21. For reasons against seeing Matthew 7:15–23 as anti-Pauline, see David Hill, "False Prophets and Charismatics: Structure and Interpretation in Matthew 7:15–23," *Biblica* 57 (1976): 327–48.

22. See, for example, W. D. Davies, *Torah in the Messianic Age and/or the Age to Come* (Philadelphia: Society of Biblical Literature, 1952).

23. See, for example, Betz, *Essays on the Sermon on the Mount,* 156–57.

24. Walter Bauer, William F. Arndt, and F. Wilbur Gingrich, *A Greek-English Lexicon of the New Testament,* 2nd ed. (Chicago: University of Chicago Press, 1979), 296–97; G. Kittel, ed., *Theological Dictionary of the New Testament* (Grand Rapids, Mich.: Eerdmans, 1964), 2:590–99.

25. Joachim Jeremias, *The Prayers of Jesus* (London: SCM, 1967), 100–101.

26. Bauer, Arndt, and Gingrich, *Greek-English Lexicon*, 297; and Kittel, *Theological Dictionary*, 2:595.

CHAPTER 7

THE COMMON
ISRAELITE BACKGROUND

The previous pages display many differences between the Sermon on the Mount and the Sermon at the Temple and show that all those variations were purposeful and consistent with the delivery of the Sermon in Bountiful. In further support of the assertion that the Sermon on the Mount appropriately appears in the Sermon at the Temple, one may wonder if Jesus did *not* change some things from the Sermon on the Mount that he should have changed in order to make the text understandable to the Nephites. Although it is impossible to know for sure how much of the Sermon at the Temple the Nephites readily recognized from their Old Testament and Israelite heritage (and 3 Nephi 15:2 makes it clear that they did not immediately understand everything that Jesus said), I conclude that there are few individual words or concepts in the Sermon at the Temple that should have been puzzling to the Nephites. In my opinion, there are no other words or phrases in the Sermon where something needed to be changed but was not.

Indeed, most of the words and phrases, images, ideas, and modes of logical expression in the Sermon on the Mount are rather universally understandable to all mankind. What person does not understand such basic words or concepts as mercy, the poor, peacemakers, salt, light, sun, wind, darkness, open, secret, treasure, heart, mote, beam, bread, serpent, tree, fruit, blossom, rock, sand, men, brother, love, hate, enemy, adversary, marriage, divorce, greet, day, tomorrow, throw, hand, pigs, dogs, grass, power, glory, rejoice, fields, barns, ask, seek, knock, listen, clothing, good, evil, sin, forgive, righteousness, obey, cut off, swear, kill, prophet, wide, narrow, parents, children, holy, stature, eye, call, judge, lamp, riches, pearls, fast, pray, law, debts, and so forth? There are some 383 Greek words in the total vocabulary of the Sermon on the Mount. Most are everyday words. The translation of these words is generally straightforward. Their overt meanings can hardly be mistaken, whether they are expressed in English, Latin, Greek, Aramaic, Nephite, or any other language.

Krister Stendahl has suggested one such translation problem in the way the Sermon at the Temple renders the fourth beatitude. It reads, "Blessed are all they who do hunger and thirst after righteousness, for they shall be filled with the Holy Ghost" (3 Nephi 12:6). He remarked that it seemed unnatural to associate the Greek word *chortazō* (physically filled) in Matthew 5:6 with a spiritual filling, since the New Testament Greek usually uses a different word, *plēroō*, when it speaks of being filled with the Spirit and since *chortazō* appears in passages about actual feedings of multitudes, eating crumbs, and so on.[1]

The problem, however, is solved when we turn to Old Testament backgrounds of the Sermon. The promise of Jesus, that those who hunger and thirst after "righteousness" *(dikaiosunēn)* shall be filled *(chortasthēsontai)*, is closely related to the last two verses of Psalm 17 (Psalm 16 in the Greek Septuagint), a rarely mentioned text that Stendahl apparently overlooked. This psalm contrasts the filling *(echortasthēsan)* of the stomach in uncleanliness with beholding the face of God in righteousness *(dikaiosunē)*: "I shall be satisfied *[chortasthēsomai]* when I awake, with thy likeness" (Psalm 17:15). Here the word *chortazō* is used to describe one's being filled with the Spirit and being satisfied by beholding the righteousness of God. The distinctiveness of this use of *chortazō* in Psalm 17 and Matthew 5:6 only increases the likelihood that Jesus' New Testament audience would have recognized his allusion to these words in the psalm, a passage that would have been quite familiar to them. It shows that the translation in the Sermon at the Temple does well by making explicit this particular understanding of *chortazō* as having reference to a spiritual filling by the Holy Ghost, such as that which comes when a person beholds the face of God in righteousness.[2]

The text of the Sermon on the Mount is steeped in phraseology of early biblical literature. Although most Christians assume that Jesus' words were completely original, in fact many of the words and phrases in the Sermon on the Mount were taken directly or proximately from the Old Testament scriptures. These expressions would have had a familiar ring to his audience in Galilee and probably also to his listeners in Bountiful, who shared the Israelite scriptural heritage up to the time of Jeremiah. The following list shows the main biblical antecedents and precedents drawn upon by Jesus in the Sermon. Some are direct quotes; others are paraphrases or closely related expressions.

Old Testament	The Sermon
"The meek also shall increase their joy in the Lord, and the poor among men shall rejoice in the Holy One of Israel" (Isaiah 29:19).	"Blessed are the poor in spirit" (Matthew 5:3; compare 3 Nephi 12–14 throughout this table).
"To comfort all that mourn" (Isaiah 61:2). "To set up on high those that be low; that those which mourn may be exalted to safety" (Job 5:11).	"Blessed are they that mourn: for they shall be comforted" (Matthew 5:4).
"The meek shall inherit the earth" (Psalm 37:11). "The meek shall eat and be satisfied: they shall praise the Lord that seek him: your heart shall live for ever" (Psalm 22:26). "The meek will he guide in judgment: and the meek will he teach his way" (Psalm 25:9). "God arose to judgment, to save all the meek of the earth" (Psalm 76:9).	"Blessed are the meek: for they shall inherit the earth" (Matthew 5:5).

Old Testament	The Sermon
"The Lord lifteth up the meek: he casteth the wicked down to the ground" (Psalm 147:6).	
"The Lord taketh pleasure in his people: he will beautify the meek with salvation" (Psalm 149:4).	
"Good tidings unto the meek" (Isaiah 61:1).	

Old Testament	The Sermon
"I shall be satisfied [chortas-thēsomai] . . . , I will behold thy face in righteousness [dikaio-sunēi]" (Psalm 17:15 LXX).	"Blessed are they which do hunger and thirst after righteousness [dikaiosunē]: for they shall be filled [chortasthēson-tai]" (Matthew 5:6).
"They shall not hunger nor thirst; neither shall the heat nor the sun smite them: for he that hath mercy on them shall lead them, even by the springs of water shall he guide them" (Isaiah 49:10).	
"The meek shall eat and be satisfied: they shall praise the Lord that seek him: your heart shall live for ever" (Psalm 22:26).	

Old Testament	The Sermon
"Who shall ascend into the hill [temple] of the Lord? or who shall stand in his holy place? He that hath clean hands, and a pure heart" (Psalm 24:3–4; see 73:1).	"Blessed are the pure in heart: for they shall see God" (Matthew 5:8).
"They shall be called [klēthē-sontai] the sons [huioi] of the living God" (Hosea 1:10 LXX). "I have said, Ye are gods; and all of you are children of the most High" (Psalm 82:6).	"They shall be called [klēthē-sontai] the children [huioi] of God" (Matthew 5:9).
"They mocked the messengers of God, and despised his words, and misused his prophets" (2 Chronicles 36:16).	"Men shall revile you, and persecute you, and shall say all manner of evil against you falsely . . . for so persecuted they the prophets which were before you" (Matthew 5:11–12).
"Neither shalt thou suffer the salt of the covenant of thy God to be lacking" (Leviticus 2:13).	"Ye are the salt of the earth" (Matthew 5:13).
"Trodden under feet" (Isaiah 14:19).	"Trodden under foot" (Matthew 5:13).

Old Testament	The Sermon
"A nation meted out and trodden under foot" (Isaiah 18:7).	
"The crown of pride . . . shall be trodden under feet" (Isaiah 28:3).	
"The Lord hath trodden under foot all my mighty men" (Lamentations 1:15).	
"Thou hast trodden down all them that err from thy statutes" (Psalm 119:118).	
"I will also give thee for a light to the Gentiles, that thou mayest be my salvation unto the end of the earth" (Isaiah 49:6; see 42:6).	"Ye are the light of the world" (Matthew 5:14) "I give unto you to be the light of this people" (3 Nephi 12:14).
"When his candle shined upon my head, and when by his light I walked through darkness" (Job 29:3). "For thou wilt light my candle: the Lord my God will enlighten my darkness" (Psalm 18:28).	"Neither do men light a candle, and put it under a bushel" (Matthew 5:15).

Old Testament	The Sermon
"Thou shalt not kill" (Exodus 20:13; Deuteronomy 5:17).	"Thou shalt not kill" (Matthew 5:21).
"Do not go hastily to court, for what will you do in the end if your neighbor puts you to shame? Argue your case [out of court] with your neighbor; and do not betray the confidence of another, lest hearing about it he may shame you and your bad reputation will never go away" (Proverbs 25: 8–9; from the Hebrew).	"Agree with thine adversary quickly, whiles thou art in [a legal dispute] with him; lest at any time the adversary deliver thee to the judge, and the judge deliver thee to the officer, and thou be cast into prison. Verily I say unto thee, Thou shalt by no means come out thence, till thou hast paid the uttermost farthing" (Matthew 5:25–26).
"Thou shalt not commit adultery" (Exodus 20:14).	"Thou shalt not commit adultery" (Matthew 5:27).
"Lust not after her beauty in thine heart; neither let her take thee with her eyelids" (Proverbs 6:25). "Seek not after your own heart and your own eyes, after which ye use to go a whoring" (Numbers 15:39).	"Whosoever looketh on a woman to lust after her hath committed adultery with her already in his heart" (Matthew 5:28).

Old Testament	The Sermon
"Let him write her a bill of divorcement" (Deuteronomy 24:1).	"Let him give her a writing of divorcement" (Matthew 5:31).
"The Lord, the God of Israel, saith that he hateth putting away" (Malachi 2:16).	"Whosoever shall put away his wife, saving for the cause of fornication, causeth her to commit adultery" (Matthew 5:32).
"Thou shalt not bear false witness" (Exodus 20:16). "Ye shall not swear by my name falsely" (Leviticus 19:12; see Numbers 30:2). "Thine enemies take thy name in vain" (Psalms 139:20).	"Thou shalt not forswear thyself" (Matthew 5:33).
"Pay thy vows unto the most High" (Psalm 50:14).	"Perform unto the Lord thine oaths" (Matthew 5:33).
"If thou shalt forbear to vow, it shall be no sin in thee" (Deuteronomy 23:22). "Better is it that thou shouldest not vow, than that thou shouldest vow and not pay" (Ecclesiastes 5:5).	"Swear not at all" (Matthew 5:34).

Old Testament	The Sermon
"The heaven is my throne, and the earth is my footstool" (Isaiah 66:1).	"Neither by heaven; for it is God's throne: Nor by the earth; for it is his footstool" (Matthew 5:34–35).
"Zion . . . city of the great King" (Psalm 48:2).	"Jerusalem . . . the city of the great King" (Matthew 5:35).
"Eye for eye, tooth for tooth" (Exodus 21:24; Leviticus 24:20; Deuteronomy 19:21).	"An eye for an eye, and a tooth for a tooth" (Matthew 5:38).
"I gave my back to the smiters [rhapismata], and my cheeks to them that plucked off the hair" (Isaiah 50:6 LXX).	"Whosoever shall smite [rhapizei] thee on thy right cheek, turn to him the other also" (Matthew 5:39).
"If thou at all take thy neighbor's raiment to pledge, thou shalt deliver it unto him by [sundown]" (Exodus 22:26). "Hath given his bread to the hungry, and hath covered the naked with a garment" (Ezekiel 18:7).	"If any man will sue thee . . . and take away thy coat, let him have thy cloke also" (Matthew 5:40).

Old Testament	The Sermon
"[Thou] shalt surely lend him sufficient for his need" (Deuteronomy 15:8).	"From him that would borrow of thee turn not thou away" (Matthew 5:42).
"Giveth unto the poor" (Proverbs 28:27).	
"If thou lend money to any of my people that is poor by thee, thou shalt not . . . lay upon him usury" (Exodus 22:25).	
"Love thy neighbour" (Leviticus 19:18).	"Love thy neighbour and hate thine enemy" (Matthew 5:43).
"In that thou lovest thine enemies, and hatest thy friends" (2 Samuel 19:6).	
"If thou meet thine enemy's ox or his ass going astray, thou shalt surely bring it back to him again" (Exodus 23:4; see Deuteronomy 22:1).	"Love your enemies, bless them that curse you, do good to them that hate you" (Matthew 5:44).
"If thine enemy be hungry, give him bread to eat; and if he be thirsty, give him water to drink" (Proverbs 25:21).	

Old Testament	The Sermon
"Ye are the children of the Lord your God" (Deuteronomy 14:1).	"That ye may be the children of your Father" (Matthew 5:45).
"Ye are Gods . . . children of the most High" (Psalm 82:6).	

"Ye shall be holy: for I the Lord your God am holy" (Leviticus 19:2).	"Be ye therefore perfect, even as your Father which is in heaven is perfect" (Matthew 5:48).
"Thou shalt be perfect" (Deuteronomy 18:13).	
"Let your heart therefore be perfect with the Lord our God" (1 Kings 8:61).	

"He went in therefore, and shut the door upon them twain, and prayed unto the Lord" (2 Kings 4:33; compare Isaiah 26:20).	"When thou prayest, enter into thy closet, and when thou hast shut thy door, pray to thy Father" (Matthew 6:6).
"He turned his face to the wall, and prayed unto the Lord" (2 Kings 20:2).	

"Yea, when ye make many prayers, I will not hear" (Isaiah 1:15).	"For they think that they shall be heard for their much speaking" (Matthew 6:7).

Old Testament	The Sermon
"I will sanctify [hallow] my great name" (Ezekiel 36:23).	"Hallowed be thy name" (Matthew 6:9).
"His name shall endure forever: his name shall be continued as long as the sun: and men shall be blessed in him: all nations shall call him blessed" (Psalm 72:17).	
"Holy and reverend is his name" (Psalm 111:9).	
"They shall sanctify my name" (Isaiah 29:23).	
"This is the bread which the Lord hath given you to eat" (Exodus 16:15).	"Give us this day our daily bread" (Matthew 6:11).
"Satisfied them with the bread of heaven" (Psalm 105:40).	
"Thine, O Lord, is the greatness, and the power, and the glory, and the victory, and the majesty: for all that is in the heaven and in the earth is thine; thine is the kingdom, O Lord, and thou art exalted as head above all" (1 Chronicles 29:11).	"Thine is the kingdom, and the power, and the glory, for ever" (Matthew 6:13).

Old Testament	The Sermon
"The whole earth is full of his glory" (Isaiah 6:3).	

"Is it such a fast that I have chosen? a day for a man to afflict his soul? is it to bow down his head as a bulrush, and to spread sackcloth and ashes under him? wilt thou call this a fast, and an acceptable day to the Lord?" (Isaiah 58:5).	"When ye fast, be not . . . of a sad countenance. . . . When thou fastest, anoint thine head, and wash thy face" (Matthew 6:16–17).
"The fast . . . shall be . . . joy and gladness" (Zechariah 8:19).	

"If a thief be found breaking up" (Exodus 22:2).	"Where thieves break through and steal" (Matthew 6:19).
"If thieves [come] by night, they will destroy till they have enough" (Jeremiah 49:9).	

"The spirit of man is the candle of the Lord" (Proverbs 20:27).	"The light of the body is the eye" (Matthew 6:22).

Old Testament	The Sermon
"And in thy seed shall all the nations of the earth be blessed; because thou hast obeyed my voice" (Genesis 22:18).	"Seek ye first the kingdom of God, and his righteousness; and all these things shall be added unto you" (Matthew 6:33).
"A blessing, if ye obey the commandments of the Lord your God, which I command you this day" (Deuteronomy 11:27).	
"Delight thyself also in the Lord; and he shall give thee the desires of thine heart" (Psalm 37:4).	
"Gather [manna at] a certain rate every day" (Exodus 16:4).	"Take . . . no thought for the morrow" (Matthew 6:34).
"Holy men . . . : neither shall ye eat any flesh that is torn of beasts . . . ; ye shall cast it to the dogs" (Exodus 22:31).	"Give not that which is holy unto the dogs, neither cast ye your pearls before swine" (Matthew 7:6).
"Those that seek me early shall find me" (Proverbs 8:17).	"Seek, and ye shall find" (Matthew 7:7).
"Ye shall seek me, and find me" (Jeremiah 29:13).	

Old Testament	The Sermon
"To seek the Lord; but they shall not find him" (Hosea 5:6).	
The Two Ways (see Deuteronomy 11:26; 30:15, 19; Jeremiah 21:8; Proverbs 28:6, 18).	The Two Ways (see Matthew 7:13–14).
"The prophet, which shall presume to speak [what] I have not commanded him to speak, . . . shall die" (Deuteronomy 18:20; see Zechariah 10:2).	"Beware of false prophets" (Matthew 7:15).
"They gaped upon me with their mouths, as a ravening and a roaring lion" (Psalm 22:13). "Her princes in the midst thereof are like wolves ravening the prey" (Ezekiel 22:27).	"Inwardly they are ravening wolves" (Matthew 7:15).
"The Lord alone shall be exalted in that day" (Isaiah 2:11, 17; see Exodus 8:22; and many others).	"In that day" (Matthew 7:22).

Old Testament	The Sermon
"[They] prophesy lies in my name" (Jeremiah 14:14; compare 14:15; 23:25; 27:15; 29:9, 21).	"Have we not prophesied in thy name?" (Matthew 7:22).
"Depart from me, all ye workers of iniquity" (Psalm 6:8; see 141:4; Isaiah 31:2; 32:6; 59:6; Hosea 6:8; Micah 2:1).	"Depart from me, ye that work iniquity" (Matthew 7:23).
"And one built up a wall, and, lo, others daubed it with untempered morter [sand]: . . . there shall be an overflowing shower; and ye, O great hailstones, shall fall; and a stormy wind shall rend it" (Ezekiel 13:10–11).	"A foolish man . . . built his house upon the sand: And the rain descended, and the floods came, and the winds blew, and beat upon that house; and it fell" (Matthew 7:26–27).
"The Lord is nigh unto them that are of a broken heart; and saveth such as be of a contrite spirit" (Psalm 34:18). "A broken spirit: a broken and contrite heart" (Psalm 51:17).	"Come unto me with a broken heart and a contrite spirit" (3 Nephi 12:19).

This list is undoubtedly incomplete, but it is striking—and I believe most readers will be as surprised as I was by the substantial number of phrases in the Sermon on the Mount that essentially repeat or allude to phrases in the Old Testament. Many other parallels can also be adduced from the Dead Sea Scrolls and other Jewish writings. Obviously, the lines of the Sermon "are not a spontaneous lyrical outbreak of prophecy, but a profound message founded on a complex network of biblical reminiscences and midrashic exegesis."[3]

My purpose in displaying these parallels and likely precedents is not to claim that Jesus quoted each of these Old Testament passages verbatim. Several of them are precise quotes; others are only paraphrases or presentations of similar concepts. My point is simply to show that Jesus' words would not have sounded strange to either his Jewish or Nephite listeners. Their common Israelite and prophetic heritages would have prepared both audiences to understand and appreciate the messages in this Sermon as Jesus transformed their old laws into new.

While we cannot know for sure how many of these Old Testament expressions were found on the plates of brass or how closely they were rendered by Jesus into the contemporary Nephite dialect, certainly many of these phrases were known to the Nephites (especially the passages in the Pentateuch and Isaiah). Accordingly, although the Sermon is often thought of as a uniquely "Christian" scripture, it is saturated with Israelite and Jewish elements.[4] Passages from the Law, the Prophets, and the Psalms; covenantal injunctions about giving to the poor (see Mosiah 4:16–26), praying, and fasting (see Omni 1:26; Mosiah 27:23; Alma 5:46); and specific references to wealth (see Jacob 2:12–19), the temple of Solomon (see 2 Nephi 5:16), and the "strait and narrow" (1 Nephi 8:20) were familiar territory to the Nephites.

An informed Israelite or a devout Nephite would have readily recognized that the Sermon took the threads of the old covenantal law and wove them into a splendid new tapestry. Once we are aware of this rich background of Israelite origins, we can hardly imagine a reaction more fitting than that of the Nephites: Their reaction was one of marvel and wonder at how all their old and familiar things had suddenly become new (see 3 Nephi 15:3).

It is not difficult to identify many ways in which the Nephites could well have recognized that Jesus was presenting ideas to them that they had known before but that now appeared in a new form or context. Their Israelite backgrounds had schooled and prepared them to recognize and finally receive the principles and ordinances of the gospel of Jesus Christ. Some of the places in the Sermon at the Temple where one can discern points of transforming continuity between the old and the new—especially seen in the temple legacy of the giving of the law of Moses in Exodus 19–24 and its connections with the Sermon at the Temple in 3 Nephi 11–18—include the following:

1. Whereas previously "the Lord descended upon [Mount Sinai] in fire" and tumult to a place set apart as holy (Exodus 19:18), now he came peacefully to the temple as "a Man descending out of heaven" (3 Nephi 11:8).

2. The old Hosanna Shout of Psalm 118 could only look forward to him "that cometh in the name of the Lord" (Psalm 118:26), but now it rang out to bless him who had finally come (see 3 Nephi 11:17). This long-awaited event must have broken forth into the lives of the people at Bountiful with the kind of unbelievable euphoria that so many people in the world experienced with the initial

opening of the Berlin Wall in 1989—they had never dared to dream that they would actually live to see it happen.

3. To take the place of the old sanctification of the people and the ritual washing of their clothes, the Nephites were given an expanded understanding of the ordinance of baptism for the remission of sins. (For widespread indications of ancient Israelite ceremonial or ritual ablutions to remove impurity both from the worshippers and temple priests, see Exodus 19:14; Leviticus 13:58; 15:17; 2 Samuel 12:20; 2 Chronicles 4:6; Psalms 24:4; 26:6; 73:13; Ezekiel 16:9.)[5]

4. Radically upgrading the nature of witnesses—which under the old law could be seventy of the elders (see Exodus 24:9), or stones (see Joshua 24:27), or the heavens and the earth (see Deuteronomy 4:26)—now the members of the Godhead themselves stood as primary witnesses of the doctrine and covenants of Jesus Christ (see 3 Nephi 11:35–36).

5. The old list of curses that for centuries had been ritually invoked upon those who privily worked wickedness (see Deuteronomy 27:11–26) were now transposed into or replaced by a list of glorious blessings upon those who secretly worked righteousness (see 3 Nephi 12:3–11; 13:4, 6, 18).

6. The old view of creation had presented the words "Let there be light" as a physical phenomenon, but now it became a personal creation, "Let your light so shine" (3 Nephi 12:16).

7. The old law of sacrifice was explicitly replaced by the sacrifice of a "broken heart and a contrite spirit" (3 Nephi 12:18–19), and whereas previously the sacrificial animal was to be pure and without blemish (*haplous*), now the disciples themselves were to become "single" (*haplous*) to the glory of God (see 3 Nephi 13:22; Matthew 6:22).

8. Similarly, old commandments regarding murder, adultery, divorce, and oath-swearing (see Exodus 20:13–17) were dramatically transfigured in the new order of Christ to promise results even more glorious than Solomon's temple of old (see Matthew 6:29; 3 Nephi 13:29).

9. In the covenant at Sinai the people covenanted to do "all the words which the Lord hath said" (Exodus 24:3; see Deuteronomy 24:1–4), and the Lord promised in return to "bless thy bread, and thy water; and [to] take sickness away from the midst of" the people (Exodus 24:25). So too the Nephites newly covenanted with blessed bread and wine to do what the Lord had commanded (see 3 Nephi 18:3–10), and he healed all their sick (see 3 Nephi 17:9).

10. Moses wrote the words of the covenant, built an altar (see Exodus 24:4), sprinkled blood on the people, and said, "Behold the blood of the covenant, which the Lord hath made with you concerning all these words" (Exodus 24:8). As the Nephites looked back on the divine and ritual-laden origins of the law of Moses, they could easily see its fulfillment in the new revelation that they received from Jesus at the temple in Bountiful, at a symbolic mount, with laws concerning sacrifice, obedience, adultery, consecration, the healing of the sick, the blessing of bread, and the drinking of the cup of the blood of the new testament.

In broad terms, the main themes of the Sermon at the Temple are also the topics treated in the book of Leviticus, regarded by Jews as the most sacred of the five books of Moses. Its main concerns are implementing the law of sacrifice (Leviticus 1–7; 17), bestowing the priesthood (chaps. 8–10), assuring purity (chaps. 11–16), holy living and loving one's neighbor (chap. 19), defining chastity (chaps. 18, 20), hallowing the Sabbath days (chap. 23), eschewing

blasphemy (chap. 24), and caring for the poor and conse-
crating property to the Lord (chaps. 25–27). Not being
steeped in the ethical and spiritual dimensions of the law
of Moses, modern LDS readers tend to overlook the profound religious legacy of these underlying purposes of the
law that have enduring relevance to the temple.

Over and over it is evident in the Sermon at the Temple
that indeed "all things had become new" (3 Nephi 15:3) in
a great and marvelous way. Jesus identified himself as the
prophet-like-Moses and said, "I am he that gave the law,
and I am he who covenanted with my people Israel"
(3 Nephi 15:5). The continuity from the law of Moses to the
law of Christ is nowhere more visible than at the temple in
Bountiful as Christ gave the Nephites laws, covenanted
with them, and made all their old things new.

Only a few passages require discussion in regard to the
Nephites' ability to understand what Jesus was talking
about. The first instance is whether the Nephites would
have understood the word *mammon*. The ancient origins
and etymology of this word are highly uncertain.[6] Around
the time of Jesus it was a frequently used Aramaic word in
Palestine, meaning "wealth, property, profit, or money,"
appearing in the Targums, the Mishnah, the Talmud, and
the Damascus Document.[7] It is unknown how far back in
history the word was known or where it came from, and
thus one cannot be certain about the nature of its occur-
rence in 3 Nephi. Aramaic is old enough that a Nephite
word for money could have been "mammon," but without
access to the original Nephite texts it is unclear if Jesus
used this Aramaic word in the Sermon at the Temple, or if
it was a part of Nephite vocabulary, or whether Jesus used
some closely comparable Nephite word for "wealth" that
was simply translated by Joseph Smith as "mammon."

Nevertheless, the context of laying up heavenly treasures and serving only one master makes it clear what Jesus was talking about. Similar things can be said of the Aramaic word *Raca*, whose antiquity and possible derivation from Hebrew is also uncertain but whose basic meaning is unmistakable in the context of calling another a fool in ridicule or derision.

The second problematic passage raises the question of whether the Nephites would have known where it was written, "Hate thine enemy" (Matthew 5:43). One searches in vain in the Old Testament for exactly such a writing; and, indeed, in this particular instance Jesus does not say to the Nephites, "It is also written *before you*" (3 Nephi 12:43), as he did with the first law against murder. Thus the Nephites may have been left to wonder who *had* written such a thing. Several scholars have suggested that Matthew 5:43 refers to a text from the community at Qumran: God commands his sons to "love everything that he has chosen but to hate everything that he has rejected."[8] Thus Jesus' listeners in Palestine may have recognized in his words a veiled criticism of that specific sect. Another possibility is that Jesus was responding to some other contemporary "popular maxim or partisan rallying cry" glossing Leviticus 19:18.[9] The roots of Matthew 5:43, however, may run much earlier, for similar sentiments are found in 2 Samuel 19:6, which criticizes the king for having everything backwards, "in that thou lovest thine enemies, and hatest thy friends." The implication is that one should hate one's enemies and love one's friends. In any event, whether or not the Nephites knew where such a saying was written, they would have had no difficulty understanding Jesus' meaning. They may have thought immediately of their own ongoing, painful problems with the Lamanites, a group that expressly taught their children to hate their enemies eternally (see Mosiah 10:17; compare Jacob 7:26).

Third, "figs" and "grapes" are mentioned in 3 Nephi 14:16: "Do men gather grapes [literally 'bunches'] of thorns, or figs of thistles?" Thorns and thistles were present in the New World, but grapes and figs are slightly more questionable. John Sorenson points out that "certain grapes were present, but we do not know that they were used for food or drink,"[10] although he reports that this is now thought to be more likely. Still, we cannot be sure what a Nephite might have thought when he heard the words *figs* and *grapes*. There are several possibilities. Certainly the words were known to the Nephites from the Hebrew records brought with them from Jerusalem, and thus these fruits may have been known to them simply as archaic terms; or perhaps the Nephites used these names for local fruits; or again, perhaps the sense behind the Greek word *staphulas* ("bunches," usually of grapes) was simply understood to mean bunches of some other kind of fruit. In any event, several varieties of figs and grapes existed in the New World (fig bark was used to make paper in Mesoamerica), and the context would have made it clear to Jesus' audience that he was talking about bunches of fruit gathered from trees.

Fourth is the "sanhedrin" mentioned in Matthew 5:22. Since the Greek word *synedrion* seems to have been first used in the days of Herod as a title for the Great Sanhedrin of Jerusalem,[11] one may wonder if the Nephites would have understood what Jesus meant when he said, "Whosoever is angry with his brother shall be in danger of his judgment [*krisei*]. And whosoever shall say to his brother, Raca, shall be in danger of the council [*synedrion*]; and whosoever shall say, Thou fool, shall be in danger of hell fire" (3 Nephi

12:22). Commentators on Matthew sometimes assert that the Greek words for *judgment* and *council* refer technically to local Jewish courts, the Small Sanhedrins and the Great Sanhedrin,[12] but the terminology is not so specific. Courts or councils of all kinds could be denoted. Strecker argues that "judgment" can be understood only "figuratively. . . . Jesus is thinking of the final judgment."[13] Alternatively, the "council" could allude to the council in heaven, which figures in God's judgments upon the world (see 1 Nephi 1:6–10),[14] or, as I have suggested above, to an apostolic council that judges mankind in this world or in the world to come (see 3 Nephi 27:27).[15] Likewise, the Nephites had synagogues, places of some kind, where they gathered together (see 2 Nephi 26:26; see also Alma 16:13), and they used a trumpet or horn to call people to repentance (see Alma 29:1). All these are concepts the Nephites would have readily understood.

The above cases are ones where a Nephite might have had difficulty readily understanding the Sermon at the Temple. Most of its common human experiences and life settings, such as thieves breaking in or going a second mile, need not presuppose anything out of the ordinary in Nephite civilization.[16] To my mind, this result is worth observing: In all the places where the two texts differ, good and sufficient reasons exist for the divergence; yet no further changes were probably needed in deference to the Nephite culture or audience, because much of the newness of the Sermon was firmly grounded in familiar terrain.

Notes

1. Krister Stendahl, "The Sermon on the Mount and Third Nephi," in *Reflections on Mormonism*, ed. Truman G. Madsen (Provo, Utah: BYU Religious Studies Center, 1978), 142. Stendahl,

an outside observer, offers several valuable insights into the Sermon at the Temple, but his explanations of them usually fall short. He notes well the emphasis on baptism, the ordination of the twelve disciples, "coming unto Jesus," and the role of the commandments (ibid., 141–43). More is involved in 3 Nephi 11–18, however, as shown above, than the mere introduction of certain literary Johannine features.

2. See numerous references to the notion of being physically "filled with the spirit" in Robert F. Smith, ed., *Book of Mormon Critical Text: A Tool for Scholarly Reference* (Provo, Utah: FARMS, 1987), 3:961 n. 287.

3. D. Flusser, "Blessed Are the Poor in Spirit," *Israel Exploration Journal* 10/1 (1960): 13.

4. In further discussions of the thoroughly Jewish character of the Sermon on the Mount, others have convincingly found Jesus the Jew at virtually every turn in the Sermon on the Mount. See, for example, Hermann L. Strack and Paul Billerbeck, *Kommentar zum Neuen Testament aus Talmud und Midrasch* (Munich: Beck, 1922), 1:188–474; Samuel T. Lachs, *A Rabbinic Commentary on the New Testament* (New York: KTAV, 1987); and "Does the Sermon on the Mount Follow a Rabbinic Pattern?" in W. D. Davies, "My Odyssey in New Testament Interpretation," *Bible Review* 5/3 (June 1989): 15.

5. Hugh W. Nibley, *The Message of the Joseph Smith Papyri* (Salt Lake City: Deseret Book, 1975), 93–96; Robert A. Wild, *Water in the Cultic Worship of Isis and Sarapis,* Etudes preœliminaires aux religions orientales dans l'Empire romain, no. 87 (Leiden: Brill, 1981), 143–48; and Thomas F. Torrance, "The Origins of Baptism," *Scottish Journal of Theology* 11 (1958): 158–71.

6. G. Kittel, ed., *Theological Dictionary of the New Testament* (Grand Rapids, Mich.: Eerdmans, 1967), 4:388–90.

7. Matthew Black, *An Aramaic Approach to the Gospels and Acts,* 3rd ed. (Oxford: Clarendon, 1967), 139–40, citing A. M. Honeyman, "The Etymology of Mammon," *Archivum Linguisticum* 4/1 (1952): 60; see Walter Bauer, William F. Arndt, and F. Wilbur

Gingrich, *A Greek-English Lexicon of the New Testament* (Chicago: University of Chicago Press, 1957), 490.

8. 1QS I 3–4, see Georg Strecker, *The Sermon on the Mount: An Exegetical Commentary,* trans. O. C. Dean Jr. (Nashville: Abingdon, 1988), 87; mentioned also in S. Kent Brown, "The Dead Sea Scrolls: A Mormon Perspective," *BYU Studies* 23/1 (1983): 65.

9. O. J. F. Seitz, "Love Your Enemies," *New Testament Studies* 16 (1969): 51. On the possible historical settings of Matthew 5:43–44 and Luke 6:27–28, see pp. 39–54.

10. John L. Sorenson, *An Ancient American Setting for the Book of Mormon* (Salt Lake City: Deseret Book and FARMS, 1985), 186.

11. Kittel, *Theological Dictionary,* 7:862.

12. Strecker, *Sermon on the Mount,* 65–67.

13. Ibid., 65, as the concluding reference to "hell fire" makes apparent.

14. Raymond E. Brown, "The Pre-Christian Semitic Concept of 'Mystery,'" *Catholic Biblical Quarterly* 20 (1958): 419 n. 10, includes the word *synedrion* among the terms used in "the vocabulary [of] the LXX to translate *sōd* where it is used of the heavenly assembly," citing, however, only Proverbs 3:32 and Jeremiah 15:17. See E. Theodore Mullen Jr., *The Divine Council in Canaanite and Early Hebrew Literature,* Harvard Semitic Monographs, no. 24 (Chico, Calif.: Scholars, 1980); and John W. Welch, "The Calling of a Prophet," in *The Book of Mormon: First Nephi, The Doctrinal Foundation,* ed. Monte S. Nyman and Charles D. Tate Jr. (Provo, Utah: BYU Religious Studies Center, 1988), 35–54.

15. On the use of the word *synedrion* in early Christianity to refer to a council of apostles, see Kittel, *Theological Dictionary,* 7:871, who points out that Ignatius spoke of a council of elders as the *topon* of the *synedrion* of the apostles and as "the council [*synedrion*] of God and the council [*synedrion*] of the apostles."

16. Ulrich Luz, *Matthew 1–7: A Continental Commentary,* trans. Wilhelm C. Linss (Minneapolis: Fortress, 1989), 326, 345.

CHAPTER 8

JOSEPH SMITH
AND THE TRANSLATION OF
THE SERMON AT THE TEMPLE

Inasmuch as the Sermon at the Temple is appropriately nuanced and subtly different from the Sermon on the Mount, as the previous chapters show, one might well wonder how this occurred. Joseph Smith explained that it came by the gift and power of God as the text was translated one line after another. The following study of events and factors involved in this translation process bear out Joseph's testimony and point strongly to the conclusion that his translation of the Sermon at the Temple was meticulously accurate.

No Time for Research

To begin with, those who reject Joseph Smith's explanation of how the Book of Mormon came forth must at least credit him with high marks for keeping many factors in mind as he allegedly modified the Sermon on the Mount to fit into a Nephite context. Given enough time and research opportunities, a reasonably intelligent person could probably work his way through the Sermon on the Mount in a similar fashion, producing something like the Sermon at the Temple; and with a little luck, such a reviser might not overlook or mistake anything important in the modification process.

Time and research, however, were not on Joseph Smith's side. The account of Jesus' ministry among the Nephites was translated before May 15, 1829, and Joseph and Oliver had commenced their work of the translation and transcription several hundred pages earlier only on April 7, 1829.[1] At this pace, assuming that they completed about eight pages per day, they could have spent only about two days on the totality of the Sermon at the Temple in 3 Nephi 11–18.

No Way to Crib

Several historical accounts of the translation process make it unlikely that any copying of a printed Bible occurred. While many have assumed that Joseph covertly took out his copy of the King James Bible and worked from it when he came to the Isaiah and Sermon on the Mount materials in the Book of Mormon, the following testimonies of people who intimately assisted Joseph Smith in the transcription process and routinely watched him work give evidence that such a thing did not occur. Emma Smith, Martin Harris, Oliver Cowdery, David Whitmer, William Smith, Lucy Mack Smith, Elizabeth Anne Whitmer Cowdery Johnson, Michael Morse, Sarah Heller Conrad, Isaac Hale, and Joseph Knight Sr. all left historical comments on what they knew of how Joseph worked when he was translating the Book of Mormon.[2] None of their statements mentions anything about the use of a Bible or allows room for it.

In an interview in 1879, Emma Smith was asked and asserted the following:

Q. Had he not a book or manuscript from which he read, or dictated to you?

A. He had neither manuscript nor book to read from.

Q. Could he not have had, and you not know it?

A. If he had had anything of the kind he could not have concealed it from me.[3]

While this interview occurred fifty years after the events it reports, Emma still had a vivid memory of many details. Her recollection can probably be trusted even more regarding things that did *not* occur than in describing the particulars of things that did occur, especially since she would have been unforgettably surprised to see Joseph cribbing from the Bible. It is unknown whether she was present when the Sermon at the Temple was translated, although she would have been somewhere in and around the cabin in Harmony, Pennsylvania, in the middle of May 1829, when Joseph and Oliver were working their way through this material.

David Whitmer and others corroborated Emma's description. For example, in 1881 the *Deseret Evening News* published an article from Richmond, Missouri, about this Book of Mormon witness. It reports, "Mr. Whitmer emphatically asserts, as did Harris and Cowdery, that while Smith was dictating the translation he had NO MANUSCRIPT NOTES OR OTHER MEANS OF KNOWLEDGE save the Seer stone and the characters as shown on the plates, he being present and cognizant how it was done."[4]

In 1834 Oliver Cowdery described the work of that period. He vividly recalled, "These were days never to be forgotten—to sit under the sound of a voice dictated by the *inspiration* of heaven. . . . Day after day I continued, uninterrupted, to write from his mouth, as he translated . . . the 'book of Mormon.'"[5] Oliver was present during all of the translation of the Sermon at the Temple. It seems highly unlikely that Joseph could have read from the Bible and Oliver not have known it—and if he knew it, not to have been irreparably disillusioned. Oliver had himself attempted to translate but had been unsuccessful (see D&C 9). Certainly he thought that more was involved in the translation process than simply reading from the Bible and making a few modifications to the text. It seems to me that Oliver would have instantly doubted Joseph's ability to translate if he ever caught him using the Bible or suspected him of relying directly on it as he translated. Oliver and Joseph were in close proximity to each other, and the use of the interpreters would have made it very awkward for Joseph to put a large Bible anywhere nearby without Oliver becoming aware of it.

Nowhere to Hide

It is possible, one may counter, that Joseph sat behind a curtain or blanket while he was translating, as is commonly imagined. But the only reports, so far as I know, that mention such a thing are from Professor Charles Anthon and Reverend John A. Clark.[6] Both of these hostile sources, even if we can trust them on this point, depend on information given to them by Martin Harris, who was scribe only in 1827 and 1828. None of the scribes in 1829 ever mentions the use of a curtain while they were present. Their silence on this point is significant. All other factors indicate that Joseph was quite open with the translation process when Oliver and the others at the Whitmer farm were present and assisting.

It appears that Joseph used the curtain only at first and perhaps because he rightly did not trust Martin Harris as much as his other scribes (see D&C 10:7, which calls Martin

Harris "a wicked man" who "has sought to destroy" Joseph's gift of translation). Oliver Cowdery, on the other hand, had used the interpreters; and the Lord, who had appeared to Oliver early in 1829 testifying of "the truth of the work" and calling him to "write for [Joseph] and translate," had already shown him the plates in a vision.[7] With such a divine endorsement for Oliver, Joseph would have had little need to use a curtain when Oliver was present. Indeed, Emma's testimony describes a similar situation, wherein she "frequently wrote day after day, often sitting at the table close by him, he sitting with his face buried in his hat, with the stone in it, and dictating hour after hour with nothing between us."[8] The recollection of Oliver's wife, Elizabeth Anne Whitmer Cowdery Johnson, written in 1870, also denies that a curtain was used while she was present during the final stages of translating at the Whitmer farm in Fayette: "I often sat by and saw and heard them translate and write for hours together. Joseph never had a curtain drawn between him and his scribe while he was translating. He would place the director in his hat, and then place his face in his hat, so as to exclude the light, and then [dictate?] to his scribe the words [he said] as they appeared before [him?]."[9]

At this time in Fayette, according to our best estimates,[10] Joseph translated the small plates of Nephi, and that section of the Book of Mormon contains several sections of Isaiah material (see 1 Nephi 20–21; 2 Nephi 7–8, 12–24). If Joseph simply cribbed from the Bible when he came to such sections on the Book of Mormon plates, one must seriously wonder how he did it.

Thus, while the theory in question—that Joseph used his family Bible in translating the Book of Mormon—may appear to solve one problem, it creates another. The idea that Joseph relied directly and heavily on his Bible may ease the minds of those who resist seeing any divine power at work in the translation process, but it creates a different concern: the historical accounts give no impression whatever that Joseph turned to the Bible when dictating the text of the Sermon at the Temple.

No Need to Assume Physical Reliance

Additional considerations also make the claim of plagiarism improbable. For example, Hugh Nibley has cogently argued that it is counterintuitive to imagine that Joseph would have included long passages in the Book of Mormon that closely resembled several chapters from Isaiah as well as the Sermon on the Mount if he did not need to. He would not have been so foolish as to copy unnecessarily and thereby create an obvious problem for the Book of Mormon: "It is hard to see why a deceiver would strew the broadest clues to his pilfering all through a record he claimed was his own."[11]

Although B. H. Roberts, Sidney B. Sperry, and others have conjectured that people might argue that Joseph made direct use of his King James Bible in order to make the difficult translation job easier, they advance this theory as an assumption.[12] Sperry was satisfied to view the Nephite scripture in 3 Nephi 12–14 as an independent text, even though it only "finds support *at times* for its unusual readings in the ancient Greek, Syriac, and Latin versions, and at other times no support at all."[13] Roberts believed that Jesus presented to the Nephites "great truths in the same forms of expression he had used in teaching the Jews, so that *in substance* what he had taught as his doctrines in Judea he would repeat in America."[14] Hence, according to Roberts, when Joseph Smith thought that the words on the Nephite record and in the King James Bible *"in substance,* in thought, . . . were alike, he adopted our English translation."[15] The conjecture that Joseph needed a rest is neither a necessary nor an exclusive explanation.

Other logical possibilities exist for the Sermon in the Book of Mormon. For instance, although very little is known about the process of translating the Book of Mormon, for one who believes that Joseph Smith received *any* part of the book through the gift and power of God, it is a relatively small step from there to believe that the Sermon at the Temple was similarly translated and dictated under the direction of divine inspiration; that is, if the spiritual mechanisms or procedures were in place to accomplish the translation of the some ninety-five percent of the book that has no biblical counterpart, those mechanisms could just as well have supplied the rest. One may thus assume that, in accomplishing this translation, God projected a text similar to the biblical texts through Joseph Smith or that the power of God brought the English texts of the Bible especially to Joseph's memory as those words were appropriate and helpful in producing the Book of Mormon translation.

At the same time, while there is no evidence that Joseph could recite verbatim long sections of Isaiah and Matthew, one may certainly assume that he had read or heard those chapters several times around the family hearth. This would make it possible for the powers of inspiration to draw these words out of his memory and put them extraordinarily at his disposal, causing him to recall them, even though they would have been buried too deep in his brain to be remembered voluntarily. As B. H. Roberts has said, "The English interpretation was a reflex from the prophet's mind," and not "an arbitrary piece of mechanical work."[16]

As Joseph studied the translation out in his mind (see D&C 9:8), the words he then thought and spoke rang true to him. I would think this occurred as the translation flowed forth, independent of immediate input but also reflexive of Joseph's vocabulary and prior knowledge, reinforced by his inspired subconscious recall of the parallel texts in the Bible.

Stylistic Similarities

Even if the claim of simple plagiarism is set aside, the question may still arise, Why, in any event, is the English translation of the Sermon at the Temple so pervasively similar to the style and language of the King James rendition of Matthew 5–7? As general Christian commitment to the King James translation wanes, and as the number of years between modern readers and the time of Joseph Smith widens, the oddities of King James language grow more glaring and the force of this question increases.

For people in 1830, however, the question was far less obvious or bothersome than it may be for people today. This concern was not an issue even for critic M. T. Lamb, who wrote in 1887 that the King James Version itself had already miraculously preserved the exact words of Jesus, penned by Matthew: "if Matthew remembered the exact words of the Savior, and wrote just as they were first spoken" or "if he only remembered the substance," in either case it was a miracle.[17]

B. H. Roberts readily and unproblematically concluded that the stylistic similarities between the Sermon at the Temple and the Sermon on the Mount were simply due to Joseph's language: "While Joseph Smith obtained the facts and ideas from the Nephite characters through the inspiration of God, he was left to express those facts and ideas, in the main, in such language as he could command."[18] As Joseph translated, the Lord spoke to him "after the manner of [his] language," as he speaks to all men, "that they might come to understanding" (D&C 1:24). Where the King James English would best communicate the thought of a passage to Joseph Smith, that would be the preferred rendition.

Hugh Nibley has suggested several other reasons that made the use of King James style important, if not necessary. One reason was Joseph's audience: "When Jesus and the Apostles and, for that matter, the Angel Gabriel quote the [Hebrew] scriptures in the New Testament, do they recite from some mysterious Urtext? Do they quote the prophets of old in the ultimate original? . . . No, they do not. They quote the Septuagint, a Greek version of the Old Testament prepared in the third century B.C. Why so? Because that happened to be the received standard version of the Bible accepted by the readers of the Greek New Testament."[19]

Another reason for the use of the style of the King James Version was the nature of the record: "The scriptures were probably in old-fashioned language the day they were written down."[20] Furthermore, "by frankly using that idiom, the Book of Mormon avoids the necessity of having to be redone into 'modern English' every thirty or forty years."[21] To such points, other explanations may be added, but the foregoing seem sufficient. The King James idiom yields a good translation of both the Sermon on the Mount and the Sermon at the Temple. In fact, a study of the Greek vocabulary used in Matthew 5–7 will show that in most cases, the traditional English translation is rather straightforward. The syntax of most of the sentences is relatively simple, the expressions are direct, and most of the words and phrases have obvious and adequate primary choices in

English as their translation (although their meaning and implications still remain profound).

Identical Wording

Points such as these may sufficiently justify at one level the similarities between the English in the Sermon at the Temple and the King's English in the Sermon on the Mount, but they do not explain the origins of the overwhelming preponderance of identical phraseology in these two translations at a more particular level. Something more than merely idiomatic usage, the needs of the contemporaneous audience, or the adequacy of the meaning is necessary to account for the nearly identical correspondence of expressions between these two texts. For example, if a person were to undertake the task of translating an ancient text that had already been translated by another, and if one assumed that this person had no familiarity with the first translation, there is no chance that the second translation would turn out word for word the same as the first. Something more is necessary to account for the verbal similarities between the Sermon on the Mount and the Sermon at the Temple. That shortfall, in my opinion, is made up in two ways: First, the problem with the case of our hypothetical translator is that it assumes something that is not in evidence regarding Joseph Smith and the Sermon on the Mount, for Joseph *was* familiar with the wording of the King James translation. Second, the model inadequately assumes a normal translation process rather than one impelled and activated by inspiration.

A Precise Translation

This last point naturally invites further reflection about a persistent question regarding the Book of Mormon—

namely, what kind of a translation is it? There are several possibilities, and it exceeds anyone's ability at the present time to say which is correct.[22] Joseph Smith himself declined to comment very much on this subject, saying that "it was not expedient for him" to give "all the particulars,"[23] although in private he apparently explained the process somewhat to David Whitmer and others who spoke about the matter.

Several factors indicate that it was quite a precise translation. A range of opinions may emerge as people try to describe the nature of Joseph's translation more explicitly. Some commentators on one extreme (position 1) may suggest that it was a grammatically literal translation, a verbatim word-for-word, form-for-form rendition. This seems, however, to leave little room for the fact that Joseph had to take the matter and "study it out in [his] mind" (D&C 9:8) in order to translate the text "after the manner of [his] language" (D&C 1:24). As the discussion in chapter 9 will show regarding some of the minute grammatical comparisons of 3 Nephi 12–14 and the Greek manuscripts of the Sermon on the Mount, I do not imagine that Joseph's translation process produced this kind of extremely strict, literal translation.

At the same time, such things as the presence of detailed chiasmus in the Book of Mormon,[24] the precise nature of the book's internal quotations (see, for example, Alma 36:22 quoting exactly from 1 Nephi 1:8; and Helaman 14:12 quoting verbatim from Mosiah 3:8), its consistent use of technical legal terminology,[25] and many other instances of remarkable textual complexity strongly indicate that most of the time the translation was probably not a very loose one either. Consequently, neither does it appear, as some may suggest on the more nebulous side of the matter (position 2), that the English translation should be understood as having only occasional, casual verbal connections with the ancient Nephite records or, even more nebulous (position 3), only rare thematic intersections with the underlying record.

Accordingly, seeking something of a solution close to position 1 but not quite so strictly grounded, it seems to me that Joseph's English translation (position 4) was more expressive than a mechanically literal rendition but that its elements still corresponded in some way, point by point, with many features of the ancient writing that was being translated. Many of the textual details discussed in this study strongly suggest that the meaning of something on the plates gave rise to each element of meaning in the translation, although one cannot know in all cases how close that relationship or connection was.

Historical evidence also bears out this view. David Whitmer described how the characters from the plates would appear to Joseph on a parchment with the corresponding English translation below them. Whitmer once explained, "Frequently one character would make two lines of manuscript while others made but a word or two words."[26] If this is an accurate statement, it confirms that the translation was rather strict, character for character, although sometimes several English words were required to express the meaning of a single inscription. So, for example, two simple characters might be translated into English as "the interpretation of languages" and two others as "the Book of Mormon," as Frederick G. Williams once wrote in Kirtland.[27] Work by Royal Skousen on the surviving portions of the original manuscript of the Book of Mormon further corroborates this view, that the translation and transcription of the Nephite record was tightly controlled by Joseph Smith.[28]

Thus, with regard to the translation of the Sermon at

the Temple, this understanding of the nature of Joseph's translation—that the English Book of Mormon reflects competently but not slavishly the meaningful details in the original record of Nephi—best accounts for the presence of consistently meaningful details that are found in that text today, as has been indicated on several counts above.

Confirmation of Chiasmus

Within the boundaries of the Sermon at the Temple itself, well-composed literary structures further confirm the elemental accuracy of the translation. The account in 3 Nephi 17:5–10 of Jesus healing the sick is a beautiful five-part literary composition (A–B–C–B'–A'). It seems natural to see its elegant and coherent chiastic structure and substructures as originating in the ancient text, for it was written with great care and reflection:

(A) It begins with three references to the eyes, as Jesus casts "his eyes round about again on the multitude," as he sees that their eyes are in tears, and as they look longingly upon him, hopeful that he will tarry with them longer (3 Nephi 17:5).

(B) Jesus next speaks to the people in balanced words that sincerely invite reciprocation:

> a Behold, my *bowels are filled*
> > b with *compassion* towards you.
> > > c Have ye any sick among you?
> > > > d *Bring them hither.*
> > > > > Have ye any that are lame, or blind, or halt,
> > > > > > e or maimed, or leprous, or . . . withered, or . . . deaf, or . . . afflicted in any manner?
> > > > d' *Bring them hither*
> > > c' and I will heal them,
> > b' for I have *compassion* upon you;
> a' my *bowels are filled* with mercy.

(3 Nephi 17:6–7)

(C) Jesus then draws himself close to the people through a series of intimate "I/you" statements. Here, too, are five elements, the symbolic number of mercy. These lines emotively and mercifully affirm God's personal relationship to mankind:

> *I* perceive that *ye* desire
> that *I* should show unto *you*
> what *I* have done unto *your* brethren at Jerusalem,
> for *I* see that *your* faith is sufficient
> that *I* should heal *you*.
>
> (3 Nephi 17:8)

(B') The people then bring forth their sick to be healed. The "one" at the beginning of this verse is found in the throng coming forward with "one accord," but at the end it is found in the individual acts of love as Jesus healed "every one":

> All the multitude, with *one* accord, did go *forth*
> with their sick and their *afflicted,* and their lame,
> and with their blind, . . . dumb, and . . . *afflicted* . . . ;
> and he did heal them every *one* as they were brought *forth.*
>
> (3 Nephi 17:9)

(A') Finally, the account concludes with three references to the feet, as the entire multitude bowed down at Jesus' feet, and many came forward to kiss his feet and "did bathe his feet with their tears" (3 Nephi 17:10).

Mentioning the feet three times in this verse echoes the threefold emphasis placed on the eyes at the beginning of this pericope, thus conveying a sense of how completely these people were engrossed with their Savior, from head to foot. Moreover, in the end, their bathing his feet with their tears brings the account full circle back to the tears in their eyes, thus tying the episode together intimately and artistically.

There is certainly nothing clumsy or out of place in the composition or translation of this record.

Translated Correctly: An Interesting Case

Finally, Joseph's translation process produced a text that, interestingly, agrees with what appears to have been the Aramaic that Jesus originally spoke in Matthew 5:10. The Sermon at the Temple comes closer to the likely original intent of Jesus in the case of this verse than does the ancient Greek of the Sermon on the Mount. It is commonly assumed that Jesus usually spoke to his disciples in Aramaic (when and by whom the Sermon on the Mount was soon translated into Greek is unknown). When Jesus spoke to these fishermen and to the popular multitudes in Judea, he probably spoke to them in their local, native language. Accordingly, some scholars have worked hard, although not definitively, attempting to put the Greek of the New Testament Gospels back into what might have been the Aramaic of Jesus in order to learn what that might tell us about the intent of his original sayings.[29] In the Sermon on the Mount, several passages have been studied along these lines, but only a few have been detected where the Greek has likely misunderstood an underlying Aramaic word or expression. In most cases the nuances are very fine and the distinctions rather inconsequential.[30]

The case in Matthew 5:10 is an interesting and somewhat exceptional example of this. Several scholars speculate that the Greek New Testament may have mistranslated the purported Aramaic original. Lachs argues that the word *saddiq* (righteous one) was in the original form of Matthew 5:10 but that it was wrongly read as *zedeq* (righteousness) and accordingly rendered into Greek as *dikaiosunē*.[31] Thus, the Greek reads "blessed are they which are persecuted for righteousness' sake." But this makes awkward sense compared with the Aramaic idea that one would be blessed for enduring persecution for the sake of the "Righteous One." The latter is far closer to the translation offered by the Sermon at the Temple: "Blessed are all they who are persecuted for *my name's sake*" (3 Nephi 12:10). Joseph's inspired translation in this detail finds significant independent support from biblical studies.

Accordingly, in the several ways explored above we gain insights that help us understand how the interesting nuances and meaningful differences between the Sermon on the Mount and the Sermon at the Temple arose. Everything we know about Joseph Smith and the translation of the Sermon at the Temple warrants the detailed analysis that is pursued throughout this study of the Sermon.

Notes

1. The chronology of events in these months is discussed in John W. Welch, "I Have a Question," *Ensign,* January 1988, 46–47; and John W. Welch and Tim Rathbone, "The Translation of the Book of Mormon: Preliminary Report on the Basic Historical Information" (FARMS, 1986), 38–39.

2. Collected in Welch and Rathbone, "Translation of the Book of Mormon."

3. "Last Testimony of Sister Emma," *Saints' Advocate* 2 (October 1879): 51; and *Saints Herald* 26 (1 October 1879): 289–90.

4. *Deseret Evening News,* 10 November 1881; capitalization in original.

5. Oliver Cowdery to W. W. Phelps, *Latter Day Saints' Messenger and Advocate* 1 (October 1834): 14; italics deleted.

6. See sources in Milton V. Backman Jr., *Eyewitness Accounts of the Restoration* (Salt Lake City: Deseret Book, 1986), 213, 218; and Royal Skousen, "Towards a Critical Edition of the Book of Mormon," *BYU Studies* 30/1 (1990): 41–69; see 68 n. 25.

7. *The Personal Writings of Joseph Smith,* ed. Dean C. Jessee (Salt Lake City: Deseret Book, 1984), 8; see *The Papers of Joseph Smith: Volume 1, Autobiographical and Historical Writings,* ed. Dean C. Jessee (Salt Lake City: Deseret Book, 1989), 1:10.

8. "Last Testimony of Sister Emma," 51.

9. Copy contained on the obverse of letter of William E. McLellin to "My Dear Friends," Independence, Missouri, February 1870, RLDS Archives P13 f19l; question marks indicate illegible words.

10. Welch and Rathbone, "Translation of the Book of Mormon," 33–37.

11. Hugh W. Nibley, *Since Cumorah* (Salt Lake City: Deseret Book and FARMS, 1988), 111.

12. B. H. Roberts, "Bible Quotations in the Book of Mormon and Reasonableness of Nephi's Prophecies," *Improvement Era* 7 (January 1904): 184, says, "This is but a conjecture," but on page 191 he is more certain: "How are these *differences* to be accounted for? They unquestionably arise from the fact that the Prophet compared the King James' translation with the parallel passages in the Nephite records, and when he found the sense of the passage on the Nephite plates superior to that in the English version he made such changes as would give the superior sense and clearness." See also B. H. Roberts, *New Witnesses of God* (Salt Lake City: Deseret News, 1951), 3:441; Sidney B. Sperry, *Book of Mormon Compendium* (Salt Lake City: Bookcraft, 1968), 507–8; H. Grant Vest, "The Problem of Isaiah in the Book of Mormon" (master's thesis, Brigham Young University, 1938), 3; Donald W. Parry and John W. Welch, eds., *Isaiah in the Book of Mormon* (Provo, Utah: FARMS, 1998); Stanley R. Larson, "A Study of Some Textual Variations in the Book of Mormon: Comparing the Original and the Printer's Manuscripts and the 1830, the 1837, and the 1890 Editions" (master's thesis, Brigham Young University, 1974), 246–47; and Robert F. Smith, ed., *Book of Mormon Critical Text: A Tool for Scholarly Reference* (Provo, Utah: FARMS, 1987), 1:ix.

13. Sidney B. Sperry, *Our Book of Mormon* (Salt Lake City: Stevens and Wallis, 1947), 177; italics added.

14. B. H. Roberts, *Defense of the Faith and the Saints* (Salt Lake City: Deseret News, 1907), 1:272; italics added.

15. Ibid.; italics added.

16. B. H. Roberts, "Translation of the Book of Mormon: Answers to Questions respecting the Theory in the Senior Manual, 1905–1906," *Improvement Era* 9 (April 1906): 433.

17. M. T. Lamb, *The Golden Bible* (New York: Ward and Drummond, 1887), 19.

18. Roberts, "Bible Quotations in the Book of Mormon," 184.

19. Hugh W. Nibley, "Literary Style Used in the Book of Mormon Insured Accurate Translation," in *The Prophetic Book of Mormon* (Salt Lake City: Deseret Book and FARMS, 1989), 215.

20. Ibid., 218.

21. Ibid.

22. For general discussions of the mechanics of the translation process, see Richard L. Anderson, "By the Gift and Power of God," *Ensign,* September 1977, 79–85; James E. Lancaster, "'By the Gift and Power of God': The Method of Translation of the Book of Mormon," *Saints Herald* 109 (15 November 1962): 798–802, 806, 817; and Stephen D. Ricks, "Translation of the Book of Mormon: Interpreting the Evidence," *Journal of Book of Mormon Studies* 2/2 (1993): 201–6. For other views to the effect that the translation was not a literal process, see Ed Ashment, "The Book of Mormon—A Literal Translation?" *Sunstone,* March–April 1980, 10–14; and Blake T. Ostler, "The Book of Mormon as a Modern Expansion of an Ancient Source," *Dialogue: A Journal of Mormon Thought* 20/1 (1987): 66–123. For comments on Ostler, see Stephen E. Robinson, "The 'Expanded' Book of Mormon?" in *The Book of Mormon: Second Nephi, The Doctrinal Structure,* ed. Monte S. Nyman and Charles D. Tate Jr. (Provo, Utah: BYU Religious Studies Center, 1989), 391–414; and John W. Welch and Tim Rathbone, "Book of Mormon Translation by Joseph Smith," *Encyclopedia of Mormonism,* 1:210–13.

23. B. H. Roberts, *History of the Church of Jesus Christ of Latter-day Saints* (Salt Lake City: Deseret Book, 1976), 1:220.

24. See several of my works on this topic, for example, "Chiasmus in the Book of Mormon," *BYU Studies* 10 (autumn 1969): 69–84; "Chiasmus in the Book of Mormon," in *Chiasmus in Antiquity: Structures, Analyses, Exegesis,* ed. John W. Welch (Hildesheim: Gerstenberg Verlag, 1981; reprint Provo, Utah: Research Press, 1999); "Chiasmus in Alma 36," (FARMS, 1989); "A Masterpiece: Alma 36," in *Rediscovering the Book of Mormon,* ed. John L. Sorenson and Melvin J. Thorne (Salt Lake City: Deseret Book and FARMS, 1991), 114–31; "Criteria for Identifying and Evaluating the Presence of Chiasmus," *Journal of Book of Mormon Studies* 4/2 (1995): 1–14; and "What Does Chiasmus in the Book of Mormon Prove?" in *Book of Mormon Authorship Revisited: The Evidence for Ancient Origins,* ed. Noel B. Reynolds (Provo, Utah: FARMS, 1997), 199–224.

25. See, for example, "Statutes, Judgments, Ordinances, and Commandments," in *Reexploring the Book of Mormon,* ed. John W. Welch (Salt Lake City: Deseret Book and FARMS, 1992), 62–65.

26. David Whitmer, "The Last Man of the Men Who Attested to the Truth of the Book of Mormon," interview by *Chicago Times,* 17 October 1881; reprinted in *Chicago Tribune,* 17 December 1885, 3; also reprinted in *Deseret Evening News,* 10 November 1881.

27. "Did Lehi Land in Chile?" in *Reexploring the Book of Mormon,* 58.

28. Royal Skousen, "Translating the Book of Mormon: Evidence from the Original Manuscript," in *Book of Mormon Authorship Revisited,* 61–93.

29. See, for example, Matthew Black, *An Aramaic Approach to the Gospels and Acts,* 3rd ed. (Oxford: Clarendon, 1967); Joseph A. Fitzmyer, *Essays on the Semitic Background of the New Testament* (London: Geoffrey Chapman, 1971); and Frank Zimmermann, *The Aramaic Origin of the Four Gospels* (New York: KTAV, 1979).

30. For example, Zimmermann argues that "bushel" is correct in Matthew 5 but was misunderstood by Luke and Mark (see Zimmermann, *Aramaic Origin of the Four Gospels,* 57); that "they shall see God" is in his opinion theologically impossible

and thus must have come about as a mistranslation of "they shall be seen of God" (ibid., 68–69); that in Aramaic the salt became "spoiled (putrid)," not "foolish" (ibid., 70); that "rust" was a mistranslation of "eater" (i.e., a weevil?) (ibid., 71); that "body" and "life" in Matthew 6 should be translated more precisely as "soul" and "nourishment" (ibid., 37, 108); and that the wise man should be understood as building his house "with" stone not "upon" stone (ibid., 66). Objections can be raised quite readily to these conjectures.

31. Samuel T. Lachs, "Some Textual Observations on the Sermon on the Mount," *Jewish Quarterly Review* 69/2 (1978): 101–2; and Georg Strecker, *The Sermon on the Mount: An Exegetical Commentary*, trans. O. C. Dean Jr. (Nashville: Abingdon, 1988), 42. Strecker agrees that *righteousness* was a favorite word of Matthew, which indicates that Matthew probably introduced this word into the text of 5:10.

CHAPTER 9

THE SERMON AT THE TEMPLE AND THE GREEK NEW TESTAMENT MANUSCRIPTS

The discussion of translation in the preceding chapter leads directly into a further area of textual study, namely, the examination of the early Greek manuscripts of Matthew. What may these precious manuscripts add to our understanding of the Sermon at the Temple?

The New Testament is one of the best documented books to come down to us from the classical world. Many manuscripts of the gospel of Matthew have survived from the second through the seventh centuries and beyond. Not all of these manuscripts are exactly the same, although in an overwhelming majority of cases they agree on the words, spellings, and conjugations in the Greek text of the Sermon on the Mount. They differ noticeably from the Textus Receptus (the Greek text from which the King James Version was translated) only in a few places. This high degree of confirmation of the received Greek speaks generally in favor of the Sermon at the Temple, for one could not have wisely gambled on such confirmation a century and a half ago, before the earliest Greek New Testament manuscripts had been discovered. In the rush of manuscript discoveries in the late nineteenth and early twentieth centuries, many people expected that the earliest texts of the New Testament would prove radically different from the traditional manuscripts handed down through the ages, but the need to revise our texts significantly did not materialize. A few interesting textual variants, however, deserve brief discussion.

Transmitted Correctly: The Omission of "Without a Cause"

In one important passage, manuscript evidence favors the Sermon at the Temple, and it deserves recognition. The KJV of Matthew 5:22 reads, "Whosoever is angry with his brother *without a cause [eikēi]* shall be in danger of the judgment" (italics added). The Sermon at the Temple drops the phrase *without a cause* (3 Nephi 12:22).[1] So do many of the better early manuscripts.[2]

This favorable evidence for the Sermon at the Temple has the support of reliable sources. While lacking unanimous consensus in the early manuscripts of the Sermon on the Mount (which is not unusual), the absence of the phrase "without a cause" is evidenced by the following manuscripts: *p*64, *p*67, Sinaiticus (original hand), Vaticanus, some minuscules, the Latin Vulgate (Jerome mentions that it was not found in the oldest manuscripts known to him), the Ethiopic texts, the Gospel of the Nazarenes, Justin, Tertullian, Origen, and others. One may count as compelling all readings that are supported by "the best Greek MSS—by the A.D. 200 *p*64 (where it is extant) and by at least the two oldest uncials, as well as some minuscules, [especially if] it also has some Latin, Syriac, Coptic, and early patristic support."[3] A survey of the list of manuscripts supporting the Sermon at the

Temple and the original absence of the phrase *without a cause* in Matthew 5:22 shows that this shorter reading meets these criteria.

Moreover, this textual difference in the Greek manuscripts of the Sermon on the Mount is the only variant that has a significant impact on meaning. It is much more severe to say, *"Whoever is angry* is in danger of the judgment," than to say, "Whoever is angry *without a cause* is in danger of the judgment." The first discourages all anger against a brother; the second permits brotherly anger as long as it is justifiable. The former is more like the demanding sayings of Jesus regarding committing adultery in one's heart (see Matthew 5:28) and loving one's enemies (see Matthew 5:44), neither of which offers the disciple a convenient loophole of self-justification or rationalization. Indeed, as Wernberg-Møller points out, the word *eikēi* in Matthew 5:22 may reflect a Semitic idiom that does not invite allowance for "'just' anger in certain circumstances" at all, but "is original and echoes some Aramaic phrase, condemning anger as sinful in any case" and "as alluding to . . . the harbouring of angry feelings for any length of time."[4] In light of Wernberg-Møller's interpretation of the underlying idiom, the original sense of Matthew 5:22 is accurately reflected in the Sermon at the Temple whether *eikēi* is included in the Greek saying or not.

In my estimation, this textual variant in favor of the Sermon at the Temple is very meaningful. The removal of *without a cause* has important moral, behavioral, psychological, and religious ramifications, as it is the main place where a significant textual change from the KJV was in fact needed and delivered.

Translated Clearly

In a few places in the Greek manuscripts of the Sermon on the Mount, the Greek itself has come down over the years in a slightly different form from that which was apparently written in the original Gospel of Matthew.[5] In each of these cases, however, the later alternative Greek variants essentially say the same thing as the probable earlier readings. Thus, while the later variants may involve slightly different Greek constructions or vocabulary words, these differences are insignificant from the standpoint of translation. Accordingly, even though the Book of Mormon text does not differ in these spots from the King James Version of the Bible, the Sermon at the Temple still presents readers with a clear and appropriate translation of the essential meaning of these passages. Because the textual issues surrounding these passages have been examined elsewhere,[6] these few points can be covered here in shorter compass.

In Matthew 5:27 we read: "Ye have heard that it was said *by them of old time*, Thou shalt not commit adultery." The best early manuscripts of this verse, however, do not contain the words *tois archaiois* ("by them of old time"). They only read, "Ye have heard that it was said. . . ." Textual purists are probably right that the phrase should be left out of our Greek texts of Matthew 5:27 today, but the meaning of this phrase is implicit in the Greek text, whether or not the words *tois archaiois* are written out. This is because the parallel sayings in Matthew 5:21 and 5:33 contain the phrase *tois archaiois*, so these words are understood in verse 27, just as they are understood in verses 38 and 43, where no Greek manuscript evinced a need to repeat the obvious either. In fact, this variant is insignificant enough that the United Bible Societies' Greek New Testament does not even note it.

It is also interesting to note that the phrase *by them of old time* does *not* appear in 3 Nephi 12:33, whereas it *does* appear in the Greek and KJV of Matthew 5:33. Thus, just as the Greek manuscripts sometimes include and other times exclude the words *tois archaiois* in the five "ye have heard" verses, so does the Sermon at the Temple. Neither the Sermon on the Mount nor the Sermon at the Temple needs to spell this phrase out each time in order to convey this meaning.

In Matthew 5:30, the better Greek manuscripts read, "lest your whole body go off *[apelthēi]* into hell," while other texts, including 3 Nephi 12:30, warn, "lest your whole body *be cast [blēthēi]* into hell." These readings also present a distinction without a difference. There is no practical difference between these two idioms. The result is the same whether one's whole body "is cast" into hell or "goes off" into hell. So this variant, too, is not significant enough to have been noted in the United Bible Societies' Greek New Testament. Furthermore, it is evident that Jesus and his early apostles intended to convey no detectable difference in meaning between these two phrases, for they are used synonymously and concurrently in Mark 9:43, 45, and 47. Thus, they work as acceptable English equivalents in translation today.

Also, while the position of the prepositional phrase *into hell* shifts around in the various Greek manuscripts, in English this phrase can stand only at the end of the sentence. Thus, our English translations put this prepositional phrase in the only place where English syntax will allow.

Moreover, although the textual evidence is on the side of *go into hell* in Matthew 5:30, it may be a quirk of fate that the oldest surviving manuscripts happened to have the reading "cast into hell" (3 Nephi 12:30). This observation receives some support from Matthew Black's argument that *cast into hell*, preferred by the KJV, fits more comfortably into the alliteration of the Aramaic of this Markan (and Matthean) passage than does *go to hell*.[7] In any event, Jesus may well have said "cast into hell" originally here.

Similarly, in Matthew 7:2 the older texts read, "and with what measure ye mete, it shall be *measured* to you" (*metrēthēsetai*; italics added), while the later ones add, "and with what measure ye mete, it shall be *measured* to you *again*" (*antimetrēthēsetai*; italics added). Like the KJV, 3 Nephi 14:2 ends with the word *again*. Since Luke 6:38 also has the word *antimetrēthēsetai* (measured again), New Testament scholars have generally concluded that the text of Matthew 7:2 was changed at some point to harmonize with Luke.

Behind the English word *again*, however, stands only the Greek intensifying prefix *anti-*. With or without this prefix on the verb, the sentence means exactly the same thing. In either case, Jesus says that the standards a person uses to judge or to measure others will be used against the person who uses them. Again, this variant was not considered significant enough to be noted in the United Bible Societies' Greek New Testament.

The texts of Matthew 5:44 present an interesting set of readings. Some texts say "love your enemies and pray for them which despitefully use you," while others add such words as "bless them that curse you, do good to them that hate you." The injunction to love one's enemies is shorter in the earlier manuscripts; the later ones seem to have incorporated the additional words from Luke 6:27–28. Here the issue is a little different. Did Joseph Smith have the shorter text on the plates and expand it in the translation process, or did the longer text appear there similar to the way Jesus had spoken in Luke 6:27–28? Either is possible. Jesus must have said something like "love your enemies" many times; he need not have said it exactly the same way every time. Moreover, as John Gee has pointed out, early Hebrew versions of Matthew 5:44 contain the longer form similar to the Sermon at the Temple.[8] These points seem to me to allow adequate room for the translation given in the Sermon at the Temple.

Likewise, in Matthew 6:4, 6, and 18 textual evidence supports the idea that Matthew 6:4, 6, and 18 originally said, "Your Father will reward you," not "Your Father will reward you *openly [en tōi phanerōi]*." The KJV and the Sermon at the Temple, however, read "openly." Again, the only possible meaning of these verses is that God will openly reward the righteous with treasures in heaven on the judgment day. This understanding is sustained by the Greek verb for *reward*, namely, *apodidomi*. It has a wide variety of meanings, including "to give retribution, reward, or punishment." Its prefix *apo* can mean, among other things, "out from." For example, in the word *apocalypse*, the prefix *apo* means "out from" that which is hidden. In the verb *apodidomi*, it may convey the idea of being rewarded *apo*, that is "out from" the obscurity of the acts themselves, or openly. Thus, one does not need the phrase *en tōi phanerōi* (translation) in order to understand that "he who sees *in secret* will reward you *apo*, openly."

God will reward the righteous openly when the books are opened at the final judgment. Contemplating an open reward of treasures in heaven is especially consistent with the increased eschatological orientation of the Sermon at the Temple.

The Long Ending of the Lord's Prayer

Finally, there is the famous textual problem at the end of the Lord's Prayer in Matthew 6:13. Did the prayer originally include the doxology "For thine is the kingdom, and the power, and the glory, for ever. Amen"? Can one assume, with Jeremias and others, that Jesus originally appended some ending to the Lord's Prayer, although it is not recorded in the earliest survivors of the Sermon on the Mount? This issue is unsettled among biblical scholars.[9]

It is well-known that the earlier Greek manuscripts have no doxology at the end of the Lord's Prayer; they end abruptly with "deliver us from evil." In this respect they resemble (and may have been changed to conform with) Luke 11:4, which also simply ends "but deliver us from evil." The Sermon at the Temple along with later Greek manuscripts and the KJV conclude with a doxology. Whether the phrase was originally present in the text of Matthew cannot be known, although most textual critics find it easiest to believe that the phrase was introduced later into that text. For many circumstantial reasons, however, no one seems to doubt that Jesus probably pronounced a doxology of some kind at the end of his prayers. The only question is how early such a thing found its way into the text of the Gospel of Matthew.

The following evidence makes it likely that Jesus indeed ended his prayers in Jerusalem and Bountiful with a doxology. First, it would have been highly irregular at the time of Jesus to end a Jewish prayer without some words in praise of God. Jeremias states: "It would be a completely erroneous conclusion to suppose that the Lord's Prayer was ever prayed without some closing words of praise to God; in Palestinian practice it was completely unthinkable that a prayer would end with the word 'temptation.' Now, in Judaism prayers were often concluded with a 'seal,' a sentence of praise freely formulated by the man who was praying."[10]

Second, Jeremias's point can be extended one step further into the temple. As pointed out above, a special acknowledgment of the glory and kingdom of God was spoken in the temple of the Jews as a benediction on the Day of Atonement. The people bowed their knees, fell on their faces, and said, "Praised be the name of his glorious kingdom forever and eternally!" In the sacred matters in the temple, one did not simply answer "Amen."[11] It is all the more unlikely that a prayer at the temple would end without some form of doxology. This may be a factor in explaining why the prayer here at the temple in Bountiful includes the doxology, but the instruction given by Jesus on prayer out in the open in Luke 11 does not.

Third, the doxology in the KJV and Sermon at the Temple seems to have followed a traditional form, reflected in 1 Chronicles 29:10–13, as is widely observed.[12] The Nephites may have known such phraseology from their Israelite traditions, for it appears in an important blessing spoken by King David, and the Nephite records contained certain historical records of the Jews (see 1 Nephi 5:12). According to Chronicles, David's blessing reads: "Wherefore David blessed the Lord before all the congregation: and David said, Blessed be thou, Lord God of Israel our father, *for ever and ever*. Thine, O Lord, is the greatness, and the *power*, and the *glory*, and the victory, and the majesty: for all that is in the heaven and in the earth is thine; thine is the *kingdom*" (1 Chronicles 29:10–11; italics added).[13]

Fourth, although a minority, several early texts in Greek, Syriac, Coptic, and in the Didache (ca. A.D. 100) also exist that include doxologies at the end of the Lord's Prayer in Matthew 6:13. These indicate that the cultic or liturgical use and acceptance of some doxology was apparently widespread at a very early time in Christianity. The form of these doxologies, however, could easily vary, as is borne out by 2 Timothy 4:18.[14]

Fifth, it can also be noted that the Lord's Prayer in the Sermon at the Temple differs in several other respects from the version of the prayer in Matthew 6, as discussed above. Like the prayer in Luke 11, the prayer in the Book of Mormon is shorter than the version in Matthew, yet it agrees substantially with Matthew's wording, a felicitous result for the Sermon at the Temple in light of Jeremias's conclusion that "the Lucan version has preserved the oldest form with respect to *length*, but the Matthean text is more original with regard to *wording*."[15]

In sum, it is hard to see that the Sermon at the Temple can be faulted. In each case where minor textual troubles prevent us from knowing exactly how the Greek text of Matthew originally read, the Book of Mormon offers an appropriately acceptable rendition of the meaning of that passage. And in the one case where the ancient manuscripts convey an important difference in meaning from the King James Version by omitting *without a cause* in Matthew 5:22, the Book of Mormon agrees with the stronger manuscript reading of that text. The Greek manuscripts of the Sermon on the Mount do not discredit the Book of Mormon, and may on balance sustain it.

Notes

1. This point was first published in John W. Welch, "A Book You Can Respect," *Ensign*, September 1977, 45–48.

2. For a discussion of this text by a scholar who challenges many normal assumptions, see David A. Black, "Jesus on Anger: The Text of Matthew 5:22a Revisited," *Novum Testamentum* 30/1

(1988): 1–8. While acknowledging that "the shorter text undoubtedly has impressive manuscript support," Black presents reasons why the longer reading "should at least be reconsidered in scholarly discussions of this passage" (ibid., 5; compare p. 2). His points, however, have not shifted the balance of scholarly opinion to favor including the word *eikē*.

3. Stanley R. Larson, "The Sermon on the Mount: What Its Textual Transformation Discloses concerning the Historicity of the Book of Mormon," *Trinity Journal* 7 (spring 1986): 43.

4. P. Wernberg-Møller, "A Semitic Idiom in Matt. V. 22," *New Testament Studies* 3 (1956): 72–73; italics deleted.

5. Of course, it is impossible to know exactly what the original copy of Matthew's Gospel was like. See J. K. Elliott, "Can We Recover the Original New Testament?" *Theology* 77/649 (1974): 343.

6. Larson originally explored the possibility of twelve such trouble spots for the Sermon at the Temple and then published his *Trinity Journal* article suggesting eleven. See his "The Sermon on the Mount: What Its Textual Transformation Discloses," 23–45. After my examination of those points in chapter 8 of my 1990 edition of *The Sermon at the Temple and the Sermon on the Mount* (Salt Lake City: Deseret Book and FARMS), Larson reduced the number to eight in "The Historicity of the Matthean Sermon on the Mount in 3 Nephi," in *New Approaches to the Book of Mormon: Explorations in Critical Methodology*, ed. Brent L. Metcalfe (Salt Lake City: Signature Books, 1993), 115–64. Those eight were dealt with again in my review of that material in "Approaching New Approaches," *Review of Books on the Book of Mormon* 6/1 (1994): 152–68. I have appreciated this stimulating and courteous exchange.

7. Matthew Black, *An Aramaic Approach to the Gospels and Acts*, 3rd ed. (Oxford: Clarendon, 1967), 171.

8. John Gee, "La Trahison des Clercs: On the Language and Translation of the Book of Mormon," *Review of Books on the Book of Mormon* 6/1 (1994): 68.

9. For a recent debate regarding the long ending of the Lord's Prayer, see Andrew J. Bandstra, "The Original Form of the Lord's

Prayer," *Calvin Theological Journal* 16/1 (April 1981): 15–37; Jacob van Bruggen, "The Lord's Prayer and Textual Criticism," *Calvin Theological Journal* 17/1 (1982): 78–87; and Andrew J. Bandstra, "The Lord's Prayer and Textual Criticism: A Response," *Calvin Theological Journal* 17/1 (1982): 88–97.

10. Joachim Jeremias, *The Prayers of Jesus* (London: SCM, 1967), 106; Ulrich Luz, *Matthew 1–7: A Continental Commentary,* trans. Wilhelm C. Linss (Minneapolis: Fortress, 1989), 385.

11. Hermann L. Strack and Paul Billerbeck, *Kommentar zum Neuen Testament aus Talmud und Midrasch* (Munich: Beck, 1922), 1:423, citing Mishnah, *Yoma* 6:2, and others. Discussed in chapter 4 concerning 3 Nephi 13:9–13. Samuel T. Lachs, "Why Was the 'Amen' Response Interdicted in the Temple?" *Journal for the Study of Judaism: In the Persian, Hellenistic and Roman Period* 19/2 (1988): 230–40, shows that the "amen" was dropped by the Pharisees, leaving only the doxology, during the Second Temple period when the High Priest was a Sadducee, whose words were not to be confirmed. In Lehi's day, and hence in Nephite culture, the "amen" was clearly added (see 1 Chronicles 16:36; Nehemiah 8:6; Psalm 106:48). Ibid., nn. 7 and 10.

12. Jeremias discusses this, as Larson too observes ("The Sermon on the Mount: What Its Textual Transformation Discloses," 35). See John W. Welch, "The Lord's Prayers," *Ensign,* January 1976, 15–17; and Strack and Billerbeck, *Kommentar zum Neuen Testament,* 1:424.

13. Italics added. Note that "for ever and ever," which appears in the JST and which Larson claims is going "in a direction away from the original text" ("The Sermon on the Mount: What Its Textual Transformation Discloses," 39 n. 34), is close to this ancient blessing of David and is also the same as the typical ending of the Jewish temple benediction. See Strack and Billerbeck, *Kommentar zum Neuen Testament,* 1:423, "immer u. ewig."

14. Ulrich Luz, *Matthew 1–7: A Continental Commentary,* trans. Wilhelm C. Linss (Minneapolis: Fortress, 1989), 385.

15. Jeremias, *Prayers of Jesus,* 93; italics in original.

CHAPTER 10

JESUS AND THE COMPOSITION OF THE SERMON ON THE MOUNT

The presence of virtually all of the Sermon on the Mount in the Sermon at the Temple, and therefore in the *ipsissima vox,* or personal voice, of Jesus, will certainly present yet a different set of improbabilities to the minds of many liberal New Testament scholars. It is widely accepted in New Testament scholarship that Matthew gave the Sermon on the Mount its final form (although there is no consensus about when Matthew worked, how much he wrote himself, or which words and phrases he drew from the variously existing pre-Matthean sources or traditions that scholars have hypothesized).

The Book of Mormon, however, presents the reader with a version of the Sermon on the Mount that is substantially identical to the Sermon in the King James Bible and that places this text entirely in the mouth of Jesus in A.D. 34. The idea that Jesus was the author of the Sermon on the Mount, let alone the author of the covenant-oriented interpretation that the Sermon at the Temple gives to the Sermon, is not likely to find many ready-made adherents among the disciples of Q or other source-critical students of the New Testament. Without purporting to deal with all the complexities of the synoptic question, I will attempt to explain to a general audience some of the very legitimate issues raised by New Testament studies and how the Sermon at the Temple has tended to shape my thinking about these scholarly endeavors.

Characteristic Words of Jesus

At the outset it is worth pointing out that there are no words in the Sermon at the Temple that Jesus *could not* have said. As discussed in chapter 6, places where scholars have found the strongest traces of later redaction in the Sermon on the Mount are not in evidence in the Sermon at the Temple. Perhaps far more of the Sermon on the Mount was original with Jesus than New Testament scholarship has come to assume; it is certainly too aggressive to date the entire Sermon on the Mount by the last element added to this sermon in the course of its transmission and transcription.

Moreover, all the themes of the Sermon on the Mount are consistent with the generally accepted characteristics of the very voice of Jesus, even judging very cautiously. Those characteristics of Jesus' personal words, as they have been identified by Joachim Jeremias,[1] are readily visible in the Sermon, namely, (1) the use of parables (for example, the salt, the light, the tree, the house on the rock); (2) the use of cryptic sayings or riddles (for example, 3 Nephi 12:17; Matthew 5:17); (3) speaking of the reign or kingdom of God (for example, 3 Nephi 11:33, 38; Matthew 5:3, 10; 6:33); (4) the use of "amen" or "verily" (over thirty times in the Sermon at the Temple); and (5) the word *Abba*, or *Father* (Matthew 6:9, and dozens of times in the Sermon at the Temple). Based on Jeremias's analysis, one may presume that New Testament phrases containing one of these five qualities are authentic to the *ipsissima vox* of Jesus.

Proceeding with Caution

For most New Testament scholars, however, the question of authorship in the Sermon on the Mount is likely to be a much greater stumbling block to the Sermon at the Temple than any manuscript or stylistic issue, for it is a very widely held opinion that Matthew or some earlier redactor compiled or wrote the Sermon on the Mount as we now know it, collecting miscellaneous sayings of Jesus and putting them together into a more or less unified sermon or series of sermonettes. The presence of this material in the Sermon at the Temple, however, commits the believing Latter-day Saint to doubt such a claim. It seems unlikely for a person to believe that the resurrected Jesus delivered the sermon to the Nephites recorded in 3 Nephi 11–18 within a year after his crucifixion and at the same time to hold that the evangelist gave the Sermon its basic form and selected its content.

It is thus necessary to ask why many scholars have concluded that Matthew composed the Sermon on the Mount. Are their assumptions and reasons persuasive? The synoptic question, which has driven an enormous amount of New Testament research, cannot be casually dismissed or lightly ignored. How the Gospels were composed, when and why they were written, how they are similar to or different from each other, and what underlying sources they drew upon, are intriguing questions. After a century of work, these issues still remain fascinating to many readers.

Over the years, a steady flow of journal articles and books have advanced various ingenious theories and have marshalled evidence for or against certain positions regarding the composition of the synoptic Gospels. Any thoughtful and well-informed Latter-day Saint can derive a wealth of information from these studies about the subtlety of these sacred records that tell us so much about the mortal ministry of Jesus Christ. But not every proposed theory regarding the synoptic question is equally persuasive. All readers must evaluate and carefully consider the evidence presented. Covert biases and assumptions are sometimes at work; and despite the overwhelming popularity of a particular hypothesis today, it may likely fall into disfavor tomorrow.[2] Surmising, extrapolating, following hunches, and outright guesswork fuel much of this research, as some forage for tidbits of information gleaned here and there from among the textual records.

With regard to the composition of the Sermon on the Mount in particular, the assertion of Matthean authorship is not a simple one. It is difficult to attack in large part because it is not very focused. The reasons for seeing Matthew's hand in the text of the Sermon on the Mount are vague and broad. They can scarcely be negated because they can hardly be verified. The theory has spawned numerous books and dissertations, developing and applying the hypothesis, but the results are still far from conclusive. This is largely because the relationships between the Sermon and the other Gospels are so complex. As Harvey K. McArthur states: "The Sermon on the Mount presents unusual complications in the matter of sources. . . . Of the Sermon's 111 verses, about 45 have no obvious parallels in Luke, 35 have loose parallels, and 31 have parallels which are close both in content and in phraseology. The curious feature of this evidence is [that] . . . [t]he close parallels are unusually close, and the loose parallels are unusually loose!"[3]

Faced with this array of difficulties, it is not surprising that nothing approaching scholarly unanimity exists over how much of the Sermon on the Mount Matthew wrote himself, or how much he took from an existing pre-Matthean text or other sources. For those who have concluded that Matthew had documents at his disposal from which he drew, there is even less consensus about where those records came from or for what purpose they were written or used in the earliest Christian communities.

The Sermon as a Pre-Matthean Text

The trend in recent years, however, has been toward seeing somewhat less Matthean influence in the composition of the Sermon on the Mount itself and toward dating large sections of the Sermon on the Mount back into the first decades of Jewish Christianity. Hans Dieter Betz, in particular, has advanced the theory that the Sermon on the Mount was a composite of pre-Matthean sources, embodying a set of cultic instructions that served the earliest Jewish-Christian community in Jerusalem as an epitome of the gospel of Jesus Christ, which Matthew later incorporated into his Gospel.[4]

Betz's thesis has much to commend it. For one thing, it finds support in the vocabulary of the Sermon on the Mount. When one compares the Greek words in the Sermon on the Mount with those used by Matthew in the rest of his Gospel, some sharp contrasts emerge. Of the 383 basic vocabulary words in the Sermon on the Mount, I count 73 (or 19% of the total) that appear *only* in the Sermon (sometimes more than once) and *never* elsewhere in the Gospel of Matthew; in fact, they often are *never* used again in the entire New Testament. In some cases, words used in the Sermon on the Mount, such as *doma* (gift,

Matthew 7:11; compare Ephesians 4:8, quoting Psalm 68:18), appear un-Matthean, for on all nine other occasions outside the Sermon on the Mount when Matthew speaks of gifts, he prefers to use the word *dōron* (gift), even where the context is similar to that of Matthew 7:11 (see, for example, Matthew 2:11; 15:5). Only two words in the Sermon, *geennan* (hell) and *grammateoi* (scribes), are used by Matthew in greater preponderance than other New Testament writers, and in only one case, *rhapizei* (smite; Matthew 5:39; 26:67), is Matthew the sole New Testament writer to use a Sermon on the Mount vocabulary word outside the Sermon.

Thus on the level of mere vocabulary, the Sermon on the Mount appears to be unlike Matthew's writings. Although this kind of straightforward word study is not conclusive of authorship, especially since the textual sample involved is statistically small, the result seems to me to be indicative.[5] If Matthew's hand played a significant role in drafting, selecting, or reworking the contents of the Sermon on the Mount, it seems odd that nearly every fifth vocabulary word is one that Matthew never had occasion to use again in his Gospel. Nevertheless, the issue is not cut-and-dried.

New Light from New Documents

I am confident that New Testament scholars are doing about the best they can with what they have. If it were not for my acceptance of the material contained in the Book of Mormon, I would readily agree with many of their conjectures. They have three synoptic Gospels—Matthew, Mark, and Luke—and it is entirely indeterminable in most passages which Gospel is the oldest or reflects the most accurate or original image of the historical Jesus. Sometimes Luke appears to give the better view, other times Mark, and still other times Matthew. Discussion and resolution of the problem, however, are prejudicially circumscribed by the documents permitted into consideration. For example, if the *Gospel of Thomas,* or another newly discovered text, were to be accepted as a very early source, it would have a tremendous impact on the question of which sayings of Jesus in the synoptic Gospels people would accept as authentic.

History is always vulnerable to the inherent weaknesses of its records.[6] For example, newspapers once reported that a cannon mounted on a monument erected by the Daughters of the Utah Pioneers in Farmington, Utah, could not have been brought across the plains, since its serial number and an 1864 date stamp indicate that it was cast in Richmond, Virginia, during the Civil War.[7] If this were the only information known about the famous pioneer cannon, we would be tempted to reject out of hand the mind-boggling stories about dragging a cannon all the way from Nauvoo to Salt Lake City in 1847 through the mud and over hundreds of trackless miles. In this case, however, the 1847 diary of Charles C. Rich removes any doubt: There was a cannon that his company fired regularly as the wagon train moved across the prairie, even though the Farmington monument may not have the right one. This serves as a sobering reminder of our inability to date historical details conclusively by relying solely on the earliest surviving artifact.

The question of which sayings of Jesus are authentic usually turns on certain assumptions people have made about which parts of the Gospel accounts were early or which came later. For example, if a person holds to the premise that Jesus neither ordained apostles nor formally organized a church in Palestine, then it is a foregone conclusion

that the person will strongly discount any sayings with ecclesiastical content in the Gospels as being later additions
by someone belonging to the settled church later in the first
century. Of course, such issues are complex and deeply in-
terwoven with other historical and literary strands. Thus,
the discussion of the Matthean composition of the Sermon
on the Mount begins, and to a large extent ends, with the
same sort of preassessment of source documents and their
possible provenances.

These points are relevant to our discussion of the
Sermon at the Temple. Most scholars are willing to change
or modify their old opinions when new, credible evidence
is discovered. My personal verdict is that the Sermon at
the Temple constitutes such evidence. If admitted into
evidence, it becomes a major factor in settling the question of who wrote the Sermon on the Mount. The problem
rests in determining whether the Book of Mormon should
be allowed to contribute any primary evidence in this discussion. Of course, for Latter-day Saints, who are con-
vinced on their own grounds of the historicity of the Book
of Mormon, the Sermon at the Temple will figure as one
of the main determining documents in their discussion of
the issue of who composed the Sermon, rather than as a
text whose character is judged as a by-product of that
discussion.

Others will likely reject the Sermon at the Temple and
the Book of Mormon as such evidence, but that rejection
will usually be made on other religious or theological
grounds, not on the alleged Matthean authorship of the
Sermon on the Mount. It would be circular, of course, to
disallow the Sermon at the Temple as evidence against
Matthean authorship by rejecting it simply on the ground
that Matthew wrote the Sermon on the Mount, for that is

the very question about which one seeks the further documentary evidence in the first place.

Rejecting Some Speculative Presumptions

Limited to the sources in the New Testament, scholars advance several theories to support the proposition that Matthew wrote the Sermon on the Mount. I have not found any of these presumptions or hypotheses compelling enough to discredit the Sermon at the Temple.

For example, many scholars assume that the sayings of Jesus started out short and simple and that they grew in complexity as they were collected, grouped, and handed down in lore and tradition until his followers canonized them. Hence, Jeremias reasons as follows: "The Sermon on the Plain [in Luke 6] is very much shorter than that on the mount, and from this we must conclude that in the Lucan Sermon on the Plain we have an earlier form of the Sermon on the Mount."[8] This view receives some support from the fact that pithy sayings of Jesus were collected elsewhere by Matthew into single chapters (as in the Parable Sermon of Matthew 13), and thus one infers that the same thing occurred with the Sermon on the Mount.[9]

This inference is not compelling, however. What apparently happened in the case of Matthew 13 need not have happened for Matthew 5–7. Moreover, movements as dynamic as early Christianity do not characteristically begin with a sputtering start. Great religious and philosophical movements typically begin with the monumental appearance of a figure who captures the spirit of his followers and galvanizes them into dedicated action. It seems more likely to me, as a hypothesis, that the words and discourses of Jesus started out profound and already well developed, than that they began as disjointed sayings or fragmented maxims. Day in and day out, Jesus spoke to his disciples and to the multitudes who flocked to see him. I doubt that they came out to hear a string of oracular one-liners. What they heard were coherent sentences projecting a vision and worldview. The Sermon on the Mount would reflect such wisdom and perspective, making it just as likely that the abbreviated excerpts of it that are scattered elsewhere in the synoptic Gospels are its derivatives.

One can hardly be unaware of the vast amount of effort that has been spent searching for Q and for the original words of Jesus.[10] The assumption here is that Matthew, Mark, and Luke had access to a common source that no longer survives. In this quest some scholars stipulate or conclude that the form of a saying of Jesus as it appears in Mark or Luke was earlier than the parallel saying in Matthew. But this discipline is far from objective or certain. For example, many have often argued that Luke 6, the Sermon on the Plain, was earlier than the Sermon on the Mount and that Matthew used the Sermon on the Plain as one of his sources in compiling the Sermon on the Mount. It is also possible, however, that Luke 6 was dependent on the Sermon on the Mount. The debate tilts both ways: Some articles advance reasons for seeing the Matthean Beatitudes and Lord's Prayer or other formulations as bearing the characteristics of earlier sayings,[11] while a minority of others advance reasons for Lukan priority of the same material.[12] To resolve these difficulties, some scholars have advanced the idea of multiple Qs. These arguments revolve around a number of assumptions about the kinds of words, expressions, themes, or issues that Jesus would most likely have used or that would have concerned him. Much of this is sophisticated, technical, informed guesswork.

Many scholars have also often assumed that Jesus said

something only once, or said it in only one form. Hence scholars launch prolonged odysseys, such as the one to ascertain the "original form" of the Beatitudes or of the Lord's Prayer. This quest, however, assumes that Jesus blessed his disciples using the words of the Beatitudes only once and taught his followers to pray using the words of the Lord's Prayer on only one occasion. If this assumption fails, then two different iterations (even though closely related to each other in form) could both be original sayings.

It should also be noted that the most persuasive evidence for the synoptic problem comes from parallel reports of events rather than sayings. In the case of singular events, which logically can be assumed to have happened only once, the differences in the accounts of Matthew, Mark, and Luke are very telling. But the same logic does not necessarily carry over into the reported speeches, all or parts of which could very well have been repeated more than once and not quite the same each time.

For example, regarding the relationship between the Sermon on the Mount and Luke's Sermon on the Plain in Luke 6, it is significant that the two speeches follow essentially the same order, making the omissions in Luke especially interesting. Luke begins with certain beatitudes, notably blessing those whose names had been cast out as evil or worthless (see Luke 6:22). There follows a set of woes or curses upon the rich, the full, those who laugh or make fun, and followers of false prophets (see Luke 6:24–26). Brief instructions are given regarding loving enemies, turning the other cheek, giving to those who ask, lending to sinners, being merciful, and doing well unto others (see Luke 6:27–36), the last point being one of the few major elements taken out of order from the Matthean text. The Sermon at the Plain then skips all of the material found in Matthew 6 (some of which is found when Jesus speaks in private to his apostles in Luke 11), and then presents most of the items found in Matthew 7, with some variations, including judge not, give and it shall be given, whatsoever ye measure, the mote and the beam in the eye, good fruit from a good tree, grapes and figs, calling the Lord "Lord," and the houses built on the rock and the sand (Luke 6:37–49).

This selection of materials can be explained by the different settings in which the two speeches were reportedly given. The Lucan speech, of course, was delivered to a much larger audience than was the Sermon on the Mount, for "a great multitude of people" had come out from all around the region, from Jewish and gentile cities, "to hear him" (Luke 6:17). Consistent with this circumstance, Jesus presents here the more public elements of his message.[13] He covers the golden rule and the principles of charity, and then he teaches the people the manner in which God will judge all people. Missing from this speech in Luke are all of the elements that one would expect to be reserved for the closer circle of disciples, such as the call to be the light unto the world and the salt of the earth; the specific laws of obedience, sacrifice, brotherhood, chastity, and consecration; instructions regarding oaths, prayer, clothing, and secrecy; and entering through the narrow gate into the presence of God. Rather than detracting from the historicity of these two speeches as independent iterations, their settings and audiences appropriately dictate what has been included and what has been omitted. Assuming that Jesus indeed spoke to a large multitude of diverse people, he would have followed his own instruction on such occasions and would not have given "that which is holy" to those who were not yet prepared to receive it (Matthew 7:6). He seems to have followed that principle exactly in determining which elements to mention in Luke 6 and which points to pass over in speaking to this particular crowd, addressing them not on a temple mount but on an ordinary level in the countryside.

Others argue that if the Sermon on the Mount had been in existence before the writing of the Gospel of Matthew, then Mark and Luke would also have used it in exactly that form. This, however, is an argument from silence. Mark's and Luke's purposes were different from Matthew's; they included different sorts of speeches and information. In Mark's case, there is reason to believe that he consciously chose not to include all that he knew of what Jesus had said.[14]

Certain passages in the Sermon on the Mount seem likely to postdate Jesus' lifetime, such as those that reflect anti-Pharisaical, antigentile, or anti-Pauline sentiments, and possibly the designation of Jerusalem as the City of the Great King. These passages have been pointed to as sure signs of late composition of the Sermon on the Mount. Strecker, for example, argues that "Matthew does not reflect a historically faithful picture" because he distinguishes between the Pharisees and scribes, when "in truth one cannot differentiate stringently between scribes and Pharisees."[15] However, such verses alone may simply be later additions. They need not point to a late composition of the bulk of the Sermon. As discussed above, all of these elements, which may be strongly suspected of being late intrusions, are absent from the Sermon at the Temple.

Finally, some scholars point to the possible presence of Greek concepts in the Sermon on the Mount and argue that only Matthew could have inserted them. These points of possible Hellenistic influence are far from certain, however; and even if they are present in the Sermon on the Mount, it is equally possible that Jesus would have known them from his own cultural surroundings, which included several neighboring Hellenistic centers. Nor must these allegedly Greek ideas in the Sermon be understood exclusively as Hellenisms in any event. Many of these ethical teachings are universally present in all kinds of centers. The foregoing discussion surveys the kinds of arguments, generally speaking, that have been advanced supporting the theory of Matthean composition of the Sermon on the Mount and why they are not necessarily persuasive.

Putting the Words of Jesus before Matthew

In addition to the rebuttals made above, several affirmative reasons can be adduced for believing that the Sermon on the Mount was not written by Matthew but existed as a pre-Matthean source. For example, the Sermon on the Mount is in tension in places with the major themes of the Gospel of Matthew as a whole. Kingsbury, for example, finds that the Sermon presents Jesus in one direction as a conciliatory teacher and a new Moses, whereas "the driving force of the plot [of the Gospel of Matthew] is the element of conflict," with this second direction culminating in the tensions of the passion narrative.[16] As discussed above, Betz and others have marshalled considerable evidence that the Sermon on the Mount is the kind of document used as a cultic text or to instruct or remind initiates of church rules, and it makes the most sense for the Sermon to have been used in that way before the time when the Gospel of Matthew was written.[17]

I would add that verbal and conceptual similarities between the epistle of James (which I believe to be early) and the Sermon further indicate that James knew something like the Sermon on the Mount when he wrote his letter.

Compare, for example, James 5:12 with Matthew 5:33–37 on oaths; James 3:11–12 with Matthew 7:16–22 on knowing a fig tree or vine by its fruit; James 1:13 with Matthew 6:13 on being led into temptation; James 4:11 with Matthew 7:1–2 on judging a brother; James 2:13 and Matthew 5:7 on showing mercy; and many other similarities.[18] Jeremias has also noted that James and the Sermon on the Mount share the same character as "the classical example of an early Christian didache,"[19] and this rings true in light of the way the early Christian Didache, discovered in 1873, quotes extensively from the Sermon on the Mount. It seems quite evident that the epistle of James was consciously drawing on a known body of basic Christian teachings already known and used in the church as persuasive, authentic sayings. Thus it seems unlikely that James could have written as he did unless something like the Sermon on the Mount was already considered authoritative, whether oral or written. In that case, is it possible that Matthew could have written the Sermon on the Mount late in the day and have pawned it off in James' community as an original? A similar point can be made with respect to Paul's letters, some of which seem to reflect parts of the Sermon, although Paul could have learned these through other channels.[20] I do not insist that these similarities prove a literary dependency on the Sermon on the Mount. In particular, the role of memory must not be discounted,[21] especially where ritual texts are involved. In light of the Jewish and Hellenistic teaching methods of his day, "If [Jesus] taught, he must have required his disciples to memorize."[22] At the time Matthew wrote, people were still alive who personally remembered Jesus. One must ask how a totally new sermon of Jesus, compiled and advanced by Matthew, would ever have been accepted. As Gerhardsson has argued, "Remembering the attitude of Jewish disciples to their master, it is unrealistic to suppose that forgetfulness and the exercise of a pious imagination had too much hand in transforming authentic memories beyond all recognition in the course of a few short decades."[23]

Emphasizing Jesus at the Temple

Although the New Testament may not tell as much as one would like about the numerous teachings of Jesus, and in spite of the different approaches taken by each of the four Evangelists, one strong thread that runs through the earliest memories about Christ in all four Gospels is the centrality of the temple for Jesus. In light of the purpose of the present book, namely, to associate the Sermon on the Mount with ancient temple motifs recognized by Latter-day Saints, it is worth revisiting the many passages in the New Testament Gospels that link Jesus deeply with the temple. By emphasizing the presence of Jesus at the temple, these passages increase the likelihood that temple elements should be found in his main teachings. The temple was important to Jesus. Finding features in the Sermon on the Mount that Latter-day Saints may follow as leading to the temple is, therefore, consonant with this significant element in the life of Jesus as reported in the New Testament Gospels.

Jesus did not reject the idea of the temple. Instead, he desired to replace the temple system in Jerusalem with a new temple order, a sacred way of holiness and purity that he promised to raise up without hands (see Mark 14:58; compare Daniel 2:34).[24] In speaking of this new temple system, of course, Jesus alluded to his body and the resurrection (see John 2:21). But what does the resurrection have to do with the temple? Through the resurrection, all mankind will be brought into the presence of God to be judged according to the fruits they have borne. Preparing people to pass that day of judgment, to be known by their fruits, and to enter into the presence of God is precisely the final objective of the Sermon on the Mount (see Matthew 7:2, 13, 20–21).

Where else in the teachings of the Savior can one find a stronger candidate than the Sermon on the Mount for instructions regarding the essential order that should take the place of the old temple system under the new covenant? Jesus promised that he would "draw all men" unto God by leading the way (John 12:32). Should readers of the New Testament assume that the new temple, which Jesus promised to build, was left by him without blueprints? I think not. Can a better source be found for such directions than the Sermon on the Mount?

The new temple, we know, would not be built with hands; instead, it would be built with the heart (see Matthew 5:8, 28; 6:21). Jeremiah had prophesied that, through a spiritually transforming experience, the new temple in the day of the Lord would write the law upon the people "in their inward parts" (Jeremiah 31:33). The new temple would thereby build a covenant people of the heart, not of outward performances of the hand only. The epistle to the Hebrews has much to say about the high priesthood of Christ and related temple imagery (see Hebrews 7–10). In the midst of this temple section of the epistle stands the fulfillment of Jeremiah's prophecy: "For this is the covenant . . . I will put my laws into their mind, and write them in their hearts: and I will be to them a God, and they shall be to me a people" (Hebrews 8:10). This shows that early Christians understood that a new temple system had in fact been established by Jesus and that it involved the covenantal transformation of the heart. This is precisely what the Sermon on the Mount strives to achieve.

It appears that Jesus discretely imbedded this new order in the words he spoke, proclaiming his new law and covenant and supplanting the old law and testament (as one sees again in the Sermon on the Mount in its antitheses, Matthew 5:17, 21–22, 27–28, 33–34, 38–39). One may thus suspect that he carried this, his central message, directly into the heart of all Israel by preaching its elements regularly in the temple. Perhaps for this reason, especially, the earliest Christians remembered with vivid particularity things that Jesus said and did at the temple. Many of their most salient recollections of his ministry were associated with the temple.

All four Gospels remember Jesus walking and teaching daily in the temple (see Matthew 21:23; 26:55; Mark 11:27; 12:35–40; 14:49; Luke 19:45–48; 20:1; 22:52; John 7:28; 10:23). This main impression about Jesus and the temple is one of the relatively few historical facts about the life of Jesus that all four Gospels share. The meanings ascribed to his presence in the temple may well be more theological than historical, but they all rest on this "issue marked as crucial in all the Gospels: Jesus' engagement with the [temple] cult."[25]

Furthermore, the three synoptic Gospels have several points in common regarding Jesus and the temple, particularly in the course of their passion narratives. In these three gospels, and told directly following Jesus' triumphal entry from the east into the temple mount of Jerusalem, Jesus surveyed the situation at the temple (see Mark 11:11) and drove out the money changers (see Matthew 21:12–15; Mark 11:15–19; Luke 19:45). These Gospels then tell how Jesus prophesied that not one stone of the temple would be left standing on top of the other (see Matthew 24:1–2; Mark

13:1–2; Luke 21:5–6). These cryptic words formed a major element in the accusations leveled against Jesus by the chief priests' witnesses in two of these accounts (see Matthew 26:61; Mark 14:58–59), and similar words were reiterated in cruel taunts against Jesus as he hung on the cross (see Matthew 27:40; Mark 15:29). Ultimately, however, the synoptic gospels do not position Jesus against the temple per se, but show him as the fulfillment of the temple. They each report that when Jesus died, the veil of the temple tore in half from top to bottom (see Matthew 27:51; Mark 15:38; Luke 23:45), effectively opening the holy of holies to all the pure in heart who would seek to see God and enter his presence through the new covenant of Jesus Christ.

The temple was seen in the Jewish world as a source of God's power. From this sacred place flowed streams of living water and divine blessing. Unlike the chief priests who had abused those powers, Jesus did not succumb to such temptations to aspire to the honors of men or to exercise unrighteous dominion. When Matthew and Luke tell how Jesus resisted the temptation to abuse his divine powers, they report how Satan took Jesus specifically to the temple, where Jesus refused to take any advantage of those powers (see Matthew 4:5–7; Luke 4:9–12).

It does not seem coincidental that the Gospel of Matthew (the tax collector) takes particular note of temple matters that have to do with money. He alone reports that Jesus encouraged his disciples to pay the temple tax voluntarily and miraculously provided a coin for them to pay this offering (see Matthew 17:24–27).[26] Those who operated the temple economy had, quite notably, violated the principle that temple offerings and transactions should be consecrated exclusively to the Lord, for which Jesus held them accountable. The story of the unforgiving steward, who himself had squandered 10,000 talents owed to his master, may well be a veiled critique of the misuse of the temple treasury, which according to Josephus amounted to the phenomenal sum of 10,000 talents.[27] This story appears only in Matthew 18. Furthermore, Matthew is the only one to point out that the thirty pieces of silver were returned by Judas to the temple treasury, where those coins apparently came from (see Matthew 27:5). Given the importance of the law of consecration, laying up treasures in heaven, and serving God and not mammon as temple motifs, it is not surprising that Jesus was so deeply troubled by money changing and commercial abuses in the temple.

Matthew adds other unique points of emphasis in reporting Jesus' program of temple novation. In Matthew, in refuting those who criticized Jesus for supposedly working on the Sabbath, Jesus responded, "Have ye not read in the law, how that on the sabbath days the priests in the temple profane the sabbath, and are blameless? But I say unto you, That in this place is one [meaning God] greater than the temple" (Matthew 12:5–6). Similarly, when Jesus taught that swearing by the temple really means swearing by God (see Matthew 23:16–17), he pointed his disciples toward the true spirit of the temple, the house of God. It is God who sanctifies all things, including the temple, not vice versa.

Mark, the Gospel of actions, uniquely states that after Jesus cleansed the temple, he "would not suffer that any man should carry any vessel through the temple" (Mark 11:16). In Mark's view, Jesus brought the old temple services "to a halt."[28] This act speaks volumes, dramatically indicating the totality of change from the old to the new.

The Gospel of Luke, the wise Greek, emphasizes the temple as a place of learning, as temples typically were in the ancient world.[29] Luke alone looks back on the time when Jesus as a youth outwitted the doctors at their own game (see Luke 2:42–50), and Luke alone notes that in Jesus' final week people came to the temple "early in the morning" to hear him preach (see Luke 21:37–38).

Recollections of Jesus at the temple are even stronger in the Gospel of John. So strong is the positive association between Jesus and the temple in the Gospel of John that John never mentions, in connection with the so-called trials of Jesus, that Jesus had ever spoken anything against that holy place. John reports that Jesus came regularly to Jerusalem for such temple festivals as the Passover (see John 2:13) and the Feast of Tabernacles (see John 7:10). He was in the temple when he found the man whom he had cleansed at the Pool of Bethesda (meaning "the house of mercy") on the Sabbath (see John 5:14–16). He was in the temple when he declared the kingdom at the Feast of Tabernacles (see John 7:28). He was in the temple when the woman taken in adultery was brought to him for judgment (see John 8:2). He spoke of the temple as "my father's house" (John 14:2), and he appropriated to himself various temple symbols such as the living water, the bread of life, the light of the world, and the true vine.[30] His final high priestly prayer blessed his apostles that they might know God and achieve unity with him and each other, echoing the blessings of the temple.[31]

For John, Jesus embodies the name and presence of God, the ascension to heaven, and rites of purification.[32] John places the cleansing at the temple at the beginning of his Gospel (see John 2:14–17), perhaps so that he can report without embarrassment all of the times that Jesus came to Jerusalem and used the temple as his base of operations. In John, immediately after Jesus drove out not only the money changers but also all the sellers and their animals, he gave as a prophetic sign the saying "Destroy this temple, and in three days I will raise it up" (John 2:19). In John are found allusions to the prophecy of Zechariah, "which presents an eschatological expectation of a restored temple,"[33] and which may also echo the prophecy of restoration for all Israel as a new people: "After two days he will revive us; in the third day he will raise us up, and we shall live in his sight ['in his presence'; literally, 'before his face']. Then shall we know [him]" (Hosea 6:2 LXX).

All this is to say that the earliest Christian memory of Jesus was deeply intertwined with the temple. The reason for this, I would suggest, has something to do not merely with the place where Jesus often stood, but even more with the things that he taught, which created a new, yet old, temple environment for his followers, complete with a new high priest, a new set of commandments adopted by way of covenant, a new order of prayer and sacrifice, and a new manner of receiving an endowment of power from on high and entering God's presence. Understanding the Sermon on the Mount as a text that has everything to do with a new order of sacred relationships between God and his people exposes the temple subtext for Jesus' program of temple novation. He did not aim his mission merely at the fringes of rural Jewish societies; he sought to recreate the very heart of all Judaism. By contemporary measures, that heart stood in Jerusalem on the Temple Mount in its holy of holies.

After the death and resurrection of Jesus, the earliest Christians continued to follow their Master by meeting at the temple. Luke reports that they assembled "continually in the temple, praising and blessing God" (Luke 24:53). In the book of Acts, the temple in Jerusalem continues to figure prominently in the religious lives of the followers of Jesus.[34] Even long after the destruction of the temple in

Jerusalem by the Romans in A.D. 70, the Christians subtly continued to envy the temple and to sense the loss of this sacred institution, righteously understood and administered, as Hugh Nibley has extensively demonstrated.[35] It is difficult to imagine that this emphasis on the temple would have arisen in early Christianity if the teachings of Jesus had not been explicitly understood by his earliest disciples as having much to do with instituting a new temple order.

In sum, these brief comments on the words of Jesus, the composition of the Sermon on the Mount and the Gospels, and the memories of the early Christians are not intended to be conclusive. By offering these thoughts, I acknowledge the vast amount of literature that exists concerning the questions of the historical Jesus and the authorship of the Sermon on the Mount. I find the questions fascinating and engaging, but most of them still remain questions. I know of no reason why Jesus could not have said all the things contained in the Sermon at the Temple or on the Mount, the many theories and treatises to the contrary notwithstanding, and, given Jesus' strong orientation toward the temple, I see several reasons to believe that he did.

Notes

1. Joachim Jeremias, *New Testament Theology,* trans. J. Bowden (New York: Charles Scribner's Sons, 1971), 29–37; see John Strugnell, "'Amen, I Say unto You' in the Sayings of Jesus and in Early Christian Literature," *Harvard Theological Review* 67/2 (1974): 177–82.

2. For a quantitative attack on the synoptic problem, see Eta Linneman, *Is There a Synoptic Problem?* trans. Robert W. Yarbrough (Grand Rapids, Mich.: Baker, 1992).

3. Harvey K. McArthur, *Understanding the Sermon on the Mount* (Westport, Conn.: Greenwood, 1978), 21–22.

4. Hans Dieter Betz, *Essays on the Sermon on the Mount,* trans. L. L. Welborn (Philadelphia: Fortress, 1985), 1–15, 55–76; and Betz, *The Sermon on the Mount,* ed. Adela Yarbro Collins (Minneapolis: Fortress, 1995), 70–80. Alfred M. Perry, "The Framework of the Sermon on the Mount," *Journal of Biblical Literature* 54 (1935): 103–15, similarly finds evidence that Matthew worked from a written source that he regarded "so highly that he used it for the foundation of his longer Sermon, even in preference to the Q discourse" (ibid., 115). On the conjectured existence of other pre-Matthean sources, see Georg Strecker, *The Sermon on the Mount: An Exegetical Commentary,* trans. O. C. Dean Jr. (Nashville: Abingdon, 1988), 55–56, 63, 67–68, 72.

5. M. D. Goulder, reply to "The Beatitudes: A Source-Critical Study," by C. M. Tuckett, *Novum Testamentum* 25/3 (1983): 211, comments that "word-counts can be used in a much more sophisticated way than is usual. . . . Over a longer passage, say the Sermon, such counting would be significant."

6. For further discussion, see Luke Timothy Johnson, *The Real Jesus* (San Francisco: Harper, 1996), 81–104.

7. *Deseret News,* 5 August 1989, sec. B, p. 1.

8. Joachim Jeremias, *The Sermon on the Mount,* trans. Norman Perrin (Philadelphia: Fortress, 1963), 15.

9. Ibid., 13.

10. For the present state of the art, see John S. Kloppenborg, *Q Parallels: Synopsis, Critical Notes, and Concordance* (Sonoma, Calif.: Polebridge, 1988).

11. Robert A. Guelich, "The Matthean Beatitudes: 'Entrance Requirements' or Eschatological Blessings?" *Journal of Biblical Literature* 95/3 (1976): 416–19; M. D. Goulder, "The Composition of the Lord's Prayer," *Journal of Theological Studies* 14 (1963): 32–45; Ernest Lohmeyer, *The Lord's Prayer,* trans. J. Bowden (London: Collins, 1965), 27–28; and Raymond E. Brown, "The Pater Noster as an Eschatological Prayer," in *New Testament Essays* (London: Geoffrey Chapman, 1965), 244. Erik Sjöberg, "Das Licht in dir: Zur Deutung von Matth. 6,22f Par.," in *Studia*

Theologica (Lund, Sweden: Gleerup, 1952), 5:89, finds that there "can be no doubt that the Matthean formulation is the original" of Matthew 6:22, as compared with Luke 11:35–36. D. Flusser, "Blessed Are the Poor in Spirit," *Israel Exploration Journal* 10 (1960): 11, concludes that it is "certain that Matt. v, 3–5 faithfully preserves the saying of Jesus and that Luke vi, 20 is an abbreviation of the original text."

12. Neil J. McEleney, "The Beatitudes of the Sermon on the Mount/Plain," *Catholic Biblical Quarterly* 43/1 (1981): 7–8; and Robert A. Guelich, "The Antitheses of Matthew V. 21–48: Traditional and/or Redactional?" *New Testament Studies* 22 (1976): 446–49.

13. Betz, *Sermon on the Mount*, 372.

14. See the discussion of the Secret Gospel of Mark, in pp. 75–76 of this book, concerning 3 Nephi 12:48.

15. Strecker, *Sermon on the Mount*, 59.

16. Jack D. Kingsbury, "The Place, Structure, and Meaning of the Sermon on the Mount within Matthew," *Interpretation* 41 (1987): 132–33; he also points out that the depiction of the disciples in Matthew 5:11–12 and 7:15–23 has "no place in the picture the narrator paints of the disciples during the earthly ministry of Jesus" (ibid., 135). See Charles E. Carlston, "Interpreting the Gospel of Matthew," *Interpretation* 29 (1975): 3–12, for a more harmonious view of the unique traditional and ecclesiastical interests of Matthew. See also C. J. A. Hickling, "Conflicting Motives in the Redaction of Matthew: Some Considerations on the Sermon on the Mount and Matthew 18:15–20," *Studia Evangelica* 7 (1982): 247–60.

17. Betz, *Essays on the Sermon on the Mount*, 55–70; and W. D. Davies, *The Sermon on the Mount* (Cambridge: Cambridge University Press, 1966), 105–6.

18. These are mentioned in John W. Welch, "Chiasmus in the New Testament," in *Chiasmus in Antiquity: Structures, Analyses, Exegesis,* ed. John W. Welch (Hildesheim: Gerstenberg Verlag, 1981; reprint, Provo, Utah: Research Press, 1999), 212; and Patrick J. Hartin, "James and the Q Sermon on the Mount/Plain," *Society of*

Biblical Literature 1989 Seminar Papers, ed. David J. Lull (Atlanta: Scholars, 1989), 440–57. John Gee, "Use of the Sermon on the Mount in the Earliest Christian Church" (FARMS, 1989), 5–9, has observed further connections between Matthew 5:48 *(teleioi)* and James 1:4 *(teleioi)*; asking of God (James 1:5–6; Matthew 7:7–11); blessed *(makarios)* in James 1:12 and the Beatitudes; lust (James 1:14–15; Matthew 5:28); good gifts and perfect *(teleion)* offerings (James 1:17; Matthew 7:11); anger and insult (James 1:19–20; Matthew 5:22); doing the word (James 1:22–25; Matthew 7:21–27); and several others. Richard Lloyd Anderson, "Paul's Witness to the Early History of Jesus' Ministry," in *The Apostle Paul: His Life and Testimony* (Salt Lake City: Deseret Book, 1994), 28, concludes that "James has used representative sections of Christ's full sermon." However, the precise nature of the relationship between James and the Sermon remains a puzzle (Betz, *Sermon on the Mount,* 6 n. 13).

19. Jeremias, *Sermon on the Mount,* 22.

20. Betz, *Sermon on the Mount,* 6 n. 12.

21. Birger Gerhardsson, *Memory and Manuscript* (Grand Rapids, Mich.: Eerdmans, 1998); and Linnemann, *Is There a Synoptic Problem?* 182–85.

22. Gerhardsson, *Memory and Manuscript,* 328.

23. Ibid., 329.

24. Bruce Chilton, *The Temple of Jesus: His Sacrificial Program within a Cultural History of Sacrifice* (University Park, Penn.: Pennsylvania State University Press, 1992), 137–54.

25. Ibid., 138.

26. Hugh Montefiore, "Jesus and the Temple Tax," *New Testament Studies* 11 (1964–65): 70–71.

27. John W. Welch, "Herod's Wealth," in *Masada and the World of the New Testament,* ed. John F. Hall and John W. Welch (Provo, Utah: BYU Studies, 1997), 81–82.

28. Chilton, *Temple of Jesus,* 115.

29. Hugh W. Nibley, "Temples: Meanings and Functions of Temples," in *Encyclopedia of Mormonism,* 4:1462.

30. On the temple in the Gospel of John generally, see

Richard Holzapfel and David Seely, *My Father's House: Temple Worship and Symbolism in the New Testament* (Salt Lake City: Bookcraft, 1994), 141–70.

31. William Hamblin, "Temple Motifs in John 17" (FARMS, 1995).

32. Mark Kinzer, "Temple Christology in the Gospel of John," in *Society of Biblical Literature 1998 Seminar Papers* (Atlanta: Scholars, 1998), 1:447–64.

33. Mark A. Matson, "The Contribution to the Temple Cleansing by the Fourth Gospel," in *Society of Biblical Literature 1992 Seminar Papers*, ed. Eugene H. Lovering Jr. (Atlanta: Scholars, 1992), 503.

34. Holzapfel and Seely, *My Father's House*, 119–38.

35. Hugh W. Nibley, "Christian Envy of the Temple," *Jewish Quarterly Review* 50 (1959–60): 97–123, 229–40; reprinted in Nibley, *Mormonism and Early Christianity* (Salt Lake City: Deseret Book, 1987), 391–434.

CHAPTER 11

THE SERMON IN LIGHT OF RITUAL STUDIES

One final approach to understanding the nature and function of the Sermon on the Mount has come recently through the channels of religious ritual studies. Taking this additional tack provides further insights into the ritual character of the Sermon. Having exhaustively plowed the fields of form, source, and historical criticism and still having come up short on completely satisfying approaches, students may find helpful insights by turning in other directions, such as to rhetorical or social scientific studies.

Seeing the Sermon through the lens of ritual studies would seem particularly promising. Several rituals were practiced by the early Christians from the first century onward, including baptism (offered by John the Baptist), almsgiving, prayer, fasting, washing and anointing (as mentioned in the cultic instructions in Matthew 6:1–18), the laying on of hands for the gift of the Holy Ghost or to ordain priesthood officers (mentioned as early as Acts 6:6; 8:17), the sacrament of the Lord's supper or the Eucharist (well established by the time of Paul's letters to the Corinthians in the early 50s A.D.), blessing the sick (James 5:14), and marriage (the most extensive evidence coming from the *Gospel of Philip*),[1] to mention only some.

Such rituals were important to early Christianity. Indeed, it seems unlikely that any new religion could successfully emerge in the ancient world without inaugurating its own rituals. All ancient religions were highly ritualistic, especially when compared with modern religions. Their individual and sometimes iconoclastic rituals served as markers to distinguish one group from the others. Cultic observances and solemn rites served to foster needed loyalty of members to the group and to enshrine the basic tenets of each religion, as well as to offer sacrifices to their gods and to pay homage to the spirits of their kindred dead. Although they were influenced to some extent by philosophical schools of thought, ancient religions were more than mere bodies of abstract teachings and more than logical systems of philosophical thought. For this reason, such religious philosophers as Philo of Alexandria did not launch a religious movement. Religions had rituals, temples, priests, regulations, and cultic systems.

Primitive Christianity, along with its host Jewish culture, soon had to deal with the loss of the temple in Jerusalem, but well before its destruction in A.D. 70, Jesus and his apostles had already begun their program of replacing that temple with a new temple concept and system. Given its Jewish antecedents and matrix, it seems unlikely that Jesus' temple program was entirely spiritualized at the beginning, as it soon would come to be. Thus, the recent search for further clues about the earliest Christian rituals is well warranted.

Studies of Ritual and Ceremony

Interest in ritual studies rose sharply among social scientists in the 1980s. Beginning in the winter of 1987, the *Journal of Ritual Studies* commenced publication on this subject under the auspices of the Department of Religious Studies at the University of Pittsburgh. This interest soon spilled over into biblical studies. In 1994 a full issue of *Semeia,* a journal dedicated to experimental biblical criticism and published by the Society of Biblical Literature, devoted its total attention to ritual elements in the New Testament. Without attempting to survey everything in this growing field of religious scholarship, I will sketch some of the basic definitions, concepts, and functions that this discipline has come to associate with rituals in general, and I will apply these criteria to the Sermon on the Mount. Seeing the Sermon as a temple text places it in a ritual context, and the plausibility of that contextualization is confirmed by the broad findings of ritual studies.

Victor Turner was among the first social scientists to analyze rituals. By *ritual* he meant any "prescribed formal behavior for occasions not given over to technological routine, having reference to beliefs in mystical beings or powers."[2] Religious rites have been classified under two headings: as rituals or as ceremonies. In general, rituals (such as baptisms) are said to occur at any time, are primarily oriented toward the future, are presided over by professionals, and transform a person from one status to another. Ceremonies (such as the observance of Passover or the sacrament of the Lord's supper) usually occur at regular times, celebrate past events, are conducted by many kinds of officials, and serve principally to reconfirm the status and role of people in the religion.[3] In reality, however, the lines between these two categories are not rigid.

Whether the Sermon on the Mount in its earliest iterations should be thought of as accompanying a transforming ritual or a repeated ceremony probably depends on developments within the lives of individual early Christians. The first time the Sermon was experienced by a disciple, either in Galilee or at Bountiful, it was generative and transformative; as a text that accompanied baptism or prepared initiates for entrance into the kingdom of God on earth, the Sermon is probably best understood as a ritual text. Subsequent reiterations of the Sermon, either by Jesus or his disciples, however, are probably best thought of in terms of ceremony. Out of the Sermon, for example, came the ceremonial use of the Lord's Prayer in the ancient Mediterranean arena and also the ceremonial sacrament prayers among the peoples of the Book of Mormon. Ceremonially rehearsing these sacred texts reminded worthy Christians of the things Jesus had said and reconfirmed their status and role as believers. Thus, the Sermon may well be seen both as ritual and ceremony.

General Functions of Ritual

According to social scientists, rituals and ceremonies serve several generic functions. Significantly, as the following discussion demonstrates, the Sermon amply serves each of these functions as articulated in the scholarly literature.

For example, one common function served by most religious rites is to give order to the community's way of life: "Societies employ rituals that express their guiding ideas . . . by dramatizing [their] world view and way of life."[4] Without doubt, the Sermon expresses the guiding ideas of the Christian's way of life. It is a guide for daily living with an eternal perspective.

Furthermore, religious rites typically derive much of their ability to link the individual with the cosmos—the particular with the general, the real with the ideal—by turning ordinary experiences into sacred symbols. "Ritual relies for its power on the fact that it is concerned with quite ordinary activities,"[5] such as eating bread, drinking wine, or being washed. Similarly, the Sermon on the Mount imbues the ordinary occurrences of daily life with sacred import, utilizing everything from salt, light, cheeks, and coats, to lilies, thistles, fish, and bread.

The ordinary, however, "becomes significant, becomes sacred, simply by being there," in a sacred place, a place of clarification, where "it becomes sacred by having our attention directed to it in a special way."[6] Functioning as a focusing lens, ritual, especially at a temple or other sacred space, is "a means of performing the way things ought to be in conscious tension to the way things are in such a way that this ritualized perfection is recollected in the ordinary, uncontrolled, course of things."[7] Throughout the Sermon, a tension tugs at us between the way things usually are and the way perfection would have us be. It presents in dramatic images the doctrine of the Two Ways and holds out to our view the contrast between our old way of seeing things and a new vision of the divine way things can and should be.

Observers also find that silence ritually heightens the ability of participants to hear these clarifying messages. Temples and rituals in general function best when, "as in all forms of communication, static and noise (i.e., the accidental) are decreased so that the exchange of information can be increased."[8] Hence, it is no idle point that the Sermon at the Temple commences in a state of utter silence (see 3 Nephi 11:8), and both Sermons admonish people to go into their quiet closets to pray behind closed doors (see Matthew 6:6; 3 Nephi 13:6).

Religious rites are not only private experiences; they are also interpersonal. One of their salient purposes is "to create social cohesion."[9] Unquestionably, the Sermon serves this purpose as well by prohibiting anger against others; by requiring people to settle their differences quickly; by demanding kindness, generosity, honesty, and forgiveness; and by abolishing judgment of a brother. The golden rule, which sums up the Law and the Prophets, is perhaps the ultimate touchstone of social cohesion.

Moreover, in implementing that social order, rituals and ceremonies unleash spiritual power from "'the generating source of culture and structure.'"[10] They provide structure and control to the social order, making important public statements "about the hierarchal relations between people."[11] Thus, scholars conclude that rituals are not only a source for setting social boundaries but are much more: they are "'models *of*' what people believe and . . . 'models *for* the believing of it.'"[12] Rituals model the behavior of believing, righteous people. Ritual texts tell the believer how to respond to certain situations and how to believe the sacred ritual itself. In this light, one may consider the functions served by the social structures, boundaries, and models that are set in and by the Sermon on the Mount. The Sermon provides fundamental rules for interpreting law and order, structuring marriages and divorce, serving masters, and rejecting false prophets; it sets boundaries by identifying improper conduct, for example, in those who love only their friends or who parade to be seen of men; and it provides many models for believing in God and his righteousness, trusting in God, going the extra mile, and giving to those who ask for help.

In addition, ritual is more than simple symbolic expression and more than a dramatic presentation. Ritual is a system of "redressing social crisis and restoring order" after disruption.[13] Reacting against the unsettling effects of change, the stability afforded by ritual rejuvenates community values and institutions. This ritual function is detectable in the Sermon's reassurance that Jesus did not come to destroy but to fulfill the law. The teachings of Jesus were unsettling to many people. He was controversial in his own lifetime, and his followers were considered blasphemers by the dominant culture. In the face of these monumental crises, the ritualized reassurances of the Sermon restored order in the lives of the early followers of Jesus. In the Sermon at the Temple, the crisis was of epic proportions, involving not only ethical and social reorientations, but also the destruction of entire cities and the obsolescence of the traditional order of temple sacrifices (see 3 Nephi 9:3–20).

Structurally, rituals of transformation then conduct the initiates through three stages. Rituals and rites of passage, according to standard theory, typically involve (1) a separation from the old society, (2) an isolation in a marginal or liminal, amorphous state, and (3) a reaggregation into a new social set.[14] Interestingly, K. C. Hanson has applied this three-stage ritual analysis fairly successfully to the Sermon on the Mount.[15] Thus, he suggests: (1) "In ritual terms, [Jesus] left the general population and gathered his disciples for instruction."[16] They are at first strongly separated from other people; they are not to be like the Pharisees or hypocrites. Thus, (2) the initiates find themselves next on the border, in a no man's land, neither Jew nor Greek, and they see themselves in a state of reflection and as a group of equal brothers and sisters, "divested of their previous habits of thought, feeling, and action," thinking about "the powers that generate and sustain them."[17] Through adherence to "keeping secret the nature of the *sacra*," which is "the crux of liminality,"[18] the result of the Sermon (3) is, finally, "the group's initiation into Jesus' teaching. . . . The master-teacher has guided the initiands into a new status."[19] Aggregation as a new group of adherents has resulted.

The contours of this three-stage ritual process are even more prominent in the Sermon at the Temple. There the traumas of destruction, loneliness, and uncertainty accentuate the stages of separation and liminality. There the rituals of baptism (see 3 Nephi 11:21–27) and taking a new name (see 3 Nephi 18:11; see also Moroni 4:3) are integrally connected with the Sermon, and the ordination of new officers (see 3 Nephi 12:1–2) overtly structures the reaggregation of the believers into a new society.

Rituals in all cultures aid in this difficult process of transformation across boundaries. They provide coherence and comfort as people walk the perilous path from one stage in life to another. With respect to the Sermon on the Mount, Philip Esler agrees with Hanson's analysis particularly with respect to this element of transformation: "There is clearly a transformation here both in the restoration to wholeness of the sick and broken who come to Jesus and the fact that, upon seeing this, the people give glory to the God of Israel."[20] The same can be said of the Sermon at the Temple, where the healing is not only verbal but also physical. In many ways, the Sermon is transformational: It turns the world upside down. Barbara Babcock has shown how effectively rites can invert an existing social or religious order, thereby introducing a new society, order, or cosmos, even as it sets aside the old.[21] What one has heard one way of old is now said another way; enemies become friends; money becomes worthless; deeds done in secret are rewarded in the open; and mortals become as God.

Imagining the Conduct of Such a Rite

No single rite or ceremony, of course, incorporates every possible performative element of ritual, but the Sermon on the Mount potentially contains many of them. Common elements in ancient rituals include such things as actual purifications, symbolic journeys, inspired lectures on future behavior, multiple levels of initiation, the giving of secrets, expositions of holy objects, and investiture or crowning. The Sermon on the Mount alludes to such items, even if only obliquely: purification ("blessed are the pure in heart"), journeys ("the way"), lectures on future behavior (see Matthew 6:19–7:12), multiple levels of initiation ("be ye therefore perfect"), giving secrets and showing holy symbols ("give not that which is holy"), and investiture ("even as Solomon").

We may even imagine the nature of ritual actions that could have accompanied a ceremonial or ritual usage of the Sermon.[22] Consider the following prospects. Is it possible that the blessings of the Beatitudes were bestowed by the laying on of hands? That the people responded with an acclamation of rejoicing? That salt was tasted or poured out on the ground and trampled underfoot? That a coat was requested and an undergarment given? That alms were actually collected? That a group prayer was recited? That people were marked as slaves of the One Master? That robes were donned? That one stood before a surrogate eschatological judge? That something belonging to the initiate was turned and rent? That people knocked three times? That the group actually ate some bread and fish? That they passed through a narrow opening, past a tree of life, into the symbolic presence of God? Any attempt to reconstruct such ritual actions is admittedly conjectural, for that knowledge became lost with the deaths of those early initiates and remains unknown to us. But it is at least fair to wonder.

Far less conjectural, however, are the general patterns and purposes that investigators have discerned in rituals across all cultures. I point to those phenomena as further support for the basic suggestion that the Sermon functions well in a temple or ceremonial context. Just as ritual provides social order to one's way of life, ritual analysis can supply a deeply needed sense of underlying, unifying order in the Sermon itself.

Notes

1. April D. DeConick, "Entering God's Presence: Sacramentalism in the Gospel of Philip," in *Society of Biblical Literature 1998 Seminar Papers* (Atlanta: Scholars, 1998), 483–523.

2. Victor Turner, *The Forest of Symbols: Aspects of Ndembu Ritual* (New York: Cornell University Press, 1967), 19. Turner's pioneering efforts have long since been refined and expanded beyond the domain of religion.

3. K. C. Hanson, "Transformed on the Mountain: Ritual Analysis and the Gospel of Matthew," *Semeia* 67 (1994): 152–54; Mark McVann, "Reading Mark Ritually: Honor-Shame and the Ritual of Baptism," *Semeia* 67 (1994): 180; and Turner, *Forest of Symbols*, 95.

4. Bobby C. Alexander, "An Afterword on Ritual in Biblical Studies," *Semeia* 67 (1994): 210–11.

5. Jonathan Z. Smith, "The Bare Facts of Ritual," *History of Religions* 20 (1980): 125.

6. Ibid., 115.

7. Ibid., 125.

8. Ibid., 114.

9. Alexander, "Afterword on Ritual," 210.

10. Tom F. Driver, *The Magic of Ritual: Our Need for Liberating Rites That Transform Our Lives and Our Communities* (San Francisco: HarperCollins, 1991), 189, quoting Victor Turner, *The Anthropology of Performance* (New York: PAJ, 1986), 158.

11. Esther Goody, "'Greeting', 'Begging', and the Presentation of Respect," in *The Interpretation of Ritual: Essays in Honour of A. I. Richards*, ed. J. S. La Fontaine (London: Tavistock, 1972), 39.

12. Carol Schersten LaHurd, "Exactly What's Ritual about the Experience of Reading/Hearing Mark's Gospel," *Semeia* 67 (1994): 204–5, quoting Clifford Geertz, "Religion as a Cultural System," in *Reader in Comparative Religion: An Anthropological Approach*, ed. William Lessa and Evon Vogt (New York: Harper and Row, 1965).

13. Alexander, "Afterword on Ritual," 211.

14. Turner, *Forest of Symbols*, 94, following the theories of Van Gennep.

15. Hanson, "Transformed on the Mountain," 154–61. Kari Syreeni, "Methodology and Compositional Analysis," pt. 1 of *The Making of the Sermon on the Mount: A Procedural Analysis of Matthew's Redactoral Activity* (Helsinki: Suomalainen Tiedeakatemia, 1987), 217, anticipated this structural analysis. Philip F. Esler, "Mountaineering in Matthew: A Response to K. C. Hanson," *Semeia* 67 (1994): 171–77, is critical of Hanson's efforts elsewhere in Matthew but finds that "the Sermon on the Mount is a little more promising for Hanson's view" (ibid., 173).

16. Hanson, "Transformed on the Mountain," 160.

17. Turner, *Forest of Symbols*, 105; italics in original.

18. Ibid., 103.

19. Hanson, "Transformed on the Mountain," 160–61.

20. Esler, "Mountaineering in Matthew," 173.

21. Barbara Babcock, ed., *The Reversible World: Symbolic*

Inversion in Art and Society (Ithaca, N.Y.: Cornell University Press, 1998). I am grateful to Richard DeMaris for this reference.

22. In general, see Caroline Humphrey and James Laidlaw, *The Archetypal Actions of Ritual: A Theory of Ritual Illustrated by the Jain Rite of Worship* (Oxford: Clarendon, 1994).

CHAPTER 12

RESULTS AND CONCLUDING THOUGHTS

This study has surveyed the terrain of the temple mount of the Sermon textually, historically, linguistically, analytically, comparatively, religiously, and ritually. In my mind, the quest has borne good fruit. If the Sermon at the Temple is to be known by its fruits, the simple fact that it lends itself rewardingly to such scrutiny should be a strong clue that much more remains to be said and thought about the Sermon on the Mount and the Sermon at the Temple.

Much more also lies ahead in thinking about the implications of this study on other areas of research. The Sermon on the Mount is a key scriptural text. How a person understands the Sermon on the Mount—when it was written, why it was given, and what it means—has a deep impact on how one interprets the entire ministry of Jesus, numerous texts of the New Testament, and many of the experiences of early Christianity. How one views the Sermon has equally far-reaching consequences for approaching the Book of Mormon—how it was translated, what it contains, and why it is important. Sooner or later, all roads in the gospel lead past this scriptural Mount.

Thus, my interpretation will surely not be the last word on the Sermon on the Mount or its ramifications. This interpretation is likely to evoke all kinds of responses—some positive and some negative. It would be a first were that not the case: Few interpretations of the Sermon have ever met with anything close to universal acceptance. I will be the first to acknowledge that important questions and historical uncertainties remain. However, in discussing this text, which for centuries has defied consensus in analysis and summation, I hope to have shown that there is room for a Latter-day Saint interpretation that places a premium on the background and contextualizing information about the Sermon provided by the Book of Mormon.

That information leads me to the conclusion that the Sermon at the Temple is a powerful and meaningful scripture. To a greater extent than has been suspected before, it contains the fulness of the gospel, both as an epitome of Jesus' teachings and as an implementation of his commandments by way of sacred temple covenant, for many elements of the new covenant Jesus brought to the temple at Bountiful are fundamentally comparable to the temple ceremony familiar to Latter-day Saints. All portions of the text— some more obviously than others—can be understood ritually. The Sermon on the Mount is a natural script for an initiation text, which means that it (like many of the parables of Jesus) may have had esoteric significance, as well as public levels of meaning, to early Christians. To see the Sermon on the Mount simply as commandments, or as ethical teachings, or as making extraordinary apocalyptic demands, or as eschatology, is to see only parts of the whole. Through symbolic representation and covenantal ritual, however, one can journey conceptually and spiritually through the sum of its truths, from one's present condition on into the blessings of eternity.

In the end, my interpretation has not yet really answered the ultimate question, "What is the meaning of the Sermon on the Mount?" That remains for the reader to discover. What I have tried to supply is a map, a few tools, and the ability to recognize some major landmarks along the way. After all is said and done, as Harvey McArthur has written, "When the reader lifts his eyes from the details and ponders the over-all meaning of what he has read, he is still confronted by [the] basic questions"—what does Jesus mean, and how should I live?[1] For a Latter-day Saint, I suggest, the answer to these questions is to be found in the same way as is the answer to a similar question, "What is the meaning of the temple?" The answer to that central Latter-day Saint concern is sought through such things as repeatedly experiencing the temple, meditation, contemplation, faith, repentance, obedience to sacred covenants, Christ-centered living, the integration of truth into the gospel and atonement of Jesus Christ, and a steadfast walk on an undeviating path toward the day of judgment and exaltation. The meaning of the Sermon will be found in similar ways.

In the course of this study, I have also explained why, in my opinion, the superficial label of plagiarism does not fit the Sermon at the Temple. I consider this an interesting secondary concern of this study. The Nephite text differs for sound reasons from the Sermon on the Mount. These differences are significant and often subtle and, along with many other factors, show that the Sermon on the Mount was not crudely spliced into the text of 3 Nephi. There is much more in the Sermon at the Temple than the theory of plagiarism can account for. Nor is the Sermon at the Temple compromised by its similarity to the King James English or by critical studies of the New Testament. Instead, there are historical and philological reasons for believing that the Sermon at the Temple bears the hallmarks of an accurate and inspired translation of a contemporaneous record of the words that Jesus spoke in A.D. 34 at the temple in Bountiful. It is hard to imagine a more suitable text that he could have used on that occasion.

My main purpose in writing and sharing this study has been to enhance the respect and appreciation of Latter-day Saints for the Sermon at the Temple and, at the same time, to improve our understanding of the Sermon on the Mount. I realize that I have broken new ground, to say nothing of breaking stride with the preponderance of New Testament scholarly opinion by taking seriously the idea that Jesus was the author of the Sermon. I am also aware that not all the points I have advanced are equally persuasive or fully developed. I hope, however, that this uphill climb has been intelligently and engagingly conducted. After the trek, it seems clear enough to me that one should not dismiss this Mount on the basis of a few partial geological reports from the bottom. Hopefully, it will give all who make the ascent a clearer view from the top.

Note

1. Harvey K. McArthur, *Understanding the Sermon on the Mount* (Westport, Conn.: Greenwood, 1978), 15.

A Comparison of the Sermon on the Mount and the Sermon at the Temple

Text that is in **bold** is unique to 3 Nephi.
Text that is in *italics* is unique to the KJV.
All other text is found in both 3 Nephi and the KJV.

Matthew 5	3 Nephi 12
1 *And seeing the multitudes, he went up into a mountain: and when he was set, his disciples came unto him:*	**And it came to pass that when Jesus had spoken these words unto Nephi, and to those who had been called, (now the number of them who had been called, and received power and authority to baptize, was twelve) and** behold, he stretched forth his hand unto the multitude, and cried unto them, saying: **Blessed are ye if ye shall give**

Matthew 5	3 Nephi 12
	heed unto the words of these twelve whom I have chosen from among you to minister unto you, and to be your servants; and unto them I have given power that they may baptize you with water; and after that ye are baptized with water, behold, I will baptize you with fire and with the Holy Ghost; therefore blessed are ye if ye shall believe in me and be baptized, after that ye have seen me and know that I am.
2 *And he opened his mouth, and taught them, saying,*	And again, more blessed are they who shall believe in your words because that ye shall testify that ye have seen me, and that ye know that I am. Yea, blessed are they who shall believe in your words, and come down into the depths of humility and be baptized, for they shall be visited with fire and with the Holy Ghost, and shall receive a remission of their sins.

Matthew 5	3 Nephi 12
3 Blessed are the poor in spirit: for theirs is the kingdom of heaven.	**Yea,** blessed are the poor in spirit **who come unto me,** for theirs is the kingdom of heaven.
4 Blessed are they that mourn: for they shall be comforted.	**And again,** blessed are **all** they that mourn, for they shall be comforted.
5 Blessed are the meek: for they shall inherit the earth.	**And** blessed are the meek, for they shall inherit the earth.
6 Blessed are they *which* do hunger and thirst after righteousness: for they shall be filled.	**And** blessed are **all** they **who** do hunger and thirst after righteousness, for they shall be filled **with the Holy Ghost.**
7 Blessed are the merciful: for they shall obtain mercy.	**And** blessed are the merciful, for they shall obtain mercy.
8 Blessed are the pure in heart: for they shall see God.	**And** blessed are **all** the pure in heart, for they shall see God.
9 Blessed are the peacemakers: for they shall be called the children of God.	**And** blessed are **all** the peacemakers, for they shall be called the children of God.
10 Blessed are they *which* are persecuted for righteousness' sake: for theirs is the kingdom of heaven.	**And** blessed are **all** they **who** are persecuted for **my name's** sake, for theirs is the kingdom of heaven.

Matthew 5	3 Nephi 12
11 Blessed are ye, when men shall revile you, and persecute *you*, and shall say all manner of evil against you falsely, for my sake.	**And** blessed are ye when men shall revile you and persecute, and shall say all manner of evil against you falsely, for my sake;
12 *Rejoice,* and be exceeding glad: for great *is* your reward in heaven: for so persecuted they the prophets *which* were before you.	**For ye shall have great joy** and be exceeding**ly** glad, for great **shall be** your reward in heaven; for so persecuted they the prophets **who** were before you.
13 *Ye are* the salt of the earth: but if the salt *have lost his* savo*u*r, wherewith shall *it* be salted? *it is* thenceforth good for nothing, but to be cast out, and to be trodden under foot of men.	**Verily, verily, I say unto you, I give unto you to be** the salt of the earth; but if the salt **shall lose its** savor wherewith shall **the earth** be salted? **The salt shall be** thenceforth good for nothing, but to be cast out and to be trodden under foot of men.
14 *Ye are* the light of *the world.* A city that is set on *an* hill cannot be hid.	**Verily, verily, I say unto you, I give unto you to be** the light of **this people.** A city that is set on **a** hill cannot be hid.
15 *Neither* do men light a candle, and put it under a bushel, but on a candlestick; and it giveth	**Behold,** do men light a candle and put it under a bushel? **Nay,** but on a candlestick, and

Matthew 5	3 Nephi 12
light *unto* all that are in the house.	it giveth light **to** all that are in the house;
16 Let your light so shine before *men,* that they may see your good works, and glorify your Father *which* is in heaven.	**Therefore** let your light so shine before **this people,** that they may see your good works and glorify your Father **who** is in heaven.
17 Think not that I am come to destroy the law, or the prophets: I am not come to destroy, but to fulfil.	Think not that I am come to destroy the law or the prophets. I am not come to destroy but to fulfill;
18 For verily I say unto you, *Till heaven and earth pass,* one jot *or* one tittle *shall in no wise pass* from the law, *till* all *be* fulfilled.	For verily I say unto you, one jot **nor** one tittle **hath not passed away** from the law, **but in me it hath** all **been** fulfilled.
19 *Whosoever therefore shall break one of these least* commandments, *and shall teach men so, he shall be called the least in the kingdom of heaven: but whosoever shall do and teach them, the same shall be called great in the kingdom of heaven.*	**And behold, I have given you the law and the** commandments **of my Father, that ye shall believe in me, and that ye shall repent of your sins, and come unto me with a broken heart and a contrite spirit. Behold, ye have the commandments before you, and the law is fulfilled.**

Matthew 5	3 Nephi 12
20 For I say unto you, That except *your righteousness shall exceed the righteousness of the scribes and Pharisees,* ye shall in no case enter into the kingdom of heaven.	**Therefore come unto me and be ye saved;** for **verily** I say unto you, that except **ye shall keep my commandments, which I have commanded you at this time,** ye shall in no case enter into the kingdom of heaven.
21 Ye have heard that it *was* said by them of old time, Thou shalt not kill; and whosoever shall kill shall be in danger of the judgment:	Ye have heard that it **hath been** said by them of old time, **and it is also written before you, that** thou shalt not kill, and whosoever shall kill shall be in danger of the judgment **of God;**
22 But I say unto you, That whosoever is angry with his brother *without a cause* shall be in danger of *the* judgment: and whosoever shall say to his brother, Raca, shall be in danger of the council: *but* whosoever shall say, Thou fool, shall be in danger of hell fire.	But I say unto you, that whosoever is angry with his brother shall be in danger of **his** judgment. And whosoever shall say to his brother, Raca, shall be in danger of the council; **and** whosoever shall say, Thou fool, shall be in danger of hell fire.
23 Therefore if *thou bring thy gift to the altar,* and *there* rememberest that thy brother hath ought against thee;	Therefore, if **ye shall come unto me, or shall desire to come unto me,** and rememberest that thy brother hath aught against thee—

Matthew 5	3 Nephi 12
24 *Leave there thy gift before the altar, and* go thy way; first be reconciled to thy brother, and then come *and offer thy gift.*	Go thy way **unto thy brother, and** first be reconciled to thy brother, and then come **unto me with full purpose of heart, and I will receive you.**
25 Agree with thine adversary quickly, whiles thou art in the way with him; lest at any time *the adversary deliver thee to the judge, and the judge deliver thee to the officer,* and thou be cast into prison.	Agree with thine adversary quickly while thou art in the way with him, lest at any time **he shall get thee,** and thou **shalt** be cast into prison.
26 Verily I say unto thee, Thou shalt by no means come out thence, *till* thou hast paid the uttermost *farthing.*	Verily, **verily,** I say unto thee, thou shalt by no means come out thence **until** thou hast paid the uttermost **senine. And while ye are in prison can ye pay even one senine? Verily, verily, I say unto you, Nay.**
27 *Ye have heard that* it *was said* by them of old time, Thou shalt not commit adultery:	**Behold,** it **is written** by them of old time, **that** thou shalt not commit adultery;
28 But I say unto you, That whosoever looketh on a woman to lust after her hath committed adultery *with her* already in his heart.	But I say unto you, that whosoever looketh on a woman, to lust after her, hath committed adultery already in his heart.

Matthew 5	3 Nephi 12
29 *And if thy right eye offend thee, pluck it out, and cast it from thee: for it is profitable for thee that one of thy members should perish, and not that thy whole body should be cast into hell.*	**Behold, I give unto you a commandment, that ye suffer none of these things to enter into your heart;**
30 *And if thy right hand offend thee, cut it off, and cast it from thee: for it is profitable for thee that one of thy members should perish, and not that thy whole body should be cast into hell.*	**For it is better that ye should deny yourselves of these things, wherein ye will take up your cross, than that ye should be cast into hell.**
31 It hath been *said,* Whosoever shall put away his wife, let him give her a writing of divorcement:	It hath been **written, that** whosoever shall put away his wife, let him give her a writing of divorcement.
32 *But* I say unto you, That whosoever shall put away his wife, saving for the cause of fornication, causeth her to commit adultery: and *whosoever* shall marry her *that* is divorced committeth adultery.	**Verily, verily,** I say unto you, that whosoever shall put away his wife, saving for the cause of fornication, causeth her to commit adultery; and **whoso** shall marry her **who** is divorced committeth adultery.
33 Again, *ye have heard that it hath been said by them of old time,* Thou shalt not forswear thyself, but shalt perform unto the Lord thine oaths:	**And** again it **is written,** thou shalt not forswear thyself, but shalt perform unto the Lord thine oaths;

Matthew 5	3 Nephi 12
34 But I say unto you, Swear not at all; neither by heaven; for it is God's throne:	But **verily, verily,** I say unto you, swear not at all; neither by heaven, for it is God's throne;
35 Nor by the earth; for it is his footstool: *neither by Jerusalem; for it is the city of the great King.*	Nor by the earth, for it is his footstool;
36 Neither shalt thou swear by thy head, because thou canst not make one hair *white* or *black.*	Neither shalt thou swear by thy head, because thou canst not make one hair **black** or **white;**
37 But let your communication be, Yea, yea; Nay, nay: for whatsoever *is* more than these *cometh of* evil.	But let your communication be Yea, yea; Nay, nay; for whatsoever **cometh of** more than these **is** evil.
38 *Ye have heard that* it *hath been said,* An eye for an eye, and a tooth for a tooth:	**And behold,** it **is written,** an eye for an eye, and a tooth for a tooth;
39 But I say unto you, That ye resist *not* evil: but whosoever shall smite thee on thy right cheek, turn to him the other also.	But I say unto you, that ye **shall not** resist evil, but whosoever shall smite thee on thy right cheek, turn to him the other also;
40 And if any man will sue thee at the law, and take away thy coat, let him have thy clo*ke* also.	And if any man will sue thee at the law and take away thy coat, let him have thy clo**ak** also;

Matthew 5	3 Nephi 12
41 And whosoever shall compel thee to go a mile, go with him twain.	And whosoever shall compel thee to go a mile, go with him twain.
42 Give to him that asketh thee, and from him that would borrow of thee turn *not thou* away.	Give to him that asketh thee, and from him that would borrow of thee turn **thou not** away.
43 *Ye have heard that* it *hath been said,* Thou shalt love thy neighbour, and hate thine enemy.	**And behold** it **is written also, that** thou shalt love thy neighbor and hate thine enemy;
44 But I say unto you, Love your enemies, bless them that curse you, do good to them that hate you, and pray for them *which* despitefully use you, and persecute you;	But **behold** I say unto you, love your enemies, bless them that curse you, do good to them that hate you, and pray for them **who** despitefully use you and persecute you;
45 That ye may be the children of your Father *which* is in heaven: for he maketh his sun to rise on the evil and on the good, *and sendeth rain on the just and on the unjust.*	That ye may be the children of your Father **who** is in heaven; for he maketh his sun to rise on the evil and on the good.
46 *For if ye love them which love you, what reward have ye? do not even the publicans the same?*	**Therefore those things which were of old time, which were under the law, in me are all fulfilled.**

Matthew 5–6	3 Nephi 12–13
47 *And if ye salute your brethren only, what do ye more than others? do not even the publicans so?*	**Old things are done away, and all things have become new.**
48 Be *ye therefore* perfect, even as your Father *which* is in heaven is perfect.	**Therefore I would that ye should** be perfect even as **I, or** your Father **who** is in heaven is perfect.
1	**Verily, verily, I say that I would that ye should do alms unto the poor; but** take heed that ye do not your alms before men to be seen of them; otherwise ye have no reward of your Father **who** is in heaven.
Take heed that ye do not your alms before men, to be seen of them: otherwise ye have no reward of your Father *which* is in heaven.	
2 Therefore when *thou doest thine* alms, do not sound a trumpet before *thee, as the* hypocrites do in the synagogues and in the streets, that they may have glory of men. Verily I say unto you, They have their reward.	Therefore, when **ye shall do your** alms do not sound a trumpet before **you,** as **will** hypocrites do in the synagogues and in the streets, that they may have glory of men. Verily I say unto you, they have their reward.
3 But when thou doest alms, let not thy left hand know what thy right hand doeth:	But when thou doest alms let not thy left hand know what thy right hand doeth;

Matthew 6	3 Nephi 13
4 That thine alms may be in secret: and thy Father *which* seeth in secret himself shall reward thee openly.	That thine alms may be in secret; and thy Father **who** seeth in secret, himself shall reward thee openly.
5 And when thou prayest, thou shalt not *be* as the hypocrites *are:* for they love to pray standing in the synagogues and in the corners of the streets, that they may be seen of men. Verily I say unto you, They have their reward.	And when thou prayest thou shalt not **do** as the hypocrites, for they love to pray, standing in the synagogues and in the corners of the streets, that they may be seen of men. Verily I say unto you, they have their reward.
6 But thou, when thou prayest, enter into thy closet, and when thou hast shut thy door, pray to thy Father *which* is in secret; and thy Father *which* seeth in secret shall reward thee openly.	But thou, when thou prayest, enter into thy closet, and when thou hast shut thy door, pray to thy Father **who** is in secret; and thy Father, **who** seeth in secret, shall reward thee openly.
7 But when ye pray, use not vain repetitions, as the heathen *do:* for they think that they shall be heard for their much speaking.	But when ye pray, use not vain repetitions, as the heathen, for they think that they shall be heard for their much speaking.
8 Be not ye therefore like unto them: for your Father knoweth what things ye have need of, before ye ask him.	Be not ye therefore like unto them, for your Father knoweth what things ye have need of before ye ask him.

Matthew 6	3 Nephi 13
9 After this manner therefore pray ye: Our Father *which* art in heaven, Hallowed be thy name.	After this manner therefore pray ye: Our Father **who** art in heaven, hallowed be thy name.
10 *Thy kingdom come.* Thy will be done *in* earth, as it is in heaven.	Thy will be done **on** earth as it is in heaven.
11 *Give us this day our daily bread.*	And forgive us our debts, as we forgive our debtors.
12 And forgive us our debts, as we forgive our debtors.	· And lead us not into temptation, but deliver us from evil.
13 And lead us not into temptation, but deliver us from evil: For thine is the kingdom, and the power, and the glory, for ever. Amen.	For thine is the kingdom, and the power, and the glory, forever. Amen.
14 For if ye forgive men their trespasses, your heavenly Father will also forgive you:	For, if ye forgive men their trespasses your heavenly Father will also forgive you;
15 But if ye forgive not men their trespasses, neither will your Father forgive your trespasses.	But if ye forgive not men their trespasses neither will your Father forgive your trespasses.
16 Moreover when ye fast, be not, as the hypocrites, of a sad countenance: for they disfigure their faces, that they may	Moreover, when ye fast be not as the hypocrites, of a sad countenance, for they disfigure their faces that they may

Matthew 6	3 Nephi 13
appear unto men to fast. Verily I say unto you, They have their reward.	appear unto men to fast. Verily I say unto you, they have their reward.
17 But thou, when thou fastest, anoint *thine* head, and wash thy face;	But thou, when thou fastest, anoint **thy** head, and wash thy face;
18 That thou appear not unto men to fast, but unto thy Father *which* is in secret: and thy Father, *which* seeth in secret, shall reward thee openly.	That thou appear not unto men to fast, but unto thy Father, **who** is in secret; and thy Father, **who** seeth in secret, shall reward thee openly.
19 Lay not up for yourselves treasures upon earth, where moth and rust doth corrupt, and *where* thieves break through and steal:	Lay not up for yourselves treasures upon earth, where moth and rust doth corrupt, and thieves break through and steal;
20 But lay up for yourselves treasures in heaven, where neither moth nor rust doth corrupt, and where thieves do not break through nor steal:	But lay up for yourselves treasures in heaven, where neither moth nor rust doth corrupt, and where thieves do not break through nor steal.
21 For where your treasure is, there will your heart be also.	For where your treasure is, there will your heart be also.
22 The light of the body is the eye: if therefore thine eye be	The light of the body is the eye; if, therefore, thine eye be

Matthew 6	3 Nephi 13
single, thy whole body shall be full of light.	single, thy whole body shall be full of light.
23 But if thine eye be evil, thy whole body shall be full of darkness. If therefore the light that is in thee be darkness, how great is that darkness!	But if thine eye be evil, thy whole body shall be full of darkness. If, therefore, the light that is in thee be darkness, how great is that darkness!
24 No man can serve two masters: for either he will hate the one, and love the other; or else he will hold to the one, and despise the other. Ye cannot serve God and mammon.	No man can serve two masters; for either he will hate the one and love the other, or else he will hold to the one and despise the other. Ye cannot serve God and Mammon.
25	**And now it came to pass that when Jesus had spoken these words he looked upon the twelve whom he had chosen, and said unto them: Remember the words which I have spoken. For behold, ye are they whom I have chosen to minister unto this people.** Therefore I say unto you, take no thought for your life, what ye shall eat, or what ye shall drink; nor yet for your body, what ye shall put on. Is not the life more than meat, and the body than raiment?
Therefore I say unto you, Take no thought for your life, what ye shall eat, or what ye shall drink; nor yet for your body, what ye shall put on. Is not the life more than meat, and the body than raiment?	

Matthew 6	3 Nephi 13
26 Behold the fowls of the air: for they sow not, neither do they reap, nor gather into barns; yet your heavenly Father feedeth them. Are ye not much better than they?	Behold the fowls of the air, for they sow not, neither do they reap nor gather into barns; yet your heavenly Father feedeth them. Are ye not much better than they?
27 Which of you by taking thought can add one cubit unto his stature?	Which of you by taking thought can add one cubit unto his stature?
28 And why take ye thought for raiment? Consider the lilies of the field, how they grow; they toil not, neither do they spin:	And why take ye thought for raiment? Consider the lilies of the field how they grow; they toil not, neither do they spin;
29 And yet I say unto you, That even Solomon in all his glory was not arrayed like one of these.	And yet I say unto you, that even Solomon, in all his glory, was not arrayed like one of these.
30 Wherefore, if God so clothe the grass of the field, which to day is, and to morrow is cast into the oven, *shall* he *not much more* clothe you, *O* ye of little faith?	Wherefore, if God so clothe the grass of the field, which today is, and tomorrow is cast into the oven, **even so will** he clothe you, **if** ye **are not** of little faith.
31 Therefore take no thought, saying, What shall we eat? or, What shall we drink? or, Wherewithal shall we be clothed?	Therefore take no thought, saying, What shall we eat? or, What shall we drink? or, Wherewithal shall we be clothed?

Matthew 6–7	3 Nephi 13–14
32 *(For after all these things do the Gentiles seek:)* for your heavenly Father knoweth that ye have need of all these things.	For your heavenly Father knoweth that ye have need of all these things.
33 But seek ye first the kingdom of God, and his righteousness; and all these things shall be added unto you.	But seek ye first the kingdom of God and his righteousness, and all these things shall be added unto you.
34 Take therefore no thought for the morrow: for the morrow shall take thought for the things of itself. Sufficient *unto* the day *is* the evil thereof.	Take therefore no thought for the morrow, for the morrow shall take thought for the things of itself. Sufficient **is** the day **unto** the evil thereof.
1 Judge not, that ye be not judged.	**And now it came to pass that when Jesus had spoken these words he turned again to the multitude, and did open his mouth unto them again, saying: Verily, verily, I say unto you,** Judge not, that ye be not judged.
2 For with what judgment ye judge, ye shall be judged: and with what measure ye mete, it shall be measured to you again.	For with what judgment ye judge, ye shall be judged; and with what measure ye mete, it shall be measured to you again.

Matthew 7	3 Nephi 14
3 And why beholdest thou the mote that is in thy brother's eye, but considerest not the beam that is in thine own eye?	And why beholdest thou the mote that is in thy brother's eye, but considerest not the beam that is in thine own eye?
4 Or how wilt thou say to thy brother, Let me pull *out* the mote out of thine eye; and, behold, a beam is in thine own eye?	Or how wilt thou say to thy brother: Let me pull the mote out of thine eye—and behold, a beam is in thine own eye?
5 Thou hypocrite, first cast *out* the beam out of thine own eye; and then shalt thou see clearly to cast out the mote out of thy brother's eye.	Thou hypocrite, first cast the beam out of thine own eye; and then shalt thou see clearly to cast the mote out of thy brother's eye.
6 Give not that which is holy unto the dogs, neither cast ye your pearls before swine, lest they trample them under their feet, and turn again and rend you.	Give not that which is holy unto the dogs, neither cast ye your pearls before swine, lest they trample them under their feet, and turn again and rend you.
7 Ask, and it shall be given you; seek, and ye shall find; knock, and it shall be opened unto you:	Ask, and it shall be given **unto** you; seek, and ye shall find; knock, and it shall be opened unto you.
8 For every one that asketh receiveth; and he that seeketh findeth; and to him that knocketh it shall be opened.	For every one that asketh, receiveth; and he that seeketh, findeth; and to him that knocketh, it shall be opened.

Matthew 7	3 Nephi 14
9 Or what man is there of you, *whom* if his son ask bread, will *he* give him a stone?	Or what man is there of you, **who,** if his son ask bread, will give him a stone?
10 Or if he ask a fish, will he give him a serpent?	Or if he ask a fish, will he give him a serpent?
11 If ye then, being evil, know how to give good gifts unto your children, how much more shall your Father *which* is in heaven give good things to them that ask him?	If ye then, being evil, know how to give good gifts unto your children, how much more shall your Father **who** is in heaven give good things to them that ask him?
12 Therefore all things whatsoever ye would that men should do to you, do ye even so to them: for this is the law and the prophets.	Therefore, all things whatsoever ye would that men should do to you, do ye even so to them, for this is the law and the prophets.
13 Enter ye in at the strait gate: for wide is the gate, and broad is the way, *that* leadeth to destruction, and many there be *which* go in thereat:	Enter ye in at the strait gate; for wide is the gate, and broad is the way, *which* leadeth to destruction, and many there be **who** go in thereat;
14 Because strait is the gate, and narrow is the way, which leadeth unto life, and few there be that find it.	Because strait is the gate, and narrow is the way, which leadeth unto life, and few there be that find it.

Matthew 7	3 Nephi 14
15 Beware of false prophets, *which* come to you in sheep's clothing, but inwardly they are ravening wolves.	Beware of false prophets, **who** come to you in sheep's clothing, but inwardly they are ravening wolves.
16 Ye shall know them by their fruits. Do men gather grapes of thorns, or figs of thistles?	Ye shall know them by their fruits. Do men gather grapes of thorns, or figs of thistles?
17 Even so every good tree bringeth forth good fruit; but a corrupt tree bringeth forth evil fruit.	Even so every good tree bringeth forth good fruit; but a corrupt tree bringeth forth evil fruit.
18 A good tree cannot bring forth evil fruit, neither *can* a corrupt tree bring forth good fruit.	A good tree cannot bring forth evil fruit, neither a corrupt tree bring forth good fruit.
19 Every tree that bringeth not forth good fruit is hewn down, and cast into the fire.	Every tree that bringeth not forth good fruit is hewn down, and cast into the fire.
20 Wherefore by their fruits ye shall know them.	Wherefore, by their fruits ye shall know them.
21 Not every one that saith unto me, Lord, Lord, shall enter into the kingdom of heaven; but he that doeth the will of my Father *which* is in heaven.	Not every one that saith unto me, Lord, Lord, shall enter into the kingdom of heaven; but he that doeth the will of my Father **who** is in heaven.

Matthew 7	3 Nephi 14
22 Many will say to me in that day, Lord, Lord, have we not prophesied in thy name? and in thy name have cast out devils? and in thy name done many wonderful works?	Many will say to me in that day: Lord, Lord, have we not prophesied in thy name, and in thy name have cast out devils, and in thy name done many wonderful works?
23 And then will I profess unto them, I never knew you: depart from me, ye that work iniquity.	And then will I profess unto them: I never knew you; depart from me, ye that work iniquity.
24 Therefore *whosoever* heareth these sayings of mine, and doeth them, I will liken him unto a wise man, *which* built his house upon a rock:	Therefore, **whoso** heareth these sayings of mine and doeth them, I will liken him unto a wise man, **who** built his house upon a rock—
25 And the rain descended, and the floods came, and the winds blew, and beat upon that house; and it fell not: for it was founded upon a rock.	And the rain descended, and the floods came, and the winds blew, and beat upon that house; and it fell not, for it was founded upon a rock.
26 And every one that heareth these sayings of mine, and doeth them not, shall be likened unto a foolish man, *which* built his house upon the sand:	And every one that heareth these sayings of mine and doeth them not shall be likened unto a foolish man, **who** built his house upon the sand—

Matthew 7	3 Nephi 14–15
27 And the rain descended, and the floods came, and the winds blew, and beat upon that house; and it fell: and great was the fall of it.	And the rain descended, and the floods came, and the winds blew, and beat upon that house; and it fell, and great was the fall of it.
28 And it came to pass, when Jesus had ended these sayings, *the people were astonished at his doctrine:*	1 And **now** it came to pass **that** when Jesus had ended these sayings **he cast his eyes round about on the multitude, and said unto them: Behold, ye have heard the things which I taught before I ascended to my Father; therefore, whoso remembereth these sayings of mine and doeth them, him will I raise up at the last day.**
29 *For he taught them as one having authority, and not as the scribes.*	

Index of Passages

SUBJECT INDEX

SM = Sermon on the Mount
ST = Sermon at the Temple